The *J.K. Lasser Pro*™ Series

J.K. Lasser Pro Advising Entrepreneurs: Dynamic Strategies for Financial Growth
Marc J. Lane
J.K. Lasser Pro Keeping Clients for Life
Karen Altfest
J.K. Lasser Pro Expert Financial Planning: Investment Strategies from Industry Leaders
Robert Arffa
J.L. Lasser Pro Estate and Business Succession Planning: A Legal Guide to Wealth Transference
Russell J. Fishkind, Esq. and Robert C. Kautz, Esq.
J.K. Lasser Pro Wealth Building: Investment Strategies for Retirement and Estate Planning
David R. Reiser and Robert L. DiColo with Hugh M. Ryan and Andrea R. Reiser
J.K. Lasser Pro Fee-Only Financial Planning: How to Make It Work for You
John E. Sestina
J.K. Lasser Pro Preparing for the Retirement Boom
Thomas Grady
J.K. Lasser Pro Advising Mature Clients: The New Science of Wealth Span Planning
Neal E. Cutler
J.K. Lasser Pro New Strategies for College Funding: An Advisor's Guide
Raymond Loewe, CLU, ChFC
J.K. Lasser Pro Real Estate Investment Trusts: New Strategies for Portfolio Management
Richard Imperiale

The *Wiley Financial Advisor* Series

Tax-Deferred Investing: Wealth Building and Wealth Transfer Strategies
Cory Grant and Andrew Westhem
Getting Clients, Keeping Clients
Dan Richards
Managing Family Trusts: Taking Control of Inherited Wealth
Robert A. Rikoon with Larry Waschka
Advising the 60+ Investor: Tax and Financial Planning Strategies
Darlene Smith, Dale Pulliam, and Holland Tolles
Tax-Smart Investing: Maximizing Your Client's Profits
Andrew D. Westhem and Stewart J. Weissman

J.K. LASSER PRO™

REAL ESTATE INVESTMENT TRUSTS

NEW STRATEGIES FOR PORTFOLIO MANAGEMENT

J.K. LASSER PRO™

REAL ESTATE INVESTMENT TRUSTS

NEW STRATEGIES FOR PORTFOLIO MANAGEMENT

Richard Imperiale

John Wiley & Sons, Inc.

Published by John Wiley & Sons, Inc., New York.
Published simultaneously in Canada.

This publication is designed to provide accurate and authoritative
information in regard to the subject matter covered. It is sold with the
understanding that the publisher is not engaged in rendering professional
services. If professional advice or other expert assistance is required, the
services of a competent professional person should be sought.

Wiley also publishes its books in a variety of electronic formats. Some
content that appears in print may not be available in electronic books. For
more information about Wiley products visit our Web site at
www.wiley.com.

Library of Congress Cataloging-in-Publication Data:

Imperiale, Richard, 1957–
  J.K. Lasser pro real estate investment trusts: new strategies for portfolio
management / by Richard Imperiale.
      p. cm.—(The J.K. Lasser pro series)
Includes index.
ISBN 0-471-21166-4
  1. Real estate investment trusts—United States.   I. Title: Real estate
investment trusts.   II. Title. III. Series.
HG5095 .I464 2002
332.63'247—dc21

                                                          2002001142

Printed in the United States of America.

10 9 8 7 6 5 4 3 2

About the Author

Richard Imperiale is president and founder of Uniplan, Inc., a Milwaukee, Wisconsin–based investment advisory firm whose clients include institutions, endowments, foundations, Taft-Hartley Plans, and high-net-worth individuals. Imperiale started his career as a credit analyst for the First Wisconsin National Bank (now Firstar). In 1983, he joined B.C. Ziegler & Company, a Midwest regional brokerage firm where he was instrumental in the development of portfolio strategies for one of the first hedged municipal bond mutual funds in the country. In 1984, Imperiale founded Uniplan, Inc., with the objective of managing investment portfolios to achieve the greatest long-term risk-adjusted return for conservative institutional clients. Using quantitative techniques similar to those used in his prior positions, Imperiale has developed a disciplined, quantitative approach to investing in stocks and bonds for the best risk-adjusted return.

In conjunction with his work, Imperiale has developed a proprietary database of statistical information on corporate valuation. The database collects and calculates 100 data items each month on over 3,000 public companies and spans a 25-year history. In addition, Imperiale maintains a database of the property ownership of 150 publicly traded equity real estate investment trusts. This database classifies and tracks the acquisition and sale of properties and the capitalization, occupancy, and financial data related to those properties.

Imperiale, a native of New Jersey, attended Marquette University Business School, where he received a B.S. in finance. In addition, he completed the postgraduate lecture series in corporate finance at the University of Chicago Graduate School of Business and received a certificate in legal research from Concordia University. He resides in Wisconsin with his wife and two daughters. In his spare time he enjoys sailing, writing, and politics.

Contents

Foreword

This book is an explanation and analysis of real estate investment trusts (REITs). REITs and real estate investing have endured a checkered history. In general terms, REITs were historically a small and misunderstood part of the real estate investment landscape. Over the past decade, however, this has changed. Now REITs are major owners of investment-quality real estate and a major force in the institutional investment arena. In addition, REITs are a viable and competitive investment option for investors who are looking to broaden and diversify their investment portfolios.

As a professional investor in REITs, I noticed that the average investor largely misunderstood REITs. Many professional investors and portfolio managers also had little knowledge of REITs. In addition, there were very few books on the subject of REITs. Those books that were available provided either a very simple overview or a highly complex academic treatment of the topic. Most books did not address the fundamental real estate concepts that underlie the basics of real estate investing or the methods of integrating REITs into an investment portfolio.

This book is an attempt to address these very issues. We begin in Part One with a general discussion of real estate as an asset class. Then the legal and financial history of REITs is examined.

The section ends with a discussion of how REITs behave as an investment class and how they are best integrated into an investor's portfolio. Part Two describes the fundamental economic issues that affect real estate in general and analyzes these issues in the context of the REIT investment vehicle. The section concludes with specific methods for analyzing REITs as an investment and advanced investment topics involving REITs. Part Three uses the theoretical constructs developed in the first two parts to examine each major property category within the REIT universe.

REITs are an emerging asset class. As in any new asset class, the opinions of observers and other professionals within the asset class often diverge. Those diverging opinions are covered in theory in each chapter. However, in order to put the issues into a more useful framework, throughout the book there are numerous interviews with industry opinion leaders. Through the use of these interviews, the reader will gain many practical insights as expressed by those who work in the REIT industry on a daily basis. These interviews provide a practical and useful overview that bridges theoretical constructs with practical industry knowledge.

In addition, the book provides some practical statistical data that is relevant to the general analysis of REITs. This appears in the numerous charts, tables, and graphs that summarize key industry data in a usable format.

I hope that this book fills a void in the available current literature about REITs and promotes a better understanding of an emerging asset class.

Richard Imperiale
Milwaukee, Wisconsin
March 11, 2002

Preface

Real estate is one of the largest and most pervasive industries in the country. Each day we are all exposed to the business of real estate. The homes and apartments in which we live, the offices and factories in which we work, the stores we shop in, the hospitals we are born in, and the nursing homes we die in are all a part of the investment real estate landscape.

This vast landscape of real estate investment takes many forms. Large institutional investors such as pension plans and insurance companies own vast portfolios of real estate holdings. Private individuals also own large and small portfolios of real estate. In fact, about two-thirds of all American households own their homes, which in many ways is a real estate investment.

In the recent past, real estate investing had gotten a bad reputation. During the inflation-prone, tax-motivated real estate days of the 1970s, many people and institutions invested and lost money in a variety of tax-motivated real estate investments. Real estate developers and promoters were often thought of as hucksters and charlatans—and many were. Developers also got a bad reputation as real estate cowboys who would build anything if they could get the money. This too was true.

Real estate promoters and developers were the dot-com executives of the 1970s. They were getting rich as investors directed an ever growing stream of capital into the industry. The Tax Reform Act of 1986 changed the real estate landscape by ending the tax incentives that were fueling capital formation in the real estate industry. The resulting bubble in real estate ended with the largest glut of property ever seen in the U.S. real estate market.

The property glut was financed in large part by the savings and loan industry. The collapse in the real estate bubble precipitated the savings and loan crisis as property owners defaulted on their highly leveraged real estate holdings. With little or no equity in these properties and falling property values and rents, there was little incentive not to turn the keys back to the mortgage holders. The Resolution Trust Company worked during the late 1980s to resolve the S&L crisis. By the early 1990s, the excesses of the 1970s had been resolved, but real estate investments continued to have a bad reputation among small investors.

The Tax Reform Act of 1986 had set the stage for a more financially rational real estate marketplace. Legendary value investors like Sam Zell and many others, seeing this rationalization of assets, invested early in what has turned out to be one of the most stable and well-defined real estate recoveries in modern history. Real estate investors have become far more disciplined, demanding returns on invested capital that reflect the level of investment risk associated with a real estate asset. Mortgage lenders are also far more conservative. They will not lend capital on projects that they do not view as highly feasible. This has brought a capital market discipline to the commercial mortgage arena. The net result has been longer, more stable real estate expansions and less severe real estate cycles.

From this crucible of industry reshaping has emerged a new real estate paradigm. Disciplined owners, rational lenders, and higher returns on capital have resulted. Among the new class of disciplined owners are real estate investment trusts (REITs), which collectively own over 10 percent of the investment-grade real estate in the United States. REITs offer the opportunity for small investors to participate in a broad range of real estate opportunities across most major property sectors and in most geographic locations. Disciplined real estate professionals whose financial interests are largely aligned with those of the shareholders generally manage REITs.

REITs provide returns that are competitive with those of both stocks and bonds, but the performance of REITs is amazingly independent of that of both stocks and bonds. This fact allows REITs to add an additional element of diversification when they become part of a portfolio along with stocks and bonds. This book describes describes these features and attempts to put them into a framework that examines the critical investment aspects of REITs and the theoretical real estate principles that drive the REIT investment decision.

Acknowledgments

Although the author ultimately gets the credit for writing a book, there is an army of others who contribute to the process. I'd like to take a page or two to recognize them.

This book is dedicated to my wife, Sue, and our two daughters, Emily and Mary, who put up with my absence from family and school functions and during many evenings and weekends. Their support and encouragement made the completion of this project possible. Every day they make me realize how fortunate I really am.

I'd like to thank my good friend and mentor, Dr. John Komives, from the Marquette University Business School. For the past twenty years we have worked together with a great sense of adventure on many business and academic projects. We have often discussed potential projects over a cold glass of beer on many Friday evenings, and this book is a result of one of those conversations.

Of course, it's not a book without a publisher. After many non-responses, about to put the outline back in my desk drawer, I was telling my friend Jerry Tweddell my tale of woe. Jerry, who is the author of several investment books, was kind enough to introduce me to his publisher, John Wiley & Sons. Through that introduction, I met David Pugh, who is now my editor at Wiley. In the middle of the dot-com frenzy, David was open-minded enough to listen to my ideas about real estate, give me critical feedback, and go to bat for me on this project. David has been an excellent coach and critic and helped me shape this book into a much better and more useful text. I now consider him a good friend and thank him for all his help.

I thought the writing was hard. But that was easy compared to the copyediting. For helping me get through that phase of the project, I want to thank Stephanie Landis. When the writing was complete, the book had run long. Stephanie's talent and skill helped to restructure the content of the book and significantly reduce the overall page count. She also patiently taught me many useful lessons about the editing and publishing process that have made me a better writer.

The book contains a fair amount of data compiled from company reports and industry trade associations. Much of that data was processed by my assistant Rochell Tillman and my research associates, Tom McNulty, Jackie Hughes, Isac Malmgren, and Jeff Lenderman, who collectively reviewed the SEC filings of over 200 real estate investment trusts and real estate operating companies. Their diligence and hard work provided consolidated data that is not found in any other single place.

In addition, I'd like to thank David Howard, Jack McAllister, Michael Grupe, and Tony Edwards, all from the National Association of Real Estate Investment Trusts. They have each assisted me with critical comments, data, and analysis, as well as industry contacts that have been helpful in providing insights and data. Much of this information can be found in the interviews at the ends of many chapters of this book. These people are the leading thinkers in the REIT industry and provided candid insights into the workings of the business of REITs.

I would also like to thank Lyn Woloszyk, who transcribed many of the interviews for the book. She often did the transcriptions on short notice and with tight deadlines, which was helpful in keeping the project on schedule due to my time constraints. And thanks to my business partner, Larry Kujawski, who covered for me at many meetings and on many projects while I was frantically working on the book.

My sincere thanks to all of you.

J.K. LASSER PRO™

REAL ESTATE INVESTMENT TRUSTS

NEW STRATEGIES FOR PORTFOLIO MANAGEMENT

Part One

Real Estate as an Asset Class

Characteristics of Real Estate as an Investment

Chapter Summary

- Real estate has been an important component of large institutional investment portfolios for the last century.

- Well-located, high-quality real estate provides excellent return on investment, high current income, and a significant hedge against inflation.

- Real estate behaves very differently from stocks and bonds. Its value is driven by supply and demand in the local real estate market. Real estate performs well in both rising and falling interest rate environments.

- Returns in the real estate asset class rival those of stocks on a long-term basis. Because it is a hard asset, real estate provides an inflation hedge, but, unlike most hard assets, real estate provides current income.

- In 1960, a vehicle was created by Congress that enabled groups of investors to collectively own real estate portfolios similar to those of institutions. This vehicle was known as the real estate investment trust (REIT).

More money has been made in real estate than all industrial investments combined.

—Andrew Carnegie, 1902

Real estate is an asset class that major investment institutions have formally embraced as a part of their portfolios for the last century. Among institutional investors it is no secret that well-located, high-quality real estate can provide an excellent return on investment, high current income, and a significant hedge against inflation.

It is estimated that institutional real estate investors own the vast majority of the $6.3 trillion of commercial real estate in the United States. (Commercial real estate is defined as all real estate excluding single-family homes and multifamily buildings up to four units, raw land, farms and ranches, and government owned properties. About half of this commercial real estate is considered to be of sufficient quality and size to be of interest to institutional investors.) By comparison, the total capitalization of all public U.S. equities is estimated to be $12.9 trillion, and the nominal value of all nongovernment U.S. bonds is estimated to be $36.4 trillion. Thus, U.S. domestic real estate as an asset class ranks third, behind stocks and bonds, and represents 11 percent of the total of the three asset classes (see Figure 1.1).

Positive Attributes of the Real Estate Asset Class

Each institution generally has its own investment policy when it comes to real estate. Normally, institutions are attempting to match the life of assets with that of forecast liabilities. Retirement funds, insurance companies, and commercial banks are among the major private sector investors in real estate. They all have projected liabilities that must be met at some future date.

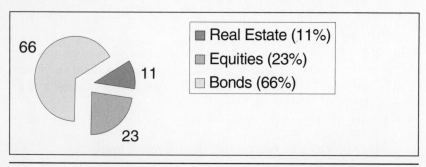

FIGURE 1.1 Commercial Real Estate versus Stocks and Bonds ($ Trillions)

The consistent and relatively predictable cash flows associated with real estate allow for a high degree of confidence when matching future liabilities.

Consistent and predictable cash flow is just one attractive feature of the real estate asset class. Real estate also tends to perform better than financial assets in an inflationary environment. In reviewing the history of real estate performance, a number of studies have found that returns from real estate were higher during times of inflation and lower during periods of disinflation. Thus, a portfolio of largely financial assets can be hedged, to some extent, against the corrosive effects of inflation through the ownership of real estate.

Taxable investors may also be able to derive some additional tax benefits from the real estate asset class. For tax accounting purposes, the value of real estate other than land can be depreciated at a rate that is generally greater than the actual economic life of the property. In most cases, the value of a well-maintained property in a good location will actually increase over time at a rate similar to inflation. This accelerated tax depreciation results in a partial sheltering of cash flow as well as the deferral of taxes, which can usually be treated as a more favorable long-term capital gain for tax purposes.

It is possible to capture some of the benefits of real estate's unique tax qualities for tax-exempt investors such as pension funds. Structuring partnerships and operating agreements in ways that allow taxable benefits to flow to those who can use them, while allocating higher levels of cash flow to tax-exempt investors, is one way tax-exempt investors can benefit from the tax advantages of real estate. In some instances the tax benefits of certain real estate projects can be sold to taxable investors by tax-exempt investors, thus allowing incremental total return to be enhanced.

There are some other primary reasons that large institutional investors are attracted to real estate. One factor that is often cited by institutions is that real estate returns behave very differently from stock and bond returns. This low correlation of returns provides an added diversification benefit. In general, adding real estate to a portfolio of stocks and bonds enhances return and lowers risk in a given portfolio.

There is a large body of academic and professional work that suggests that investing 5 to 15 percent of a portfolio in real estate increases the total return and lowers the portfolio risk. This is consistent with the fact that the largest 200 retirement plans have an average total of 17 percent of their assets invested in real estate.

Attribution of Return in Real Estate

The return attribution of real estate can be identified by a number of features, some of which are unique to real estate and some of which are common to other classes of investments. As discussed previously, the value of well-maintained real estate in a good location will actually increase over time. This capital appreciation aspect of real estate is similar to the long-term growth in value seen as a primary component of return in the equity asset class.

Real estate also has some bondlike characteristics. The consistent and predictable cash flow associated with rents paid on real estate is the primary focus of most institutional investors. This steady stream of rental income attributable to a given property or portfolio is much like the regular interest paid as the coupon of a bond. The terms of these bondlike payments are typically detailed in a lease agreement between the owner of the real estate and the user or tenant of the real estate. It is the quality and completeness of these terms and conditions as stated in the lease that allow for the analysis of the underlying cash flows of a given property.

The *term,* or length, of the rental payments as stated by the lease also produces duration characteristics similar to those of a bond investment. In a bond, the duration is, in part, a function of the term remaining before the bond matures. In real estate, the duration of the rental income is a function of the length of the underlying lease or remaining period of the rental stream. Rents derived from hotel and motel properties—which can change on a daily basis—have the shortest duration, followed by apartment rents, which are generally set for a term of one or two years. Office, retail, and industrial properties tend to have longer-duration leases that can extend for a term of 10 to 30 years or more.

Real estate also has a credit profile, much like the credit rating of a bond. This credit profile is determined by the credit quality of the underlying tenants that pay the lease and occupy the real estate. For example, an office building with 50,000 square feet leased on a long-term basis to IBM will have a much better credit profile than the same space leased to Bob's Pretty Good Computer Company, a new enterprise with an operating history of less than five years. Similarly, an IBM bond would presumably have a better credit rating than a loan to Bob's Pretty Good Computer Company, which would most likely be considered a high-risk proposition.

There are also return attribution features that are unique to the real estate asset class. The physical attributes of a given piece of real estate can have an impact on value. For example, visualize two suburban office buildings, of the same size and age, in a similar location. One is built of brick and stone, the other using simple wood construction. It is likely that because the brick and stone office building has a higher replacement cost, it may also have a higher value than the wood frame office building. Thus a building's physical quality can have a unique impact on its value.

Location is also a unique feature that can ascribe greater or lesser value to real estate. Because any given piece of real estate can only occupy a single location, each piece of real estate is in essence unique. Thus, real estate in a highly desirable location may have a much greater value than identical real estate in a different, less desirable location.

There is also the situation of what are called *externalities* in the economics of real estate. An externality occurs when an activity or event affects (for good or bad) another that is external to it. For example, if Donald Trump builds a shining new skyscraper in the middle of a marginal neighborhood, this is a positive externality for the owners of many adjoining properties, who see the value of their holdings increase overnight as a result of no direct activity on their part. Conversely, if the house next door to an apartment building in a pleasant suburban neighborhood is converted to a homeless shelter, it is likely to be considered a negative externality that lowers the value of the apartment building.

Because the problem of externalities is so crucial to real estate value, a high degree of zoning and entitlement exists in the real estate marketplace. Normally zoning considers what is commonly referred to as *highest and best use*. This is a use that is economically and physically feasible when considered relative to other adjoining real estate, economic activities in the area, the size of the site, and the intended design and use of the new building. Zoning and entitlement also extend to the regulatory level when examining real estate. Many localities have low- or no-growth policies that make it difficult to develop new real estate. Some localities adopt master plans that strictly limit the size, style, design, and use of a building in any given area of the planned community.

In some communities there is simply no more available vacant space on which to build. These are referred to as *urban infill* or *redevelopment* communities. Any entitlement in these areas becomes part of the removal and redevelopment of an existing site or the expansion and refinement of an existing property. The ever growing sentiment of "not in my backyard" among the residents of many communities often creates a situation of externalities that can have significant positive or negative impact on the value of a property. These are unique aspects of the real estate asset class.

The features that are unique to real estate—physical attributes, location, local externalities, zoning, and entitlement—contribute to real estate's low correlation of return relative to stocks and bonds. The value of real estate is driven by supply and demand in the local real estate market. The best building imaginable might sit empty in a market where supply exceeds demand for that type of real estate. Because of its permanent physical nature, real estate cannot be moved to a market where the demand is greater than the supply. In its simplest terms, real estate is a very local asset class driven by all the macroeconomic and microeconomic factors of the local and regional marketplace.

This is not to say that real estate is insulated from more national economic factors. The aggregate demand for real estate in general is driven by the overall growth in the national economy. Population demographics, job creation, and the general business cycle all have an impact on the final demand for real estate. However, this demand manifests itself in very local ways. For example, the internet frenzy that gripped San Francisco and

San Jose in the late 1990s had a huge impact on the final demand for real estate in those cities, driving real estate prices to unsustainable levels. During the same time period, real estate prices in Atlanta, Georgia, remained relatively soft due to an excess supply of local property, which had to be absorbed before prices could again advance.

Real estate seems to have a litany of positive investment characteristics. It has both stock- and bond-type attributes as well as performance features that enhance portfolio diversification. It tends to perform well in an inflationary environment and achieves good outcomes in both rising and falling interest rate environments. Taxable investors also enjoy certain tax advantages when investing in real estate. These are the beneficial features that have made real estate a favorite among institutional investors.

Negative Attributes of the Real Estate Asset Class

Although real estate has a long list of positive investment attributes, there are also some negative characteristics related to direct investments in real estate. Lack of liquidity is the largest single negative factor that goes along with owning a real estate investment portfolio. The process of buying and selling real estate can be long and involved. An investment-class property can easily take six months to a year to sell, depending on market conditions and the prevailing economic environment.

The marketability of a property will often depend on the terms and conditions of a sale. The terms are often subject to negotiation—at times, lengthy negotiation—between any given number of potential buyers and the seller. Because real estate is often financed in part with debt, the type and amount of financing that is readily available for a given property or in a given marketplace will often affect these negotiations. This lack of liquidity when compared to other financial assets such as stocks or bonds adds to the potential risk inherent in the real estate asset class.

An investor in a share of IBM common stock is buying one share out of millions of identical common shares that trade freely on a daily basis. The buyer of an office building in Detroit faces an entirely unique set of facts and circumstances that are largely different from the facts and circumstances that may affect a similar office building in Denver. Furthermore, office buildings in Detroit and Denver similar to those described may only change hands every few years. Thus, at times it may be difficult to establish a relevant market price with which to compare similar real estate.

This lack of liquidity, when coupled with the local market nature of real estate, can create a situation where real estate is a less efficient asset class. This is due in part to the uniqueness of each property as it is situated in each market. Local economic factors can lead to real estate values rising in one area of the country while falling in others. These same factors can lead to rising prices for industrial buildings and falling prices for office buildings in the very same market. The uniqueness of real estate causes these inefficiencies.

The lack of liquidity and the less efficient local characteristics of real estate also create problems when attempting to measure the performance of real estate. Performance is most accurate when measured over the period the real estate is owned, which may be 5 to 10 years or longer. Measuring annual or quarterly returns from a property or a portfolio can be difficult given the lack of market information. Appraisals are sometimes used to estimate periodic values over shorter periods of time, but this is not as accurate as the data from actual transactions. And it still leaves unanswered the question of how a real estate portfolio is performing relative to other similar portfolios.

These inefficient aspects of direct real estate investment manifest themselves in the higher potential returns that result from superior market knowledge. The inefficiencies create advantages for investors who have cultivated local market knowledge and use it to the disadvantage of the less informed owner. This use of material inside information that may be gleaned from political and business relationships is not illegal in real estate transactions, as it is in securities transactions. On this basis, some observers argue that real estate is a less than level playing field for the small investor. This perception may have some basis in the recent history of the small investor and real estate.

The late 1970s and early 1980s saw a confluence of events that hurt the general credibility of the real estate asset class in the eyes of the small investor. The federal tax code had created a situation of positive incentives for the ownership of investment real estate. The inflationary environment of the period led to ever escalating real estate prices, which in turn led to an excess amount of capital from small investors flowing into the real estate market. This took the form of a large number of private limited partnerships that were created to invest in real estate.

Federally insured savings and loan institutions became lenders to the partnerships in an environment where lenders had little incentive not to lend. There was little regulatory oversight of the situation and a great deal of leverage and liquidity. This led to a speculative real estate bubble that resulted in a real estate crash during the mid 1980s and a near-collapse of the entire U.S. savings and loan system.

It took nearly a decade for the economy to absorb the excess supply of real estate, and an entire generation of small investors was left with painful financial losses and a negative outlook on real estate as an investment. Many small investors view real estate as an institutional arena. Given the large amount of capital required to buy a real estate portfolio diversified by property type and geography, it is easy to understand the continuing negative sentiment of the small investor.

The aftermath of the limited partnerships and the savings and loan crisis has led to a real estate market with a new sense of order. Tax law changes have resulted in more modest capital formation in the real estate markets. The increased regulation and scrutiny of lenders and their loan portfolios has lowered the propensity for excess leverage in the real estate sector by requiring more equity and higher loan underwriting standards. This has resulted in a more balanced real estate economy.

Wall Street has also made a contribution to the real estate sector. The growth in securitization of real estate assets through such vehicles as commercial mortgage-backed securities (CMBS) and real estate investment trusts (REITs, pronounced *reets*) has created a public market discipline that has resulted in better transparency of the real estate markets and a more moderate real estate cycle.

The growth of REITs as an asset class has created an opportunity for small investors to participate in the ownership of institutional-quality real estate. REITs have created a solution to the lack of liquidity, lack of efficiency, and lack of relevant performance measurement that confront real estate investors in general. In addition, they provide an efficient mechanism for small investors to participate in real estate portfolios that offer diversity by property type and geography. The advantages and benefits of REITs as an asset class and how to integrate them into a portfolio strategy are the focus of this book.

Interview with Sam Zell

Sam Zell was one of the first institutional real estate investors to recognize the opportunities that resulted from the collapse of the real estate markets in the mid-1980s. He was also among the first to realize the operating advantage of the REIT structure in the post–Tax Reform Act of 1986 real estate environment. He acquired massive portfolios of office, apartment, and manufactured home community properties at below replacement cost during the depths of the real estate downturn. He later brought these public in the form of the three REITs—Equity Office, Equity Residential, and Manufactured Home Communities— which he now oversees as chairman.

Richard Imperiale: As one of America's largest real estate investors, what characteristics of real estate as an investment do you find most attractive?

Sam Zell: As an investor, I look at real estate as an area where we're dealing with hard assets and brick and mortar. There may be a lot of people who get a lot of joy out of virtual assets, but somehow or other, there's a great deal of comfort that comes from being able to see and touch and understand. Let's take the office building business. There are very few businesses where on January 1 a company can identify where 90 percent of its revenue is going to come from and what it's going to be. So, because in a very unsophisticated way, as a landlord I am the intermediary in the tenant space and certainly in evaluating real estate, obviously credit quality becomes very much of an issue. For example, ours is a high-credit portfolio and therefore we have the unique position of being able to know where 90 percent of revenue is

going to come from on January 1. I like cash flow characteristics. I think futures are terrific and presents are often more
comforting. I've been in the real estate business for 40 years
and I've always been fascinated by its creativity, its evolu-
tions. I probably have been a significant factor in this most
recent evolution revolution. It's brought all kinds of new
issues from liquidity issues to deal with financing agencies,
structuring debt in very different ways than was historically
the case, operating at lower debt levels, which is also a very
different and new experience. And, although obviously it's
less risky, it's also more challenging to produce results
because you're dealing with 60 percent equity instead of 10
percent equity. With 10 percent equity, you look like a real
genius. I think all of those things, in combination with probably a long-term penchant toward some level of inflation in
our economic system, will over time significantly reward the
owner of well-located bricks and mortar.

Imperiale: You mentioned in one of your interviews that it's
supply and demand that makes real estate appreciate, not
inflation.

Zell: That is correct.

Imperiale: And capital has been restricted in the real estate
industry in various ways—for example, public discipline
and the commercial mortgage–backed securities market—
and when new supply is restricted, rents go up. What are
the long-term trends that you see impacting real estate in
REITs that result from those kind of factors?

Zell: Well, I think we are definitely in a consolidation phase
where a higher and higher percentage of high-quality assets
will be owned and controlled by a much smaller number of
people, thereby providing a little rationality to a highly
fragmented market, which, if you think about it, is probably one of the few capital-intensive markets that isn't an
oligopoly. That's one of the evolutionary trends in real
estate. By the way, all forms of real estate, whether it be
shopping centers or somebody like Simon, are good at the
mall business today. Simon, General Growth, Maserich,
Taubman, and maybe two others probably have 85 percent

of all the malls in America. They've all been rationalized, and I think we're going to see more and more of that. I think we're going to see a higher and higher percentage of what I would call investment-grade real estate on the public markets. The process of the survival of the fittest will ultimately prevail, and we'll see 216 REITs go to 210, then to 190, and then at some point—maybe 5 or 10 years from now—we'll have probably 15 to 20 relevant REITs.

Imperiale: Do you think that'll be the end game for the industry?

Zell: Yes. I think they'll have 15 or 20 major players divided by industries and maybe there'll be three, four, or five big players in each segment, but when it's all said and done, the future of the public market is going to be about 20 companies. As significant as commercial real estate is in the U.S. economy, probably 12 to 15 percent—216 companies on the New York Stock Exchange—are significantly overweighted. When you divide it by total assets of $150 billion, it's crazy.

Imperiale: There are a lot of companies with a small number of assets.

Zell: Exactly. Over time, some of these companies will merge, some will go private, some will trade by appointment, and more and more there will be a series of major players with liquidity in the market. I don't disagree that when it's all said and done, supply and demand are the near-term factors that influence value. You could have 20 percent inflation and 20 percent vacancy and rents would go down and inflation would go up, and vice versa. But if you think not quarterly, but in 5- or 10-year increments, prior to the 1990s or the late 1980s there was inflation of give or take 3 percent, which was affecting the replacement cost. In the interim there were supply and demand cycles, but each new cycle still undertook a higher cost of replacement that ultimately became the rope that pulled up all real estate. If the kind of stimulus that I think we're going to see in the next year does lead to a recovery that may look more like stagflation than growth—but nonetheless recovery from today anyway—then maybe that step-by-step process that for so many years was part of the real estate business will return in terms of what it's going to cost to replace and build new structures to be competitive. As for overall supply and demand, I would not expect supply and demand in apartments, industrial, and office—probably in all forms of real estate—to exceed what I call the job growth level. The job growth level is the ultimate governor, and consequently, if we create new product at a modest pace, we will keep the supply/demand scenario in line and we'll get more efficient, so in theory there probably is some percentage number of real estate need for every growth in the overall market.

Imperiale: The markets have to figure that out?

Zell: Sure.

Imperiale: The discussion often revolves around the first wave of this movement from private to public real estate. As you point out, from the early 1990s through the current date, there was a vast expansion, and it seems that now the markets for public real estate have stabilized at this level. If we say that approximately 10 percent of investment-quality commercial real estate is owned by REITs now, what's going to make that go to 30 percent? What's going to create those oligopolies and that rationalization of property categories that you discuss?

Zell: It's all about creating opportunity. If Equity Office or Equity Residential had a real opportunity today, we would have no problem getting the capital. We haven't been participants in the capital market in the last couple of years because we've seen less of an opportunity. I think the publicly held REIT universe will double in size in the next 10 years. The doubling will come from new supply created by more and more owners throwing in the towel and saying, "You know, it really doesn't make any sense if I can have liquidity, or if my children can have liquidity, or if I don't have to divvy up an office building in New York, but if I can get 10 million shares and give 3 million each to my three kids . . ." I think over time, that's got to happen, and it's going to happen.

Imperiale: So in many ways the liquidity needs of the current generation of real estate owners might drive some of that along with the development?

Zell: Well, remember that so much of this is tax driven that it was very important to keep the base to cover the taxes. Obviously the world has changed dramatically since 1986, and certainly the creation of new tax liabilities has dramatically decreased because you can't use them the way you used to.

Imperiale: So the tax-motivated era of real estate really ended with the Tax Reform Act of 1986?

Zell: Yes, but it will take a generation to unwind it.

Imperiale: What are the most important factors investors should keep in mind when they're investing in REITs?

Zell: Well, it's like any company, it comes down to the management. So the first question I'd ask would be, Is management alive? Assuming that the answer is yes, then the next question is, Does management have a vision, do they know where they're going, do they know what they want to do? Next, Does management have a record of execution, predictability, accountability? As an investor, I would want broad exposure. In each of the areas of real estate of public companies, there are opportunities to invest in the best companies, and over time, that's what I think works. I don't believe in local sharpshooter mentalities. If there was ever a diversification strategy, it ought to be in real estate—take your bets in check, cover your back.

Imperiale: And the diversification in real estate is because there are so many local markets operating independently of one another that you want to diversify your geographic as well as property exposure?

Zell: I can give you examples today where we're renting apartments and getting 5 percent rental increases in Southern California and we're losing our shirt giving away 5 percent in Northern California. I've got great stuff happening in Washington and Maryland and Virginia and D.C. and I'm getting hurt in Atlanta. But broadly speaking, I've got a positive scenario, and that's what you want when you invest in real estate. To some extent, people have to understand that these kind of securities are not really geared toward speculation, nor should they be. They really are geared toward income and preservation of capital and appropriate leverage going forward. Sure, we could go to 80 percent leverage and have this extraordinary volatile equity strip, but maybe someday somebody will approach this business and say, "I'm going to go furthest out, so maybe you give me a low multiple, but I create enormous leveraged results." And maybe someday they'll be an all-cash portfolio or maybe there is already. But I think that's 10 to 15 years away. This is still a terribly embryonic market and a terribly cynical environment. You're still dealing with people who remember 1972, 1974—you're still dealing with people who remember 1985. Before 1992, the REIT law was used, in my opinion, to screw the investment public, to create retail scenarios that retail salesman could hawk that had no quality and no discipline, and that wasn't very far from a reflection on what that arena was like.

Imperiale: How does this embryonic market graduate to a more institutional marketplace? I know you've had a great accomplishment getting REITs into the S&P 500 index.

Zell: There are major institutions that six weeks ago would not take a call from a REIT analyst. Now, every institution takes calls from REIT analysts. Getting into the S&P index for Equity Residential and Equity Office has broadened dramatically the world of potential REIT investors. In the years to come, I suspect we're going to see some of those shadow S&P investors in effect building REIT positions specifically to compensate against something else. Up until now, since they never had any motivation to look at this sector and therefore to understand it, their interest in, say, the secure size with REITs versus utilities versus something else, was nonexistent. That's part of the evolutionary process.

Imperiale: Other than liquidity and diversification, are there other key advantages to owning REITs over direct real estate investment?

Zell: Let's talk about the debt markets. In July, Equity Office had a global bond offering that raised $1.4 billion dollars in 48 hours but was subscribed five to one. If an institutional investor did it at 187 over the curve, a private investor would do the exact same transaction at 350 over the curve, assuming they could get it done.

When it's all said and done, the petroleum of the real estate industry has always been capital. These vehicles have superior long range and very clear advantage in the cost of capital. Thus, public REITs have a tremendous cost of capital advantage over private real estate owners.

I think scale is also an issue. I'm sitting here in an Equity Office of a $30 billion company, which means that we can have all kinds of economies of scale, of purchasing, of management. Those economies were never available in the past, because the companies that were capable of amassing large portfolios would amass them and then manage one building at a time. They would have a massive portfolio, and they had you managing in Chicago and someone else managing in Atlanta and another local person managing in Washington D.C. The assumption had to be that there were no potential economies of scale—but I believe there are very significant economies of scale both in EQR and EOP. So because you're a public company, the scale potential has changed the rule of the possible. Nobody could have had a $30 billion portfolio as part of one company before this.

I also think talent is an issue. The classic format was the entrepreneur developer and the brother-in-law manager, but the public model is much more management focused than developer focused. The skill of getting along with the zoning board is a lot less relevant in a public company than it was when it was the entrepreneur, his brother-in-law, and somebody else building buildings. The key is managerial sophistication. For example, we're in the process of working on a succession plan for Doug Crocker at EQR.* We've been interviewing potential candidates and what we see is that

---

*Since this interview, Bruce W. Duncan has been named president of EQR.

they're all in awe of the idea of running a company of this scale, size, and quality. That means we're getting real top-notch talent managing our business, as opposed to a drift of talent away from management prior to the new evolution of the companies. At Equity Office, we run a program where we meet twice a year with our top 40 customers. We work with them and tell them what we're doing, and they tell us what they're doing. This is extraordinarily important because these people represent a big chunk of our business. When they look in the mirror and see that they're renting 3 million square feet of Equity Office, Equity Office is a serious vendor as opposed to six owners in five different locations that don't mean anything to them. Also, the fact that they can look at Equity Office's balance sheet and know exactly their capabilities really increases our creditability. It's a very different level of sophistication. Major corporations are much more comfortable having a nationwide joint venture with Equity Office than they would be with Harry So-and-so in one place and Charlie Something-else someplace else. We did 60 leases with a consulting firm. The first year it took six months, and the next six were done in two days. The clients liked the idea that they could deal with one company with no pain and no problems, negotiated and done.

Imperiale: So the paradigm of the big companies makes it much easier for them to do a broad-range real estate deal rather than negotiate it once and repeat it across the entire spectrum.

Zell: Yes. Also, in periods where employees are tough to get, the big company has the advantage of creating a sense of security, particularly after what's gone on now. Remember this generation of people being laid off are the largest and all first-timers. They've never seen this before. On the elevator the other night, one of the kids who works for me said, "You know, I think I'm the only one who's left of my friends who likes her job, and nine friends of mine have gotten laid off." This is all new for this generation. When the markets were very tight, the public company had a little advantage, but next time around it is going to have a great big advantage.

It's going to be very relevant that these people continue to prosper and take advantage of it and stepped in. There are lots of reasons for the big companies to have the advantage, some of which weren't possible any other way.

Imperiale: You've pioneered in many ways bringing some asset classes into the public real estate venue, particularly manufactured homes. You had an early vision of that asset class. In the long run, do you think there are other real estate asset classes, like timber or any others, that will come into the public arena or become more visible?

Zell: I think it's more a function of the particular management opportunities than anything else. Somebody came to me just recently and we talked about putting together a nationwide farm REIT that would own a diverse crop position and the land, so there would be an operation on a daily basis and the theoretical land appreciation. I think the only reason it hasn't been done is because there isn't anybody out there yet who has figured out a way to get it done and make it work.

I think they just did the first timber deal recently. I don't think the taxable REIT subsidiary would allow a timber deal to be a growing REIT and a slicing or sawing taxable REIT subsidiary. I don't see any reason why that wouldn't be interesting, and I suspect that there are other potential scenarios that might also work well. I think Prologis and AMB, to name two, are going to revolutionalize the warehousing business by changing the way it works by virtue of scale. So I wouldn't refute the possibility of other options at all. You know, in Brazil, they sell hotel rooms to investors. They haven't done that in the United States yet, but maybe somebody's going to go out and buy a billion dollars worth of condominiums and rent them and then turn it into a REIT. I think there's a myriad of possibilities.

Imperiale: It just takes a little imagination.

Zell: And usually it takes events. It takes something happening that creates an opportunity.

Imperiale: Can I get you to venture some brief comments on the whole real estate accounting issue? We saw the three big Wall Street firms want to go to EPS [earnings per share] and the whole debate surrounding FFO [funds from operations].

Zell: I think the industry will generally move toward dual reporting—EPS and FFO—and then you make all of the adjustments you want. But I do not believe that EPS is a clear reflection of anything in particular, other than that it's a statement. In my opinion, it's more about going through the deal using GAAP [generally accepted accounting principles] than about the results.

Imperiale: So it's more that the event is really the process.

Zell: Yes. I think FFO is a very reflective way of valuing, providing of course that there is consistency. In any deal where there are terms that aren't defined, there isn't any consistency, which forces everybody who follows FFO to fully disclose information. You may or may not agree with the capitalization of this or the application of that, but as long as there's full disclosure you can be very comfortable. I think that we're all going to report EPS.

Imperiale: Are there any other issues that you want to get on the record? I know there are so many out there, but in the context of REITs as an asset class and this whole sea change we've seen . . .

Zell: I think that the essence of the sea change is the entry of the real estate industry into the general arena, so that we as an industry, for the first time, must meet the standards of every other industry or of the market for accessing capital. Historically, our industry has had its own dedicated lenders that to a large extent have operated impervious to the rest of the economy. This has led to much steeper cycles, and I think that will always be the case. But the underlying story of this whole revolution is the real estate industry being forced to justify its capital requirements against performance in the true open market environment.

Imperiale: That was hard for a lot of people in real estate to accept.

Zell: It's not a question of accepting, it's a question of whether you had a deal. I started on the private side. I didn't join the public side until 1993. When you were borrowing 90 and 95 percent, it was all mostly nonrecourse. You had tax benefits. The private side of real estate was truly an extraordinary place for a long time.

CHAPTER 2

A Brief History of Real Estate Investment Trusts

Chapter Summary

- A real estate investment trust (REIT) is a company dedicated to owning and managing income-producing real estate, such as apartments, shopping centers, offices, and warehouses.
- REITs are legally required to pay virtually all of their net income (90 percent) to their shareholders each year in the form of dividends.
- REITs confer all the advantages and characteristics of owning real estate. In addition, REITs provide current liquidity for shareholders because their shares are freely traded on major stock exchanges. Thus, an investor can obtain all the benefits of owning real estate and enjoy complete liquidity of the investment.
- The Tax Reform Act of 1986 radically changed the investment landscape for REITs. The new laws drastically reduced the potential for real estate investment to generate tax shelter opportunities by limiting the deductibility of interest and lengthening and restricting the use of passive losses. This meant that real estate investment had to be economic and income oriented rather than tax motivated.
- When commercial property values dropped in the early 1990s, it became difficult to obtain credit and capital for commercial real estate. Many private real estate companies decided that the best

way to access capital was through the public marketplace using REITs.

There are two areas where new ideas are terribly dangerous—economics and sex.

—Felix Rohatyn, 1984

In 1960 the concept of real estate investment trusts (REITs) was a new and in many ways a bold advance. The idea was to allow groups of small investors to pool their resources to invest in large-scale, income-producing commercial property, which had historically been the domain of wealthy investors and large institutions. The enabling legislation for REITs was modeled after the registered investment company (RIC), more commonly known as a mutual fund.

A REIT begins as a simple business trust or corporation. If a number of requirements are met on a year-by-year basis, the business trust or corporation may elect to be considered a REIT for federal income tax purposes. The general requirements fall to four areas:

1. *Organizational structure.* The REIT must be organized as a business trust or corporation. More specifically, it must be managed by one or more trustees who have fiduciary duty over the management of the organization. The organization must have evidence of beneficial shares of ownership that are transferable by certificates. The beneficial ownership must be held by a minimum of 100 persons, and the five largest individual shareholders in the aggregate may not own more than 50 percent of the shares outstanding.

2. *Nature of assets.* The company's assets are primarily real estate held for long-term investment purposes. The rules require that at the end of each taxable year, at least 75 percent of the value of a REIT's total assets must be represented by real estate assets, cash, and government securities. Also, a REIT may not own nongovernment securities in an amount greater than 25 percent of the value of REIT

assets. Securities of any single issuer may not exceed 5 percent of the total value of the REIT's assets or more than 10 percent of the securities of any corporate issuer, other than taxable REIT subsidiaries.

3. *Sources of income.* At least 75 percent of the company's income is derived from real estate or real estate–related investments. A REIT must actually satisfy two income tests. First, at least 75 percent of a REIT's annual gross income must consist of real property rents, mortgage interest, gain from the sale of real estate assets, and certain other real estate–related sources. Second, at least 95 percent of a REIT's annual gross income must be derived from the income items from the preceding 75 percent test plus other passive income sources such as dividends and any type of interest.

4. *Distribution of income.* Ninety percent of net income must be distributed to shareholders. This is defined as net taxable income as determined by the Internal Revenue Code.

If the required conditions are met, a REIT may deduct all dividends paid to its shareholders and avoid federal taxation at the corporate level on the amount distributed. Thus, unlike the case for other corporations, which tend to retain most of their earnings and pay tax at the corporate level, the income tax burden for REITs is substantially shifted to the shareholder level. The REIT will only pay federal income tax on any of the 10 percent of undistributed net income it elects to retain. Unlike partnerships, REITs cannot pass losses through to their investors.

Despite the legislative intent of the REIT structure, the industry experienced a tortuous and checkered history for its first 25 years. In the early days, REITs were seriously constrained by policy limitations. REITs were mandated to be passive portfolios of real estate and were allowed only to own real estate, not to operate or manage it. This early requirement dictated that REITs needed to use third-party independent contractors to operate and manage their investment properties. This arrangement often came with built-in conflicts of interest, and the investment marketplace did not easily accept this passive paradigm.

As mentioned in Chapter 1, during these early years the real estate investment landscape was driven by tax shelter–oriented investment characteristics. Overvalued properties, coupled with the use of high debt levels, created a significant artificial basis for depreciation and interest expense. These interest and depreciation deductions were used to reduce or eliminate taxable income by creating so-called paper losses used to shelter an individual taxpayer's earned income. In an era of high marginal tax rates, the idea of using these real estate tax shelters became an industry unto itself. Investment real estate was analyzed, developed, packaged, and sold on the basis of its ability to structure and generate paper losses, which were used to shelter ordinary taxable income. This environment removed any sound economic rationale from the real estate investment equation.

Since REITs are most often geared specifically toward generating taxable income on a regular basis, and a REIT, unlike a partnership, is not permitted to pass losses through to its owners, the REIT industry simply could not compete effectively for investment capital against tax shelters. And the idea of receiving regular income from an investment was not usually considered favorable unless there were losses available to offset that income, because most individual investors were subject to high marginal tax rates.

The REIT industry has suffered some debacles that resulted from the tax environment of the early years. Because of the inability to pass losses through, many REITs focused on making mortgages of various types during the tax-motivated era in real estate. A large number of mortgage REITs made loans to builders and developers who in turn developed property that was intended for use as tax shelters. When interest rates rose to double-digit levels in the mid-1970s, many mortgage REITs were unable to access capital and collapsed, leaving the REIT industry with a bad reputation. The bankruptcies included many REITs that were associated with large, well-known (and allegedly conservative) financial institutions.

The tax-motivated environment also led to the creation of finite-life real estate investment trusts (FREITs). The idea behind these was to create a type of REIT that would liquidate its property portfolio (assumably for a large gain) at some certain time in the future. The FREIT would then use a very high degree of leverage to buy properties. The high interest expense would substantially reduce the REIT's current income available for distribution. Then the portfolio would be liquidated and the capital gains would be distributed to shareholders. Most FREITs were not able to liquidate their holdings for any meaningful gain. In fact, most lost all the equity of the shareholders.

Perhaps the most infamous aspect of REIT history is the story of the paired-share and stapled REITs, which were also born in the era of tax-motivated investing. For a more detailed discussion, see Chapter 10.

With the Tax Reform Act of 1986, Congress changed the entire dynamic of the real estate investment landscape. By limiting the deductibility of interest, lengthening depreciation periods, and restricting the use of passive losses, the 1986 Act drastically reduced the potential for real estate investment to generate tax shelter opportunities. This policy change at the legislative level meant that the new dynamic in real estate investment needed to be on a more economic and income-oriented footing. More importantly, as part of the 1986 Act, Congress also modified a significant policy constraint that had been imposed on REITs at the beginning. The new legislation modified the passive aspects of the original REIT rules. The change permitted REITs not simply to own, but also to operate and manage most types of income-producing commercial properties by providing "customary" services associated with real estate ownership. This new legislation finally allowed the economic interests of the REIT's shareholders to be merged with those of its operators and managers. The change applied to most types of real estate other than hotels, health care facilities, and some other businesses that provide a high degree of personal service.

The results of the new legislation in 1986 set the stage for significant growth of REITs as an asset class. From a policy standpoint, the new legislation achieved three important milestones:

1. It eliminated the artificial tax-motivated capital flows to the real estate sector that skewed the investment rationale and distorted the economic basis for real estate activities.

2. It eliminated any artificial bias in the formation of capital by applying uniform policy guidelines to all real estate,

thereby leveling the playing field for all participants in the real estate capital market.

3. It eliminated the inherent conflict of interest that kept REIT property owners from managing their own portfolio holdings, thus removing one of the key public market objections to the REIT structure.

Suddenly, dispassionate, rational economic operation returned to the world of real estate.

The New REIT Era

The Tax Reform Act of 1986 dramatically realigned the economic and legislative policy forces that shape the real estate markets. The new economics of real estate and the positive changes to the REIT format set the stage for the modern era of the REIT. But, as with any new market dynamic, it took time for the market participants to analyze and understand the new market forces. In addition, the excesses of the old real estate markets needed to be cured.

The aftermath of the change in tax policy was the real estate recession of the early 1990s. Until the late 1980s, banks and insurance companies continued real estate lending at a significant pace. Foreign investment in U.S. real estate, particularly from Japan, also continued to distort the market dynamics in the late 1980s.

By 1990, the combined impact of the savings and loan (S&L) crisis, the 1986 Act, overbuilding during the 1980s by non-REITs, and regulatory pressures on bank and insurance lenders led to a nationwide recession in the real estate economy. During the early 1990s, commercial property values dropped between 30 and 50 percent. Market conditions largely impeded the availability of credit and capital for commercial real estate. As a result of the recession and the ensuing capital crunch, many real estate borrowers defaulted on loans. The resulting losses by financial institutions triggered the S&L crisis and created a huge expense for the federal government. In order to maintain confidence in the banking system, the Federal Deposit Insurance Corporation (FDIC) undertook a massive bailout of the nearly bankrupt

S&L system. Under government oversight, many insolvent S&Ls were forced to merge with stronger, better-capitalized S&Ls. In order to induce this consolidation, the government guaranteed the financial performance of the insolvent S&Ls. In many other cases, insolvent S&Ls were liquidated with government oversight. The massive restructuring of the S&L system flooded the market with nonperforming real estate assets during the late 1980s. This major dislocation of the real estate markets exacerbated the decline in commercial property values during the early 1990s.

The real estate market excesses of the 1980s began to fade by the early 1990s. A higher standard was now required of real estate lenders. Market participants were no longer artificially motivated by tax policy to invest in real estate. This marked the starting point for what is considered by most industry observers to be the modern era of REITs. Starting in November 1991 against this backdrop, many private real estate companies decided that it might be more efficient to access capital from the public marketplace utilizing REITs. At the same time, many investors, realizing that recovering real estate markets were just over the horizon, decided that it was potentially a good time to invest in commercial real estate. This has led to fairly stable, long, sustained growth in the REIT asset class.

Since 1992, many new publicly traded REITs have infused much needed equity capital into the overleveraged real estate industry. As of December 31, 2001, there were over 200 publicly traded REITs and real estate operating companies, with an equity market capitalization exceeding $180 billion. This compares with $16.4 billion of market capitalization at the start of 1992. The dramatic growth can be seen in Figure 2.1.

Today, REITs are essentially owned by individuals, with 50 percent of REIT shares owned directly by individual investors. In addition, 38 percent of REIT shares are owned by mutual funds, whose shares are in turn primarily owned by individual investors. But REITs certainly do not just benefit individual investors, nor should they be considered as investments only suited for retail-type individual investors.

The debt levels associated with new-era REITs are lower than those associated with overall real estate investment. This has had

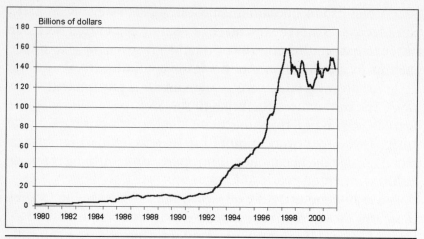

FIGURE 2.1 Equity Capitalization of REITs (Source: NAREIT)

a positive effect on the stability of the REIT asset class. Average debt levels for REITs are typically 45 to 55 percent of market capitalization, as compared to leverage of 75 percent and often higher when real estate is privately owned. The higher equity capital level of REITs helps to cushion them from the negative effects of the cyclical fluctuations in the real estate market that have historically occurred. The ability of REITs to better withstand market downturns creates a stabilizing effect on the real estate industry and its lenders, resulting in fewer bankruptcies and loan defaults. Consequently, the general real estate industry has benefited from reduced real estate losses and more consistent investment returns. This has helped real estate regain credibility with the investing public. In addition, it has fostered continued capital flows to the REIT sector and real estate in general.

REITs currently own approximately $270 billion of commercial real estate. This represents less than 10 percent of the estimated $3 trillion of institutional-quality U.S. domestic real estate. Consistent with the public policy underlying the REIT rules, many industry observers believe that the trend over time will continue to show the U.S. commercial real estate economy moving toward more and more ownership by REITs and publicly traded real estate operating companies. This public securitization of real estate is the hallmark of the new REIT era. With the current trend in place, there are very few reasons to believe that the growth in public real estate will not continue.

The 1986 Act effectively married REIT management to REIT assets, and the Taxpayer Relief Act of 1997 included additional helpful REIT reforms, but members of the REIT industry still believed they were required to operate under limitations that increasingly made them noncompetitive in the emerging customer-oriented real estate marketplace. They believed that the real estate industry, like other major businesses in the United States in the 1990s, was rapidly evolving into a customer-oriented service business. REIT landlords that provide new services to their tenants only after such services have become "usual and customary" risk losing their competitive edge in attracting and retaining top-quality tenants. But regulations restricted what services REITs could offer. As REITs grow larger, they automatically affect what services are considered customary in a geographic locale. Under the old rules, some services might never be considered customary because REITs are prevented from providing leading-edge services. Businesses have also discovered that providing ancillary services with good quality control produces customer loyalty. Under the law as it existed, a REIT was required to use independent contractors to provide noncustomary services to its tenants, so REIT management had little control over the quality of the services rendered by the independent contractor to the REIT's tenants. Income from these potential revenue-producing opportunities would accrue to the benefit of a third party, not to the REIT's shareholders.

The ability to provide potential new services to tenants would have three key benefits for the competitive posture of REITs within the real estate industry:

1. The availability of the new service to the tenant would generate greater customer loyalty and allow the REIT landlord to remain competitive with non-REIT owners that had no limitation on the type of services they could offer.

2. The new services (offered either by the landlord or by a third party licensed by the landlord) could generate an additional stream of income for the REIT shareholders.

3. The REIT management could maintain better quality controls over the services rendered to its tenants.

Over the last decade, new-era REITs have performed services for their tenants so well that third parties began to retain REITs for that purpose. The original REIT legislation contemplated that REITs could earn up to 5 percent of their income from sources other than rents, capital gains, dividends, and interest. However, many REITs were now being presented with the opportunity to maximize shareholder value by earning more than 5 percent from managing joint ventures with service providers and from selling other third-party services.

Prior to the most recent changes in REIT rules, many REITs invested in non-REIT C corporations to capture part of this income flow. These corporations provided to unrelated parties services that were already being delivered to a REIT's tenants, such as landscaping or the management of a shopping mall in which the REIT owned a joint venture interest. These arrangements often involved the use of a REIT's management personnel and were often constructed in very complex ways in order to maintain REIT status.

The industry argued that these rules were too restrictive and put REIT operators (and their shareholders) at a distinct disadvantage against non-REIT operators in the industry. At the time, the REIT asset rules were patterned after the asset diversification rules applicable to mutual funds. Under those rules, a REIT could not own more than 10 percent of the voting securities of another company (other than a "qualified REIT subsidiary" or another REIT), and the securities of another company could not exceed 5 percent of the value of a REIT's total assets.

In response to these constraints, Congress enacted the REIT Modernization Act (RMA) in late 1999. The centerpiece of this legislation was the creation of rules and guidelines for taxable REIT subsidiaries (TRSs). The legislation allows a REIT to own 100 percent of the stock of a company know as a TRS. The TRS can provide services to REIT tenants and third parties within certain limitations without jeopardizing the REIT status of the parent. The limitations contained in the TRS rules provide for size limits on TRSs to ensure that REITs continue to focus on property ownership and operation. The key provisions are that the TRS may not exceed 20 percent of a REIT's assets and the amount of debt and rental payments from a TRS to its affiliated REIT are limited. The TRS rules and a series of minor technical adjustments to the old rules should allow REITs to enjoy the same advantages and benefits of service and operating strategies that non-REIT real estate competitors may employ.

These legislative initiatives, along with the steady growth in REIT assets, have not gone unnoticed by the institutional investment community. Modern-era REITs now have sufficient size and history to be considered a viable alternative to direct real estate investments. Institutional investors have also acknowledged the advantage of the liquidity characteristic that REITs bring to the real estate asset class. In the next chapter we will explore the modern REIT as an independent asset class and the impact of REITs in a multiasset portfolio.

REITs as an Asset Class

Chapter Summary

- In the public market there are about 180 publicly traded real estate investment trusts (REITs) that deal with office, industrial, apartment, shopping center, regional mall, hotel, health care, and specialty properties. Their holdings include some of the finest properties in America, such as Mall of America in Minneapolis and the Embarcadero Center in San Francisco.

- Because real estate values are driven by local supply and demand factors, REITs allow an investor to isolate property categories and local market conditions that are improving while avoiding markets and properties that are deteriorating.

- It is possible to gain investment exposure to most regional markets or major cities and property categories within those areas simply by investing in REITs.

- Because local supply and demand factors drive the performance of specific REITs, REITs generally behave more as a function of local market conditions and less as a function of the stock and bond markets.

- Because REITs have a low correlation to both stocks and bonds, they provide additional diversification to an investment portfolio.

The best investment on earth is earth.

—Louis Glickman, 1957

Behind bonds and stocks, real estate is the third-largest asset class available to investors. It is estimated that there is $6.2 trillion of commercial real estate in the United States. *Commercial real estate* is described as all nonpublic real estate excluding one through four family homes and owner-occupied farms. Institutional-quality real estate—the real estate large enough for institutional buyer to consider purchasing—is estimated to be worth $3 trillion, or approximately half the value of the commercial real estate universe. Real estate investment trusts (REITs) and real estate operating companies (REOCs) own and operate approximately $270 billion worth of institutional-quality investment real estate, or roughly 10 percent of the total.

As discussed in Chapter 1, real estate is an asset class that has provided institutional investors with many positive attributes over time. Real estate investment trusts are competitors with other institutional investors in the real estate market. They pool the financial resources of a large number of investors for the specific purpose of investing in real estate. In many ways, a REIT is like a mutual fund, except that it invests in real estate. As discussed in Chapter 2, companies that meet certain requirements can qualify as REITs and avoid federal taxation on all net income that is distributed as dividends to their shareholders.

REITs that directly own real estate share the principal investment benefits of real estate ownership that all other institutional real estate owners enjoy. The three key investment benefits provided by most real estate are:

1. *Cash flow.* Consistent and predictable cash flow generated from rents paid is an attractive benefit of the real estate asset class.

2. *Inflation hedging.* Real estate tends to act as a hedge against inflation, increasing in value at a rate faster than inflation over the long term.

3. *Portfolio diversification.* The independent local market nature of real estate causes it to produce returns that behave very independently from both stocks and bonds. This low correlation of return provides an added diversification benefit when real estate is added to a multiasset portfolio.

Real estate is also subject to some potentially negative qualities. As discussed in Chapter 1, here is a brief summary of these negative attributes:

1. *Real estate lacks liquidity.* Because the process of buying and selling real estate is negotiated directly between buyers and sellers in local markets and often involves financing arrangements, transactions can be long and involved. Six months to a year is not an uncommon transaction time.

2. *Real estate's performance is difficult to measure.* Because real estate values are determined upon sale, it is difficult to calculate performance of a real estate portfolio prior to the sale of the properties.

3. *Real estate cannot be moved.* With few exceptions, such as mobile homes, it is not feasible to relocate existing real estate to markets where demand is better or supply is constrained.

4. *Real estate is unique.* The physical attributes of a building and its location are unique to that building. This can have both positive and negative aspects when dealing with a specific piece of real estate.

5. *Real estate is subject to externalities.* Events or activities beyond the control of the property owner affect (for good or bad) the value of a property.

As stated before, real estate is also subject to some *potentially* negative qualities. The emphasis on the word *potentially* is added because, as a substitute for the direct ownership of real estate, the unique characteristics of REITs solve some of these problems. In addition, the remaining potential problems can be effectively managed in the REIT format. These benefits give REITs a series of distinctive qualities that make them in many ways superior to direct real estate investment.

The biggest issue solved by the REIT asset class is that of liquidity. Unlike direct real estate investments, REITs are generally public companies. They trade on major stock exchanges such as the New York Stock Exchange and the American Stock Exchange as well as on the NASDAQ and over-the-counter markets. The dramatic growth in the number of publicly traded

REITs and the related growth in public equity market capitalization, as seen in Figure 2.1, have converged to make the liquidity benefit of REITs a major differentiating factor for the asset
class. As seen in Figure 3.1, the average daily trading volume in
REITs exceeds $400 million. The public markets have provided
between $300 million and $500 million of daily liquidity since
1996. When compared to a six-month liquidity window for direct
real estate investment, the advantage of daily liquidity becomes
apparent.

The liquidity advantage becomes a useful tool for the REIT
investor under a number of different circumstances. The daily
liquidity of REITs allows an investor to move into or out of a
property category such as apartments. This can be useful to the
institutional investor that wants to diversify an existing portfolio
of direct real estate investments. For example, an institution that
directly owns an interest in a portfolio of shopping centers can
easily add apartments, industrial buildings, or other property sectors that are represented by REITs trading in the public markets.
This ability to "tilt" the sector exposure of a direct real estate
portfolio by adding REITs to a real estate allocation is an area of
growing interest for institutional real estate investors.

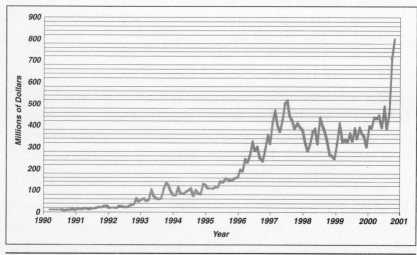

FIGURE 3.1 Monthly Average Daily Trading Volume of REITs
(Source: NAREIT)

The liquidity advantage of REITs extends in the same way to the geographic diversification of a direct real estate portfolio. As mentioned, the physical attributes of real estate preclude moving property from a local market where demand is falling or supply is in excess to a location where supply and demand characteristics are better. However, REITs provide the direct property owner with the option of diversifying a portfolio by geography. By simply adding REITs with exposure in other geographic regions, additional geographic diversification can be achieved. For example, an institution that directly owns an interest in a diversified portfolio of investment real estate in the Chicago area can add property in other locations, such as California or New York City, by adding to the portfolio REITs that have property holdings in those geographic markets. This ability to tilt the geographic exposure of a direct real estate portfolio by adding REITs to a real estate allocation allows direct real estate investors to gain exposure in locations that have better fundamental supply and demand characteristics than those in their current portfolio.

When applied to a portfolio made up exclusively of REITs, the liquidity advantage of REITs becomes even more pronounced. A pure REIT portfolio can largely eliminate the liquidity issue involved with direct real estate investments, while retaining the positive attributes of cash flow, creating an inflation hedge, and providing the additional portfolio diversification of similar direct real estate investments. In addition, the liquidity advantage of REITs allows an investor to easily add sector tilt or geographic tilt within a portfolio of REITs. The ability to migrate easily between geographic regions and property categories should not be underestimated.

Over time the property types and geographic regions most favored by direct institutional investors have shifted. These shifts are often dictated by changes in supply and demand, which are driven by local market events and macroeconomic trends. During the 1970s, regional malls were highly sought after by direct institutional investors. But in the late 1970s growth in retail sales began to fall behind the rate of inflation and the general economy began to enter a recession in 1979. This resulted in regional malls falling out of favor with direct institutional investors. Office buildings went through a similar cycle during the 1980s. Similar local market and macroeconomic trends related to the Internet revolution made San Jose and the San Francisco Bay area a highly regarded and popular geographic region for direct real estate investors during the second half of the 1990s. The collapse of the dot-com economy during 2000 resulted in a change in investor sentiment toward the region and a corresponding change in the valuation levels of properties within the region.

The ability to migrate easily between geographic regions and property categories can allow the REIT investor to capitalize on the shifts in property types and geographic regions that are the result of local market events and macroeconomic trends. The direct institutional investor can make similar portfolio changes; however, the lack of liquidity and the high frictional cost of making those changes often preclude an active management style at the direct investment level. For a few cents per share, a REIT investor can actively change geographic or property exposures with a phone call to a brokerage firm. Chapter 6 will create a framework for the geographic and sector decision-making process that supports such real estate portfolio changes.

The measurement of period-to-period performance in a direct real estate portfolio is difficult. Information about specific real estate market performance is harder and more expensive to obtain than that about the performance of stocks and bonds. Because real estate values are determined upon sale, the only way to know the true performance of a direct real estate investment is to calculate it at the time of sale of the portfolio or a particular property within the portfolio.

Data for developing performance measures over shorter periods in the direct portfolio, such as quarterly or annual returns, is often the result of estimates. These estimates are often based on capitalization rates derived from examining sales of similar properties in the local market. When used prudently, these estimates can help assess the performance of a direct real estate portfolio, but they tend to smooth out the fluctuations that might be observed in the actual values. Thus, the estimate approach tends to understate the measurement of risk or the standard deviation of returns. The true performance results will only really be known at the time of sale.

Because of the long-term policy mandates of many institutional portfolios, a periodic estimate of value in the real estate allocation is often sufficient for fiduciary purposes. However, the real performance measurement problem begins to surface when a fiduciary must assess how a particular real estate portfolio is doing relative to other real estate portfolios. Because other direct real estate portfolios are subject to the same estimate bias, it is not possible to rank the performance of a given portfolio until the portfolios in question have been liquidated. This makes the assessment of relative portfolio performance particularly difficult.

By contrast, REITs pose far fewer performance measurement issues. Because REITs and related securities trade like stocks, it is relatively simple to calculate the periodic investment returns. In addition, the same periodic pricing data can be used to calculate risk or standard deviation of returns for any given period. The readily available pricing data makes the calculation of periodic performance and portfolio risk a simple matter in a portfolio comprised of REITs and REOCs.

The assessment of relative portfolio performance is also readily available for the REIT investor. There are a large number of real estate securities indexes that are generally available through various sources on a daily real-time basis. These indexes, which are described in more detail later in this chapter, are typically unmanaged or passive in construction and are composed of broad-based aggregates of REITs and REOCs. Some also include real estate service companies. When used as an appropriate benchmark, these indexes can help in assessing the performance of a REIT portfolio or its manager.

In addition, there are over 70 funds that invest specifically in REITs or more generally in the real estate sector. These funds are listed in the appendix. Performance data on these funds is widely available in various publications such as *The Wall Street Journal* or through mutual fund rating services such as Morningstar and Weissenberger's. The performance data from these funds can also be used to make comparative measurements of the performance of actively managed real estate securities portfolios. The fund companies themselves can also be a source of additional performance-related data, including operating expenses and comparative portfolio characteristics.

The unique positive characteristics of the REIT asset class help it overcome the liquidity and performance issues related to direct real estate investment. As discussed, the liquidity advantage also mitigates the negative issues regarding the fixed physical nature of property. Thus the issues of uniqueness and externalities remain. These issues can have both good and bad aspects. Like any real estate investor, the REIT investor can attempt to manage the risks of uniqueness and employ strategies to defend against and monitor possible externalities.

The physical attributes of a building and its location that are unique to that building can have both positive and negative aspects when dealing with a specific piece of real estate. Some buildings are built with very specific objectives in mind. When given the right mix of circumstances, this can justify a higher expected return from a given real estate project. Conversely, the wrong mix of circumstances can quickly create an underperforming asset. For example, a Wal-Mart store is physically a very specific type of real estate project. That said, owning a portfolio of Wal-Mart stores that are leased on a long-term basis to Wal-Mart might be a good investment. The credit quality of Wal-Mart helps to overcome the specific physical limitations of the actual real estate. Conversely, owning a portfolio of industrial warehouses that were designed and built specifically to accommodate the Internet grocer Web Van might not be as appealing. The credit quality of Web Van is likely not sufficient to overcome the negative attributes of the physical real estate. The various aspects of managing these types of physical issues are discussed in detail in Section 3, which deals specifically with each property category available in the public REIT format.

Externalities are a group of risk factors that are difficult to manage. An *externality* is an activity or event that affects (positively or negatively) something that is external to the activity. The fact that they are external to the activity makes the management of externalities a defensive process, because the causal agent is external and beyond the control of the affected items.

The best defense against externalities in real estate is location. The externalities that will negatively affect a class A high-rise office building on Park Avenue in New York City are far fewer than those that could affect a class B office building at a little-known intersection in suburban Cleveland. The highest and best use doctrine will likely prevent a garbage dump or chemical factory from appearing in Manhattan, but this may not be the case in Cleveland. These risk factors are discussed at more length at the property-specific level in each chapter of Section 3. The old real estate adage, "Location, location, location," is a key factor when anticipating external effects.

REITs have a particular type of risk that is less of a factor in the direct real estate sector. *Systematic risk* or *market risk* is a form of risk that the direct real estate investor never encounters. This market risk affects REITs because they are part of a group of companies within a larger asset market known as the stock market or the public capital markets. Events that may be completely unrelated to REITs or the local real estate markets in which they operate can have a negative (or positive) affect on the value of publicly traded REIT shares. For example, the unexpected default of Russian government bonds in 1998 caused a severe dislocation in the world capital markets. This resulted in a sharp decline in stock prices across global markets, including a decline in the market price of REIT shares. Although the default may have had some negative implications for the price of real estate in general, the direct real estate investor did not suffer the immediate market price decline that impacted REIT shares. It could be argued that systematic risk is an externality in real estate that is specific to publicly traded REIT shares.

Public Market Real Estate Indexes

There are a large number of real estate securities indexes that are generally available through various sources on a daily real-time basis. These indexes are typically unmanaged or passive in construction and are composed of broad-based aggregates of REITs and REOCs. Some also include real estate service companies and a large number of REOCs. The following is a brief description of the major public market real estate indexes.

The National Association of Real Estate Investment Trusts (NAREIT) is the primary trade association for REITs. It is recognized as the leading public resource on the REIT industry and has performance data on REITs extending back to 1972. The organization compiles and publishes a group of indexes that are composed exclusively of publicly traded REITs. They are as follows:

- *The NAREIT Index.* This is NAREIT's index of all publicly traded REITs. It is the best known and most referenced index of REIT performance. It is the broadest pure REIT index because it includes all publicly traded REITs in relative market weightings. This index is available on a real-time basis. It rebalances on a monthly basis for new and merged REITs and new issuance of equity by existing REITs.

- *The NAREIT Equity Index.* This is the same as the NAREIT Index, except that it excludes mortgage REITs to reflect a pure equity real estate benchmark. This index is available on a real-time basis. It rebalances on a monthly basis for new and merged REITs and new issuance of equity by existing REITs.

- *The NAREIT 50 Index.* This is an index of the 50 largest publicly traded REITs. It is a benchmark more suited to the institutional investor because of the liquidity issues surrounding smaller-capitalization REITs. This index is available on a real-time basis. It rebalances on a monthly basis for new and merged REITs and new issuance of equity by existing REITs.

- *The NAREIT Mortgage Index.* This is an index of all publicly traded mortgage REITs. This index is available on a real-time basis. It rebalances on a monthly basis for new and merged REITs and new issuance of equity by existing REITs.

Other financial organizations also track and publish statistics on REITs and publicly traded real estate securities. They are as follows:

- *The S&P REIT Composite Index.* This index comprises 100 REITs, including mortgage REITs. It covers approximately 75 percent of REIT market capitalization. This index requires high-quality financial fundamentals, good liquidity, and strong earnings and dividend growth as characteristics for inclusion.

It is reweighted on a quarterly basis, and returns are computed on a daily basis.

- *The Morgan Stanley REIT Index.* This is a tradable real-time market index. It is constructed by Morgan Stanley and is tradable on the American Stock Exchange. This index has a laundry list of inclusion requirements, such as minimum market capitalization, shares outstanding, trading volume, and share price. To be included, a REIT must have a six-month trading history and must be listed on a major exchange. This index is rebalanced quarterly and does not include mortgage or health care REITs. Its ticker symbol on the AMEX is RMS.

- *The Wilshire Real Estate Securities Index.* This index is composed of REITs and REOCs. The composition is determined on a monthly basis by Wilshire Associates. This index includes hotel operating companies and development and home-building companies. It does not include specialty, health care, or mortgage REITs. Wilshire publishes returns on a monthly basis, with details available on a subscription basis. There is no real-time information available on this index.

The public market real estate indexes are primarily derived from the approximately 190 publicly traded REITs and other REOCs that invest primarily in real estate but for various reasons have not elected REIT status. As seen in Figure 3.2, Equity REITs and REOCs provide investment opportunities in all property types. The large number of publicly traded REITs provides real estate exposure in most major geographic regions. Table 3.1 describes the distribution of properties owned by publicly traded REITs by geographic region and property type.

It comes as no surprise that the distribution of REIT assets is skewed toward the largest major metropolitan markets. In fact, about 50 percent of public REIT property holdings are in the top 25 metropolitan markets. This gives the REIT investor the potential to diversify widely by geographic location and to focus on major markets with the most favorable supply and demand characteristics.

These local supply and demand factors tend to drive the performance of specific REITs. Performance is generally more of a

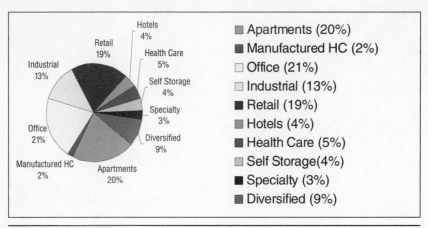

FIGURE 3.2 Distribution of REITs By Property Type as of December 31, 2001 (Source: NAREIT)

function of local market conditions and less a function of the stock and bond markets. Because REITs have a low correlation to both stocks and bonds, they provide additional diversification to an investment portfolio. It is this diversification benefit as it fits into the framework of modern portfolio theory that REITs provide in a multi-asset-class portfolio. In the next chapter we will examine these aspects of the REIT asset class.

Interview with Michael Grupe

Michael Grupe is senior vice president of research and investment affairs at NAREIT.

Rick Imperiale: Tell us about NAREIT, the history of the organization, and your history at NAREIT.

Michael Grupe: Well, the first thing to note would be that NAREIT was created in 1960, when the law that created the REIT structure under the tax code was enacted. So the association for the industry has been around as long as the industry. At that time, the intent of Congress was to provide an opportunity for small investors to participate in the economic returns of real estate investing that had been available to wealthy individuals, families, institutions, partnerships,

TABLE 3.1 REIT Property Distribution by Geographic Region as of 09/30/2001

Region	Residential Units	Retail ft²	Office ft²	Industrial ft²	Hotel Rooms	Health Care Rooms
Pacific	8%	17%	21%	22%	17%	11%
Mountain	4%	19%	5%	5%	11%	8%
West North Central	7%	3%	1%	1%	7%	7%
East North Central	23%	6%	16%	34%	10%	7%
Southwest	20%	11%	18%	16%	3%	25%
Southeast	16%	24%	12%	12%	16%	20%
Mideast	7%	13%	17%	6%	14%	9%
Northeast	14%	6%	9%	2%	22%	14%
Total*	100%	100%	100%	100%	100%	100%

Region 1—Pacific	Region 2—Mountain	Region 3—West North Central
Alaska	Arizona	Iowa
California	Colorado	Kansas
Hawaii	Idaho	Minnesota
Oregon	Montana	Missouri
Washington	Nevada	Nebraska
	Utah	North Dakota
	Wyoming	South Dakota

(continued)

47

TABLE 3.1 *Continued*

Region 4—East North Central	Region 5—Southwest	Region 6—Southeast
Illinois	Arkansas	Alabama
Indiana	Louisiana	Florida
Michigan	Oklahoma	Georgia
Ohio	Texas	Mississippi
Wisconsin		North Carolina
		South Carolina
		Tennessee

Region 7—Mideast	Region 8—Northeast
Delaware	Connecticut
District of Columbia	Maine
Kentucky	Massachusetts
Maryland	New Hampshire
Virginia	New Jersey
West Virginia	New York
	Pennsylvania
	Rhode Island
	Vermont

*May not total 100% due to rounding.

Source: Uniplan Consulting, LLC, and Uniplan Real Estate Advisors, Inc., "The Geographic Distribution of REIT Property Holdings—2001."

and so on for a long time. That was very clearly articulated in the legislation. We actually have a slide show available at our Web site www.NAREIT.com that details some of the history of the industry, including quotes from the legislation.

Imperiale: So, the original intent was to give smaller investors an opportunity to become involved in real estate as an asset class. Institutional investors have known the benefits of real estate for a long time, and one thing we've noticed was that early on, there were some structural issues with REITs that made them a little less investor friendly than they are now.

Grupe: Yes. On our Web site we have a chart book that we update every month and that can be downloaded. One of the charts is a history of the total equity market capitalization of the industry. If you look at that, it becomes very apparent that something happened beginning in 1993. For most of the period from 1960 through the early 1990s, there was very little growth, and the line for the total market cap just bounces along, not much above zero. For the first 30 to 35 years of our history, there wasn't much going on, so the questions that arise are what changed and why. There are a number of factors to explain what was happening. First, when the tax law was changed to allow for REITs, the model that was created was intended to follow the outlines of the Investment Company Act of 1940.

Imperiale: Which would cover mutual funds.

Grupe: Yes. But one of the notable characteristics of mutual funds is that they're structured in a sense as pass-through vehicles, and part of that character is that they're relatively passive investment vehicles. That same kind of passive nature was imposed on the REIT code, and it prohibited the companies from both owning and operating their properties. They could own the properties, but they were required to hire the services of an outside third-party operator to come in and manage the tenant relationships and the performance of the properties and things like that. As you might imagine, that kind of structure created the potential for significant conflicts of interest between the owners and the operators of the properties. That built-in conflict was never particularly popular with Wall Street or the investment community and tended to place a damper on the appeal of electing to operate as a REIT.

Another factor is that REITs are basically intended as vehicles for raising equity. A REIT is chartered as a business trust or a corporation like any other publicly traded company, and it elects either to operate as a REIT or not operate as a REIT. That is simply a tax election. Since a REIT has the same structure as a typical publicly traded corporation, it should be able to go out to the public and raise equity. But for most of the history of commercial real estate in the United States, properties were financed almost entirely with debt, not equity. The amount of leverage on commercial properties was very large, and there probably are a number of reasons for that. One is from a cash flow perspective. You could look at the rental income being generated by the property as being a fairly stable and dependable source of income that could be passed through the ownership structure to cover the debt service payments or the interest payments on the debt that helped finance acquisition of the properties. In many practical respects, there was a true cash flow matching situation there. The second reason was that, like the real estate taxes, all of the interest payments on the debt would be tax deductible.

Imperiale: So there were some tax motivations that went hand in hand with the structure?

Grupe: That's right. But also, as with our property finance system as a whole, a lot of this debt that was used to finance the acquisitions of these properties was secured debt. These were commercial mortgages. This is not like general corporate liabilities. This is actually secured by these properties, and there's a one-to-one relationship here, so carrying a relatively high level of debt on the property is not out of the ordinary. But when you add up all those aspects, it makes for a relatively favorable environment for financing primarily with debt rather than equity, which dampened the appeal of an equity vehicle. Then the third most important reason there was so much leverage on commercial properties was the fact that properties for many years were owned primarily through a variety of closely held and private structures. One of those, of course, was the partnership structure. One of the disadvantages of operating as a REIT compared to operating as a partnership is that partnerships, through the late 1980s, could pass losses through to the limited partners, and those passive losses could then be used to offset or to deduct from other sources of active income.

Imperiale: Other than real estate income.

Grupe: So there was that tax shelter aspect, which created a noneconomic incentive to invest through limited partnerships. The incentive was that you didn't really care if the demographics, the economics, and the supply and demand characteristics for space argued that you supply additional space to the market or not. All you wanted to do was create the property that would then generate real estate taxes and depreciation and perhaps some interest expense. All of those deductions, if there were not offsetting revenues, would simply generate losses. Those losses could then be passed through to limited partners, who could dump that on their 1040 and reduce their other taxable income. But REITs cannot pass losses through. So you had this unfair playing field where REITs were at a disadvantage because they essentially had to make their investment decisions on a solid economic basis. The other competing vehicles could ignore that.

There were a number of changes made over the years. One change, as part of the 1986 Tax Reform Act, was that the tax advantages of the partnerships were eliminated, so you could continue to operate a partnership but you could not use the losses from that to offset other sources of active income. So that competition disappeared. Congress also changed the law to allow most REITs to both own and manage their properties, so the requirement to go out and hire an external third-party property manager was eliminated. That brought a better alignment between the interests of the owners and the interests of the operators.

Then, as a result of the huge amounts of real estate investment that took place in the mid- to late 1980s, we had this huge excess supply of space by the end of the 1980s and the early 1990s. We had five or six years' worth of supply. As a result, there were what we called "see-through buildings." Those buildings had no tenants, they were generating no income, they were creating significant losses. As a result, the four primary sources of capital—the pension funds, the insurance companies, the commercial banks, and the savings and loans—completely pulled away from the market. Because that commercial property was heavily leveraged and heavily financed with debt, a lot of that debt was coming due. That debt was still maturing and rolling over, and in many cases needed to be refinanced. If they weren't going bankrupt, property owners were being forced to the brink of bankruptcy. The market was sending signals that the total amount of leverage on commercial real estate needed to be reduced and replaced with more equity, and that there needed to be a more balanced capital structure in the industry. Those four primary sources of debt were saying, "We're not going to refinance these outstanding debts, we're certainly not going to refinance them at the terms that we were lending originally, and so you property owners have two choices. You can either find equity someplace and repay our loans, or you can give us your properties." So the market, in its infinite wisdom, was sending out this signal that the old way of doing business in commercial real estate was no longer acceptable, that some major structural changes needed to be made. There had been some other changes to traditional forms of financing and to the tax code, the REIT tax code, and so on, that made the REIT choice much more appealing. Beginning in 1993, what began to happen was that property owners who still were solvent and still had equity in their portfolios began to reorganize their operations in the form of REITs, take their companies public, raise significant amounts of equity, and reduce the leverage on their properties and pay down the debt.

So the three basic pre-1993 problems were either eliminated or reduced, and that changed the economic landscape
to make equity financing or equity vehicles far more appealing and attractive. There was one other factor that helped to
provide liquidity for this whole process, and that was the
creation and introduction of the UPREIT [umbrella partnership REIT]. That created a mechanism whereby owners
that had owned properties for a long period of time and had
a sufficiently depreciated cost basis could hand over their
properties to a partnership in which REIT is the covenantal
partner in exchange for what are called OP [operating part-
nership] units. Through that process, they could avoid having the transaction treated as a sale of assets, which would
trigger the tax liability based on the capital gain, which
would be huge.

Imperiale: So they could defer this taxable event by virtue of the
new structure?

Grupe: Right. The ownership of properties could be transferred
from private partnerships and other ownership structures
to a REIT without generating tax liability.

Imperiale: So those factors coalescing in the early 1990s created
the new era for the REIT?

Grupe: Correct. Another thing that I think is worthwhile pointing
out is that while the market was making room for a publicly
traded vehicle to generate equity, the same thing was happening on the debt side through the CMBS [commercial
mortgage–backed securities] market. Again, there was a
need to restructure significant parts of the industry, to
develop new markets and new pricing mechanisms for debt,
and to be able to significantly expand the market for commercial real estate debt financing. The bankers looked at our
experience in the residential mortgage–backed securities
market and said, "Let's do the same thing on the commercial
side that we've been pretty successful at on the residential
side." We began to take what had been a privately owned,
privately financed industry and change over to a public paradigm, where we would raise debt in public markets on the
CMBS market and equity through public real estate companies, many of which elected to operate as REITs.

Imperiale: So those market changes helped the total capitalization of the REIT sector begin to grow in the early 1990s, and that impressive growth continued throughout the 1990s.

Grupe: It continued until the end of 1997, and since then it's been kind of bouncing around $130 billion to $150 billion.

Imperiale: Why is that? Do you see another leg of growth to this whole arena and asset class?

Grupe: Yes, but I can't tell you when or how it's going to develop. My sense is that it's a reflection of how our economy works. There are some very powerful forces in our open market—open access, open information, free markets that force companies and industries to continually look for more efficient methods of operation. I would argue that what has been happening in real estate in the last 10 years is not unlike the kind of repositioning we're going through right now in our health care delivery system. Medical practices, hospitals, and research institutes have been basically privately owned and privately financed. But it became pretty apparent in the 1980s that the costs of delivering health care were skyrocketing completely out of control. So there's been this movement toward alternative means of delivering health care services through managed care type providers, such as HMOs [health maintenance organizations]. There's a parallel here in that some powerful factors are coming to bear to address the issue that business as usual just doesn't work. We can't afford it. We need an alternative method of disciplining and allocating health care services. Of course, health care can be a far more emotionally involved subject than real estate, because people's welfare and lives are at stake, but the economic forces at play are similar.

I don't know exactly how the movement toward increasingly publicly owned and financed real estate will play out, but my sense is that the forces pushing us in that direction are very powerful, and that's not going to stop. It probably will never again go at quite the pace it did in the 1990s, but that's because we had a very unusual set of circumstances then. Basically, though, the economy is committed to making the industry more accountable, more transparent, more responsible, more responsive to supply and demand indicators. It's very similar to what we did 30 and 40 years ago, when we started to develop the residential mortgage–backed securities market. There too, the primary means for providing for mortgage finance had been the savings and loan industry. As interest rates would rise and fall, there'd be this tremendous amount of intermediation and disintermediation of funds from the thrift industry, and when those funds would be disintermediated, the housing industry would grind to a halt. So you had this huge part of the economy subject to these market forces, which created a real estate cycle that had very large amplitude. The social and economic costs of that grew to the point where policymakers said, "We can't afford to do business this way anymore." The whole process of developing a publicly traded mortgage-backed securities market was to broaden and diversify the sources of capital for housing finance. That way it would become less relevant whether interest rates were high or low. Mortgage capital would always be available; only the cost would change. That's what's happening on the commercial side now. Any elasticity in the supply of real estate will probably always mean that we're going to have real estate cycles, it's just how large the amplitude is.

I think broadening and diversifying the sources of capital allows the economy to allocate that capital more efficiently and to allocate it at a lower cost. In that sense, there are macroeconomic benefits that help everybody. If you go to the Web sites of the Federal Reserve Board and the Federal Deposit Insurance Corporation and look at some of the data that they have on the history of mortgage delinquencies, what is interesting is that all of their series begin in 1991. What that tells you is that before we were aware of the risks of real estate lending, before we were aware of the implications of huge amounts of leverage, before we fully appreciated the importance of having more equity in the system and so on, nobody bothered to measure anything. One of the reasons for the big real estate depression in the late 1980s and early 1990s was that nobody knew what was happening, because nobody bothered to measure anything—nobody was accountable to anybody. One of the benefits of having a publicly traded industry is that you have equity and debt analysts who track the performance of the companies, so everybody's collecting a lot more data now. That makes everybody far more accountable, it makes the whole system far more transparent, and it's a different ballgame.

Imperiale: That sets the stage for the next question I'd like to ask you. Since the real estate asset class in general now is more rational economically as a result of all these things, what advantages do REITs offer over the direct real estate investment paradigm or model?

Grupe: If you discriminate between institutional investing and individual investing, the first advantage is that investing in publicly traded real estate securities is possible for small investors.

Imperiale: With a modest amount of money?

Grupe: Right. If they don't have the money to invest in real estate directly, they can choose whether they're going to invest in individual stocks or companies or in a variety of sector mutual funds. This provides individual investors with access that is not there on the other side. For institutional investors, we don't see one option as necessarily being better than the other.

Imperiale: So, for an institution, direct investment in real estate and investment in REITs are not replacements for one another, but rather complementary?

Grupe: Exactly. One of the clear advantages of investing in publicly traded securities is liquidity. But liquidity means different things to different investors. If you're talking about a very large plan sponsor, for example CALPERS, and they're running $150 billion and they want to allocate 5 or 6 percent to real estate stocks or to real estate, it's going to be very difficult for them to get in and out of a market easily with a total market cap of $150 billion dollars. For somebody like that, the idea of executing an entire real estate investment strategy through publicly traded securities at this time is challenging at best. Another aspect to that is that CALPERS is a very large organization that has significant resources to oversee and professionally manage all its core assets. So the cost of a direct real estate investing program can be managed. On the other end of the spectrum, this past spring, the city of Dallas, Texas, made a decision to invest 10 percent of their portfolio, or about $200 million, in real estate entirely through real estate stocks. For them, investing and managing a $200 million real estate allocation in public securities makes sense. It's very easy for them to get in and out and to manage their positions, and it probably makes no sense to take on the costs of hiring a professional staff of real estate investors to oversee a $200 million real estate allocation. For others who are in between, some kind of combination is probably appropriate.

I know CALPERS has real estate stocks as part of their real estate allocation. I know that the third largest institutional investor in the United States, ABP Investments, decided maybe five or six years ago that they were going to terminate their direct investment program in the United States and do all of their U.S. commercial real estate allocation through REIT stocks. They've got a $4 billion portfolio and liquidity is not a problem. My point is that you can have some fairly large funds invested in public real estate stocks and be quite comfortable with the amount of liquidity that the market offers. You have to decide on some combination of direct versus indirect investments. And my view is that that's appropriate, because they are complements.

Imperiale: When you start to count the number of organizations out there that have the kinds of assets to invest directly in real estate, that's a short list. So there's an opportunity for everyone else to invest in real estate, going back to the original intent of the legislation. This creates a venue where people can be on equal footing with the major pension plans and have some of those same opportunities.

Grupe: Probably one of the biggest areas in which this needs to be addressed is defined contribution plans.

Imperiale: Which have been growing very rapidly.

Grupe: Not only are they most rapidly growing, they're now larger than defined benefit plans. The defined benefit plans have professional investment managers running their assets, and for years, they've been well aware of the diversification benefits of having real estate as part of their allocation. When you look at most defined contribution plans, such as 401(k)s, there are almost none that offer any kind of real estate as an investment choice for their plan participants.

Imperiale: That's remarkable, isn't it?

Grupe: There has been work done that has compared the performance of defined benefit plans with that of defined contribution plans, and, not surprisingly, it shows that defined contribution plans significantly lag defined benefit plans. Part of that is because many employees making these investment decisions for their 401(k)s don't have the background, the resources, or the interest to make sound decisions. But in many cases, they don't even have adequate opportunity, so they couldn't make good decisions even if they wanted to. For instance, look at the federal thrift savings plan. Up until last year, there were only three choices. Now there are five.

It became clear to us that, for a variety of reasons, real estate investing was not particularly well understood outside the professional investment community. In many cases, it's probably fair to say that it wasn't particularly well understood even within some sectors of the professional investment community! Unfortunately, the data are quite limited—the most commonly used data are the NACRIEF [National Council of Real Estate Investing Fiduciaries] returns, and we know they've got all kinds of problems.

But on the public side, NAREIT has been calculating performance benchmarks of REIT stocks since 1972. So the thought was that we ought to be able to bring to bear some more rigorous analytics to quantify the returns on those kinds of investments and how they complement returns in a portfolio of other diversified investments. So we asked Ibbotson to apply their asset allocation techniques to include real estate stocks and quantify what the benefits might actually be. They came up with results that have been echoed by quite a number of others. What the results show, very unambiguously, is if you build a diversified portfolio of stocks and bonds, and then include real estate stocks, that boosts the efficient frontier. The correlations between the period-to-period returns on real estate stocks and on most other investment types are relatively low.

So we spent the balance of the year making people aware of this, and we've found that in this particularly challenging and turbulent market that we've been in, this story really resonates. We've clearly gotten over the fixation on large-cap technology—that bubble has burst. This has introduced a sobering element into the market and opened people's minds to the importance of having well-diversified portfolios. And public real estate securities can play an important role in that kind of diversification.

Imperiale: In your opinion, why do REITs behave so independently from stocks and bonds?

Grupe: I think there are a number of reasons. One of the things that clearly distinguishes REIT returns is the fact that such a high proportion of their annual total returns comes from the income component. This is important because while other stocks are bouncing around a lot because most of their total return comes from price, the the periodic total return from REITs come mostly from dividends, and so that makes it a much more stable sort of total return. By having that strong source of income, you protect the downside of your periodic performance, and you're able to preserve some of the compounding benefits that you get from long-term investing. For example, The NASDAQ Index was up 85 percent in 1999, then it was down 35 percent in 2000, and down another 25 or 30 percent in 2001. That whole 85 percent upside vanished. That means investors lost the compounding benefits of long-term investing. Why is that? Well, there's no income there. Because of the volatility, you keep losing those compounding benefits, whereas if you build in something that protects you on the downside, you preserve some of that compounding benefit.

As far as pricing is concerned, the way stock prices behave is going to be affected by two general influences. One is the factors that are unique to a stock's industry. There are certain demand/supply characteristics of any industry that help to determine the operating performance of a company. Second, you've got public markets that look at those factors and at the operating performance and put some multiple on that to come up with a market price. But real estate has a high income component and a different set of supply and demand factors. These differences are reflected in the market price and in periodic total returns that are relatively uncorrelated with those of other stocks and bonds. Over the last five to seven years, the correlation has only been about 0.25. Of course, that masks the fact that even different industries have significantly different correlations between them.

Imperiale: For example, the energy complex has a very low correlation with the technology complex, and this shows that energy as a group has characteristics that are highly non-correlated to other asset classes.

Grupe: The correlation between the NAREIT Equity Index and the S&P 500 as a whole was 0.21. The individual industry correlations within the S&P 500 go from a high of 0.76 between consumer discretionary and industrials to a low of −0.16 between information technology and utilities. The correlation of the NAREIT Equity Index between those 10 or 11 separate categories within the S&P ranges from a high of 0.38 for the energy sector to a low of 0.01 for information technology. Why has the correlation between equity REIT returns and the S&P 500 declined? One of the reasons is because of the technology component. REIT returns have the lowest correlation with the information technology component of the S&P 500, and the information technology component grew in the 1990s from about 8 percent to 40 percent. The question is, now that the information technology component has been reduced to a little under 20 percent, what does that imply for the correlation between REIT stocks and S&P 500 stocks? It would suggest that the correlation should go back up, but we haven't seen that yet.

Imperiale: It's important to understand that that correlation is the cornerstone of the whole premise of having REITs as an asset class. Now, let's talk about the future. NAREIT has made significant progress in changing the legislative environment for REITs so that some of the shareholder interests are better aligned with those of management. What are some important things as a trade organization that you'd like to accomplish for the REIT asset class?

Grupe: One of our highest priorities is to foster and promote widespread understanding and awareness of what publicly traded real estate companies are all about, how they operate, and what it means to invest in their stocks. Many people don't realize that investing in the stock of a REIT is no different than investing in the stock of General Motors or IBM, it's just that the business is real estate service. Part of the confusion comes from the term REIT. People associate lots of things with the word *trust* that are not a part of their thought process when they think of other types of corporations. So we're very focused on trying to make sure that people understand this is an industry sector like any other, and that they can use the same techniques they use to evaluate investments in other stocks. By doing that, we will help to accomplish one of our other priorities of broadening and diversifying the investment base for the industry. It's important for all industries to have as stable a source of capital as possible, so you want to avoid having the capital available to your industry dominated by a particular type of investor.

Another goal is to make sure that, as part of Congress' original intent, people have an opportunity to invest in real estate stocks through their 401(k) programs. If your primary source of retirement savings is through your defined contribution plan, and the plan doesn't offer you all the choices you need to have an appropriately diversified port-folio, you are almost guaranteed to suffer real economic loss over the course of your lifetime. The access to real estate investing that Congress had intended isn't really there because the normal way of investing savings today is through mutual funds and your defined contribution plan. This situation inhibits the efficient allocation of capital within the economy and has a desperate impact on certain sectors. We would like to see that remedied.

REITs as a Portfolio Diversification Tool

Chapter Summary

- Asset allocation is the cornerstone of modern portfolio theory.
- Long-term returns, volatility, and correlation of returns among portfolio holdings affect total portfolio performance.
- Real estate investment trusts (REITs) offer competitive returns, reasonable volatility, and low correlation with other financial assets.
- Real estate investment trusts lower volatility and increase total return when added to a multi-asset-class portfolio.
- When considered in a constrained investment equation, REITs continue to improve performance outcome in multi-asset-class portfolios.
- An allocation of 5 to 20 percent in REITs will increase return and lower risk in most portfolios.
- Understanding REITs as an asset class is important for anyone who deals with investments within a multi-asset-class portfolio setting.

Never have so many been paid so much to do so little.

—Investment manager
commenting on consultants at a
client meeting

Asset Allocation and Modern Portfolio Theory

Over the past 20 years an entire industry has been born of the simple concept that the majority of the total performance of a portfolio results from the mix of investment asset classes contained in the portfolio. This simple concept is the cornerstone of modern portfolio theory (MPT). The industry spawned by the advent of MPT is known as the investment management consulting industry. This group of consultants stands ready to advise the investing world at large on the correct allocation of different investment vehicles that should be held in a portfolio to achieve the stated investment policy with the least risk to principal and the lowest volatility. As is true of most objectives, there is normally a multitude of ways to achieve the stated goal. Through careful study and analysis, the investment consultant will craft a portfolio allocation model that will drive the portfolio returns to the stated goal. For a modest additional fee, the consultant will assist the investor in developing a stated goal or policy that is consistent with the asset allocation model.

Large investors such as pension plans, endowments, and wealthy individuals have historically engaged investment consultants to address long-term investment objectives and policy questions related to those issues. These large investors have a fiduciary obligation to protect the interests of their investors, and one way to accomplish this (as well as reduce their own potential liability) is to hire a consultant to monitor investment-related issues. The consultant's job is to advise the client on the correct mix of investments and monitor the underlying performance of those investments to be certain they remain consistent with the objective.

In the past, the high level of math embedded in the consultants' practice, along with the myriad of data required to make the analysis, limited the accessibility of investment consulting to larger institutions. However, the rapid growth in the power of the personal computer, along with the democratization of data via the Internet and the availability of modestly priced software, have combined to put asset allocation modeling within the reach of even the smallest investor. Web sites offering asset allocation advice and online calculators have proliferated. Modestly priced financial planning and asset allocation software is widely available. Traditional Wall Street brokers as well as discount brokerage firms all have asset allocation investment programs available to their investment clients. Mutual fund complexes and 401(k) providers offer asset allocation advice to their clients. And, although the conceptual theory of asset allocation is simple, the practical application and administration of the process is much more difficult than most people grasp. As mentioned, there are often many ways to arrive at the same goal, but the devil is in the details.

Asset Allocation Theory and REITs

Total portfolio performance is impacted by three variables that can be attributed to any given investment asset class: (1) long-term expected and historical rate of return; (2) volatility of return, often referred to as the *standard deviation of return;* (3) correlation of returns. When consultants consider an asset class as a possible investment in a portfolio, they first study the rate of return to determine if the historic and expected returns are high enough to compete with other available investments. This return analysis is tempered with a review of how volatile the return patterns are over time. The higher the volatility of a potential return (often called *risk*), the higher the required rate of return becomes in order to achieve a slot in the investment program. Finally, the pattern of returns, or the correlation of the asset class as it compares to all other asset classes in the portfolio, must be considered. If the correlation is sufficiently different from the other asset classes in the portfolio, the returns are high enough, and the volatility is low enough, then the investment class might gain an allocation position within the portfolio.

The classic implementation of asset allocation is in the stock and bond mix of a typical balanced portfolio. The stock and bond asset classes both have reasonable expected and historical rates of return. Over the long term, bond returns are lower than stock returns, but bond returns are far less volatile than stock returns. And the correlation between stocks and bonds is relatively low. Thus, when stocks underperform their historical expected rate of return, bonds tend to outperform theirs. This trade-off between risk and return tends to lower the volatility of the entire portfolio and increase the total return per unit of risk undertaken.

As seen in Figure 4.1, the return for real estate investment trusts (REITs) has historically been higher than that for bonds and slightly lower than that for stocks over most periods of time. We can conclude by studying the numbers that the REIT asset class has historically provided competitive returns when compared to stocks and bonds. And, it would be expected that in the future REITs will continue to provide returns that are higher than bond returns and slightly lower than common stock returns.

Volatility is measured by calculating the standard deviation of the quarterly returns, in percent, over a given period of time for a particular asset class. The volatility of REITs is compared to that of large and small stocks and bonds in Table 4.1. As you would expect, because REIT returns are higher than those of bonds, the volatility of REITs is higher than that of bonds when measured over most time periods. REIT volatility is slightly lower than that of large stocks and significantly lower than that of small-cap stocks, while the returns are only slightly lower.

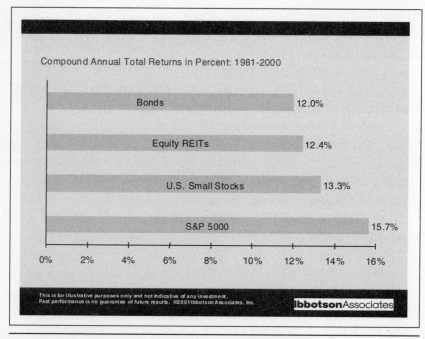

FIGURE 4.1 REITs Measure Up over Time

TABLE 4.1 Standard Deviation of Quarterly Returns

	REITs	**Large Stocks**	**Small Stocks**	**Bonds**
1972–2000	14.7	16.2	24.9	11.9
1972–1992	15	17.1	26.3	12.7
1993–2000	14.2	13.7	21.1	9.5

Source: REITs—NAREIT Equity Index; Small stocks—Ibbotson U.S. Small Stock Series; Large stocks—Standard & Poor's 500®; LT Bonds—20-year U.S. government bond.

When looking at the data, it could be concluded that REITs offer returns competitive with those of stocks, while involving substantially less risk or volatility than stocks in general.

Correlation is where REITs clearly distinguish themselves as an asset class when compared to stocks and bonds. The correlation coefficient of REITs compared to large and small stocks and bonds is surprisingly low. As summarized in Figure 4.2, REITs have a low correlation to stocks and bonds, and over the 1970s, through the 1990s, the correlation has continued to decline.

When measured in rolling five-year periods, the correlation of REITs to small and large stocks has been steadily on the decline since the early 1990s. This roughly corresponds to the modern

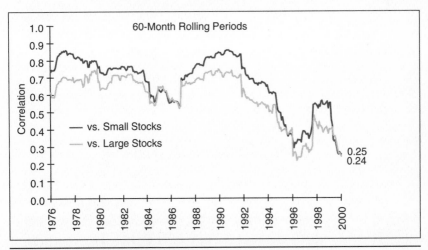

FIGURE 4.2 Declining Equity REIT Correlation
(Source: NAREIT)

TABLE 4.2 Monthly Correlation of REIT Total Returns to Other Types of Investments

	1972–2000	1970s*	1980s	1990s	1993–2000
Small stocks	0.63	0.74	0.74	0.58	0.26
Large stocks	0.55	0.64	0.65	0.45	0.25
Bonds	0.20	0.27	0.17	0.26	0.16

*1972–1979.

Source: REITs—NAREIT Equity Index; Small stocks—Ibbotson U.S. Small Stock Series; Large stocks—Standard & Poor's 500®; LT Bonds—20-year U.S. government bond.

era in REITs as discussed in Chapter 2. Table 4.2 shows the declining trend in REIT correlation.

When linked with competitive returns and reasonable volatility, investment return correlation provides the basic rationale for asset allocation and portfolio diversification. The highly noncorrelated nature of the REIT asset class provides a powerful means of additional portfolio diversification. In the now famous study "Determinants of Portfolio Performance" (*Financial Analysts Journal,* July/August 1986), Gary Brinson makes the case that asset allocation policy determines 91.5 percent of the investment performance of a given portfolio. In other words, the mix of assets in the underlying investment portfolio determines most of the investment performance. The actual security selection process, which most people consider paramount to investment performance, contributes a mere 4.6 percent of portfolio return. So it's not which stocks you own, but the fact that you own stocks, that determines most of the return in a portfolio. Simply put, asset allocation drives portfolio return.

The Portfolio Contribution of REITs

In Figure 4.3 we return to the classic balanced portfolio. For this example we use a portfolio policy of 50 percent large stocks as defined by the S&P 500 Index, 40 percent 20-year U.S. Government Bonds, and 10 percent 30-day U.S. T-Bills. For the period from 1972 through 2000, the portfolio returns 11.8 percent annually and has a volatility of 11.2 percent. When the stock and bond

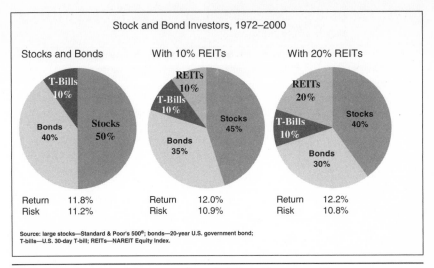

FIGURE 4.3 Diversify to Reduce Risk or Increase Return

allocation are each reduced by 5 percent, and 10 percent REITs as defined by the NAREIT Equity Index are added, the return over the same period rises to 12 percent and the risk or volatility drops to 10.9 percent. Taking the experiment one step further, when the stock and bond allocation are each reduced by 10 percent and a 20 percent REIT allocation is added, the return over the same period rises to 12.2 percent and the risk or volatility drops to 10.8 percent.

Figure 4.4 examines the potential investment contribution of REITs in a classic bond portfolio. For this example we use a portfolio policy of 90 percent 20-year U.S. Government Bonds and 10 percent 30-day U.S. T-Bills. For the period from 1972 through 2000, the portfolio returns 9.5 percent and has a volatility of 11.3 percent. When the bond allocation is reduced by 10 percent, and an allocation of 10 percent REITs as defined by the NAREIT Equity Index is added to the portfolio, the return over the same period rises to 9.9 percent and the risk or volatility drops substantially to 10.6 percent. Taking the experiment one step further, when the bond allocation is reduced by 20 percent and a 20 percent REIT allocation is added, the return over the same period continues to rise to 10.3 percent and the risk or volatility drops to 10.3 percent.

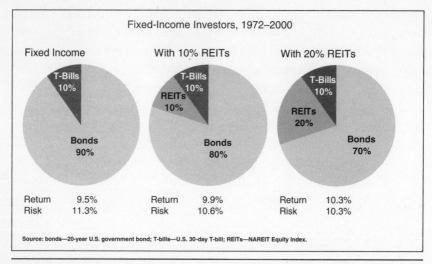

FIGURE 4.4 Diversify to Reduce Risk or Increase Return.

This type of what-if simulation demonstrates the beneficial effect of noncorrelated asset classes. In this instance REITs are examined, but the analysis can extend to other noncorrelated asset classes such as small stocks and international stocks. The examples are designed to be simple and to prove the case that REITs as an asset class add value in a multi-asset-class portfolio. In most real-life situations, investors and consultants put constraints on the minimum and maximum asset allocation for a given asset class. The specific investment policy and nature of the portfolio dictate these constraints. The tax status of the portfolio has an effect on the allocation and constraints of income-producing assets. In a taxable portfolio it is normally preferable to minimize ordinary income and maximize capital gains to lower the current tax burden and defer taxes into the future at the lower capital gains rate. Conversely, owners of tax-exempt portfolios will be more willing to hold a larger percentage of assets that produce high current income, because current taxation is not a factor in calculating actual net return. Total asset size is also a potential constraining factor. Very large institutional portfolios may not be able to effectively use smaller or more illiquid asset classes as a part of their overall strategy due to their sheer size or need for liquidity.

A simple way to explore the potential investment contribution of REITs in an allocation-constrained setting (again, while avoiding complex math) is to construct a set of what-if portfolios using REITs and other asset classes that are constrained at levels that are common among institutional investors. These what-if simulations take constrained portfolio allocations and add REITs in varying amounts over differing time periods in an attempt to determine their potential investment contribution to portfolio performance. In this simulation the following portfolio constraints are used for the following asset classes:

- *Small stocks.* Ibbotson U.S. Small Stock Series; minimum 0 percent; maximum 20 percent

- *Large stocks.* S&P 500; minimum 15 percent; maximum 60 percent

- *Bonds.* 20-year U.S. Government Bonds; minimum 5 percent; maximum 40 percent

- *International stocks.* Morgan Stanley Capital International's Europe Asia Far East Index; minimum 0 percent; maximum 20 percent

- *T-Bills.* Minimum 0 percent; maximum 15 percent

Using these constraints for the period from 1972 through 2000, an allocation of 10 percent and then 20 percent REITs is added into the portfolio while adjusting all other asset allocations to create a series of return and risk (standard deviation) outcomes within the constraints described previously. This process of optimization then creates a series of outcomes while increasing risk as defined by standard deviation in 1 percent increments. This is the type of what-if analysis a consultant might create for an institutional client. Table 4.3 shows the outcomes with a 10 percent REIT allocation over an increasing risk spectrum, and Table 4.4 shows the same outcomes with a 20 percent REIT allocation.

This data is then used to plot two efficient frontiers using possible risk and return outcomes with and without REITs in the portfolio allocation. As can be seen in Figure 4.5, REITs in a typical multi-asset-class portfolio help add return across the efficient frontier.

TABLE 4.3 Efficient Portfolios Including REITs (Constrained Optimization, 1972–2000)

	Portfolio					
	1	**2**	**3**	**4**	**5**	**6**
Small stocks	0%	3%	5%	7%	9%	18%
Large stocks	19%	27%	31%	35%	41%	37%
Bonds	26%	15%	16%	17%	9%	5%
International stocks	20%	20%	20%	20%	20%	20%
T-bills	15%	15%	8%	1%	0%	0%
REITs	20%	20%	20%	20%	20%	20%
Expected return	11.9%	12.6%	13.1%	13.6%	14.1%	14.5%
Standard deviation	9.0%	10.0%	11.0%	12.0%	13.0%	14.0%

Maximum constraints—small stocks 20%; large stocks 60%; international stocks 20%; T-bills 15%; REITs 20%. Minimum constraints—bonds 5%.

Source: small stocks—Ibbotson U.S. Small Stock Series; large stocks—Standard & Poor's 500®; bonds—20-year U.S. government bond; international stocks—MSCI EAFE Index; T-bills—U.S. 30-day T-bill; REITs—NAREIT Equity Index.

TABLE 4.4 Efficient Portfolios Including REITs (Constrained Optimization, 1972–2000)

	Portfolio					
	1	**2**	**3**	**4**	**5**	**6**
Small stocks	4%	8%	10%	12%	14%	17%
Large stocks	16%	25%	30%	34%	39%	45%
Bonds	35%	22%	19%	20%	17%	8%
International stocks	20%	20%	20%	20%	20%	20%
T-bills	15%	15%	11%	4%	0%	0%
REITs	10%	10%	10%	10%	10%	10%
Expected return	11.7%	12.4%	12.9%	13.5%	14.0%	14.4%
Standard deviation	9.0%	10.0%	11.0%	12.0%	13.0%	14.0%

Maximum constraints—small stocks 20%; large stocks 60%; international stocks 20%; T-bills 15%; REITs 10%. Minimum constraints—bonds 5%.

Source: small stocks—Ibbotson U.S. Small Stock Series; large stocks—Standard & Poor's 500®; bonds—20-year U.S. government bond; international stocks—MSCI EAFE Index; T-bills—U.S. 30-day T-bill; REITs—NAREIT Equity Index.

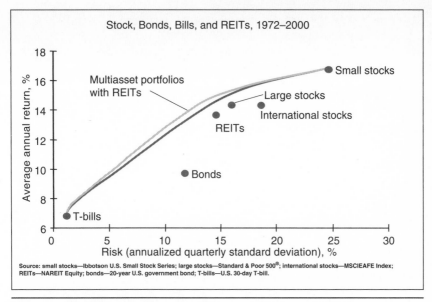

FIGURE 4.5 Efficient Frontier With and Without REITs

These outcomes used a long-term time horizon stretching from 1972 to 2000. As discussed earlier in the chapter, measured in rolling five-year periods, the correlation of REITs to small and large stocks has been steadily on the decline since the early 1990s. This decline in correlation roughly corresponds to the modern era in REITs discussed in Chapter 2. The argument could be made that as the correlation of REITs to stocks has declined, their contribution to portfolio risk reduction and return should become greater. To examine this theory, we performed the same efficient frontier analysis using 10 and 20 percent REIT allocations. Using the same minimum and maximum asset class constraints as in the 1972 to 2000 analysis, the risk outcomes were examined for the modern REIT era of 1993 through 2000. Although this is a much shorter period, due to the declining correlation of REITs to large and small stocks, the risk and return outcomes improve dramatically (see Figure 4.6). As seen in Tables 4.5 and 4.6, adding 10 and 20 percent REIT allocations significantly reduces risk as measured by standard deviation of return and increases total return in the portfolios.

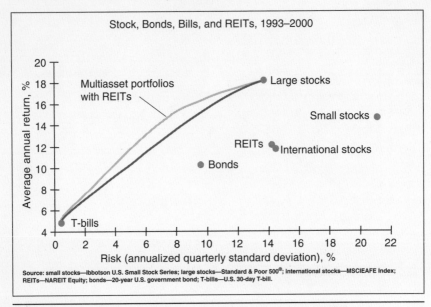

FIGURE 4.6 Efficient Frontier With and Without REITs

TABLE 4.5 Efficient Portfolios Including REITs (Constrained Optimization, 1993–2000)

	Portfolio					
	1	**2**	**3**	**4**	**5**	**6**
Small stocks	0.0%	0.0%	0.0%	0.0%	6.0%	14.0%
Large stocks	26.0%	33.0%	45.0%	56.0%	60.0%	60.0%
Bonds	19.0%	22.0%	17.0%	9.0%	5.0%	5.0%
International stocks	20.0%	20.0%	18.0%	14.0%	9.0%	1.0%
T-bills	15.0%	4.0%	0.0%	0.0%	0.0%	0.0%
REITs	20.0%	20.0%	20.0%	20.0%	20.0%	20.0%
Expected return	12.2%	13.4%	14.5%	15.4%	15.8%	16.1%
Standard deviation	5.5%	6.5%	7.5%	8.5%	9.5%	10.5%

Maximum constraints—small stocks 20%; large stocks 60%; international stocks 20%; T-bills 15%; REITs 20%. Minimum constraints—bonds 5%.

Source: small stocks—Ibbotson U.S. Small Stock Series; large stocks—Standard & Poor's 500®; bonds—20-year U.S. government bond; international stocks—MSCI EAFE Index; T-bills—U.S. 30-day T-bill; REITs—NAREIT Equity Index.

TABLE 4.6 Efficient Portfolios Including REITs (Constrained Optimization, 1993–2000)

	Portfolio					
	1	**2**	**3**	**4**	**5**	**6**
Small stocks	0.0%	0.0%	0.0%	0.0%	2.0%	11.0%
Large stocks	19.0%	33.0%	39.0%	53.0%	60.0%	60.0%
Bonds	36.0%	27.0%	31.0%	22.0%	11.0%	5.0%
International stocks	20.0%	18.0%	20.0%	15.0%	17.0%	14.0%
T-bills	15.0%	11.0%	0.0%	0.0%	0.0%	0.0%
REITs	10.0%	10.0%	10.0%	10.0%	10.0%	10.0%
Expected return	11.5%	12.8%	13.9%	14.9%	15.6%	15.9%
Standard deviation	5.5%	6.5%	7.5%	8.5%	9.5%	10.5%

Maximum constraints—small stocks 20%; large stocks 60%; international stocks 20%; T-bills 15%; REITs 10%. Minimum constraints—bonds 5%.

Source: small stocks—Ibbotson U.S. Small Stock Series; large stocks—Standard & Poor's 500®; bonds—20-year U.S. government bond; international stocks—MSCI EAFE Index; T-bills—U.S. 30-day T-bill; REITs—NAREIT Equity Index.

Conclusion

In reviewing the data presented in this chapter, it is easy to conclude that REITs offer an attractive risk-reward trade-off. With a risk profile slightly higher than that of bonds and a return profile slightly lower than that of stocks, REITs offer competitive returns for the risk assumed. Further analysis shows that in addition to competitive returns, REITs as an asset class offer a low correlation to other financial assets, including large and small stocks, bonds, international stocks, and T-Bills. This low correlation of returns to those of other asset classes has continued to increase over the modern REIT era (the last 10 years). Attractive returns and low correlation help reduce risk and increase total return when REITs are added to a multi-asset-class portfolio. An allocation of 5 to 20 percent in REITs will increase return and lower risk in most portfolios, which makes owning and understanding REITs as an asset class important for anyone who deals with investments within a multi-asset-class setting.

Integrating REITs into an Investment Portfolio

Chapter Summary

- An allocation of 5 to 20 percent in real estate investment trusts (REITs) will increase return and lower risk in most portfolios.
- An investment policy statement reflects the long-term needs and objectives of the investor.
- Rational investors seek to increase total return while decreasing total risk within a portfolio.
- Real estate investment trusts lower volatility and increase total return when added to a multi-asset-class portfolio.
- There are four basic strategies for integrating REITs into a diversified portfolio: (1) direct investment; (2) managed accounts; (3) mutual funds; and (4) unit investment trusts (UITs).
- Portfolio policies are influenced by investor expectations, and REITs should be viewed in that context.
- Real estate investment trusts have a low sensitivity to changing interest rates.
- Real estate investment trusts act as a hedge against inflation.
- Real estate investment trusts have a negative correlation to certain stock market sectors.
- Real estate investment trusts may offer a modest tax advantage to certain taxable investors.

Real estate is the closest thing to the proverbial pot of gold.

—Ada Louise Huxtable, 1970

As discussed in Chapter 4, the addition of a 5 to 20 percent allocation of real estate investment trusts (REITs) in the typical diversified portfolio will lower volatility, increase total return, and normally increase risk-adjusted return in the portfolio over most time horizons. That said, the question often arises as to how to best integrate REITs into an investment portfolio. For the large institutional investor, this is an asset class decision that is often incorporated into a portfolio through the use of an investment policy statement. The policy objective gives careful consideration to the specific objectives, constraints, and goals of the investor. These same considerations apply to smaller institutional investors and individual investors as well.

All investment policies, whether simple or complex and whether for large or small institutions, should reflect the needs of the people who are represented within the pool of assets. Many of the policy objectives are qualitative and some are quantitative, but the goal of both is to create an efficient portfolio that addresses the needs and objectives of the individuals who are reflected in the policy statement.

Rational investors always seek higher returns and lower risks in their investment portfolios. Integrating REITs creates an opportunity to gain higher returns with a lower risk profile. There are four basic strategies for integrating REITs into a diversified portfolio:

1. *Direct investment in REITs.* For investors who wish to make their own decisions on REITs, the prospect of selecting and owning individual REITs can be of interest. This process entails the selection of an adequate number of REITs to create and maintain diversification by property type and geographic location. In most instances this requires 7 to 10 REITs. Chapter 9 deals extensively with the fundamental concepts used in analyzing REITs. The direct investor monitors the ongoing business activities of the REITs.

2. *Managed real estate accounts.* Under this alternative centage of the value of a diversified portfolio is targe REITs and that amount of money is managed by a lio manager at a firm that has a specialized real estate investment portfolio. This is typically how most institutional investors would undertake the addition of REITs into their broader portfolio allocation. A list of investment management firms specializing in the management of REIT portfolios or real estate securities portfolios is listed in the appendix.

3. *Real estate mutual funds.* For the smaller investor, this option allows the opportunity to invest in real estate securities in a professionally managed portfolio. There are currently over 60 mutual funds dedicated to real estate securities and the real estate sector. These funds usually focus on investing in REITs, real estate operating companies, and housing-related stocks. In most cases the portfolio is actively managed to take advantage of emerging trends in the real estate markets. In the aggregate, these funds had $18 billion of shareholder assets as of December 31, 2001. The appendix contains a list of publicly traded mutual funds that focus on the real estate sector.

4. *Real estate unit investment trusts (UITs).* Much like mutual funds, these trusts offer small investors the advantage of a large, professionally selected and diversified real estate portfolio. However, unlike the case for a mutual fund, the portfolio of a UIT is fixed upon its structuring and is not actively managed. It is a self-liquidating pool that has a predetermined time span. After issue, shares of UITs trade on the secondary market much like shares of closed-ended mutual funds. Under this scenario, it is sometimes possible to buy shares of a UIT at a discount on the underlying value of the actual shares contained within the trust on the open market.

Relevant Characteristics of REITs

Investors' portfolio policies and strategies are often influenced by their capital market and economic expectations. These expectations are a reflection of the relevant social, political, and economic data that are available to investors at any given time. To the extent that investors monitor these economic and market factors and modify their portfolio allocations according to their perceptions, it is important to consider the key factors that may impact REITs as an asset class.

Interest Rates and REITs

Because of a generally higher than average dividend yield, many investors consider REITs to be bondlike in their characteristics. To some extent, this is true with regard to the fact that REITs provide a high level of current income, as do bond investments. However, REITs are not like bonds in their response to changing interest rates. In fact, REITs tend to be less sensitive to changes in the interest rate environment than both bonds and the broader equity market.

Real estate investment trusts and many other high-yielding stocks, such as utility and energy stocks, are often perceived to be substitutes for fixed income securities. Conventional wisdom about interest rate sensitivity suggests that, compared to fixed-income investments such as bonds and Treasury Bills, high-yielding stocks are attractive during periods of declining interest rates and in low interest rate environments. Many investors believe that during periods of increasing interest rates, high-yielding equity securities and REITs are relatively less attractive because the rising interest rate environment might have a negative impact on the underlying value of the stock's price. Just as rising interest rates diminish the current value of a bond's market price, investors perceive that rising interest rates will have the same impact on the underlying price of a stock. However, numerous studies have shown that the total returns generated by the NAREIT Equity Index have a lower correlation to changing interest rates than the S&P 500 or long-term government bonds. For example, a study completed by Uniplan Real Estate Advisors indicates that for the period of January 1989 through September 2001, the correlation coefficient between government bonds and the S&P 500 was measured at 0.42, as compared to the correlation coefficient of total return from the NAREIT Equity Index and government bonds, which was 0.24. This suggests that,

contrary to popular belief, REITs are less sensitive to chang
long-term interest rates than the broader equity market.

Correlation of REITs to Other Market Sectors

As was discovered in Chapters 3 and 4, REITs as an asset class
provide a low correlation to the equity market in general and to
large-capitalization equities in particular. It's worth noting that
when the large-cap equity market as represented by the S&P 500
is divided into its various subgroups, it is possible to further compare the correlation of REITs to other subsectors of the market.

In reviewing Table 5.1, it is interesting to note that REITs had a
lower correlation to technology stocks than to any other industry
sector in the S&P 500. In theory, the lack of correlation between
asset classes provides the ability to combine those securities into
portfolios that reduce risk without sacrificing return. This, as discussed in Chapter 3, is the cornerstone of modern portfolio theory.
Securities that show a negative correlation provide the highest
level of benefit when used to reduce portfolio risk. Negative correlation means that when returns are up on one security, they are
negative or down on the other security. It is interesting to note that
the correlations between REITs and technology stocks as well as
between REITs and communication services and REITs and the
health care sector provide a negative correlation coefficient during some periods. This relationship is particularly significant to
investors whose portfolios may include high exposure to technology, communications, or health care-related industries.

Inflation and REITs

Real estate and REITs provide a hedge against inflation. In an
environment where inflation is rising, the value of real estate and
real estate securities can be expected to increase as well. In times
of high and rising inflation, investors have historically been
rewarded by changing their asset allocation strategy to increase
their investment in the real estate asset class. In contrast, treasury securities and fixed-income securities such as bonds have
performed poorly during periods of high and rising inflation.
Therefore, fixed-income portfolio investors may want to consider REITs as a substitute for a fixed-income portfolio during
periods of expected and high inflation.

TABLE 5.1 Correlation Coefficients of Total Returns, January 1995–October 2001

	NAREIT Equity	S&P 500	Energy	Materials	Industrials	Cons. Disc.	Cons. Staples	Health Care	Financials	Info. Tech	Telecom Systems	Utilities
NAREIT Equity	1.00											
S&P 500	0.24	1.00										
Energy	0.39	0.56	1.00									
Materials	0.37	0.62	0.63	1.00								
Industrials	0.33	0.87	0.64	0.76	1.00							
Cons. Disc.	0.19	0.85	0.41	0.60	0.78	1.00						
Cons. Staples	0.24	0.47	0.32	0.38	0.49	0.35	1.00					
Health Care	0.11	0.51	0.34	0.19	0.41	0.31	0.65	1.00				
Financials	0.34	0.78	0.56	0.59	0.74	0.69	0.59	0.54	1.00			
Info. Tech	0.02	0.79	0.28	0.32	0.57	0.63	0.04	0.16	0.34	1.00		
Telecom Systems	0.06	0.61	0.12	0.19	0.41	0.55	0.26	0.37	0.42	0.42	1.00	
Utilities	0.37	0.22	0.48	0.23	0.37	0.08	0.29	0.32	0.38	-0.08	0.02	1.00

Source: National Association of Real Estate Investment Trusts®.

Just like bonds, REITs derive a large percentage of their total returns from the dividend component of the investment. However, unlike the case with bonds, the dividend component of REITs tends to increase over time. Since 1981, the average annual income return on equity REITs has been 8.54 percent (Figure 5.1). In addition, the dividend growth rate of the NAREIT Equity Index has exceeded the growth rate of inflation in every year since 1994 (Figures 5.2 and 5.3).

Considerations for Taxable Investors

The high current dividend yield of REITs may be somewhat of a disadvantage to taxable investor portfolios. For income tax purposes, dividend distributions from REITs may consist of ordinary income, return of capital, and long-term capital gains. When not held in nontaxable accounts, REITs have a disadvantage with respect to other common stocks. For the taxable investor, the greatest portion of total return expected by REIT holders consists of dividend yield, whereas common stock returns consist largely of appreciation. An appreciated stock that is held long enough to meet the holding period requirements for long-term capital gains is currently taxed at a maximum rate of 20 percent. Returns on REITs, having such a high portion of dividend income reflected as current income, may increase a taxable investor's marginal tax rate.

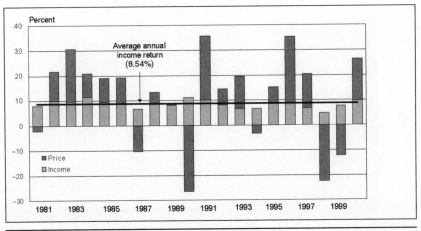

FIGURE 5.1 NAREIT Equity REIT Annual Returns, 1981–2000

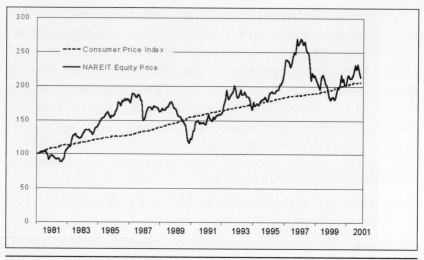

FIGURE 5.2 Equity REIT Price Index versus Consumer Price Index, monthly, 1981–2001 (Source: NAREIT)

However, REIT shares do offer taxable investors some advantages over dividends from other high-yielding stocks and dividends from corporate or government bonds. It is not unusual to have a high percentage of the dividends received each year from a REIT issued as a return of capital. This return of capital portion of the

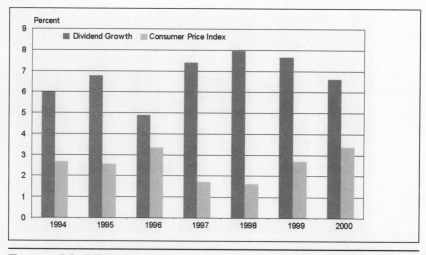

FIGURE 5.3 REIT Dividend Growth versus Consumer Price Index, 1994–2000 (Source: NAREIT)

dividend is not currently taxable to the shareholder, but rather reduces the shareholder's cost basis in the shares and defers the tax liability until the shareholder ultimately sells those shares. If the holding period of the shares is long enough to meet the requirements for long-term capital gains, then the maximum tax rate on that portion of the dividend return, which was used as a reduction in cost basis, would currently be 20 percent. This presents an advantageous situation to the extent that income-oriented investors can spend their current interest income now and may have the opportunity to defer a portion of the taxes on that current income until a later date. In fact, not only are the taxes deferred, but the investor may have the opportunity to pay taxes on the return of capital portion of the dividend at the long-term capital gains rate.

As discussed, for income tax purposes, dividend distributions paid to shareholders of REITs can consist of ordinary income, return of capital, and long-term capital gains. If a REIT realizes a long-term capital gain from the sale of a property in its real estate portfolio, it may designate a portion of the dividend paid during a tax year as a long-term capital gains distribution. This portion of the dividend is taxed to the shareholder at the lower long-term capital gain rate.

Historically, it is estimated that the return of capital component of REIT dividends has typically been approximately 30 percent of the total dividend return. It is important to note that this aggregate percentage has declined somewhat in recent years as a result of REITs reducing their overall payout ratio to investors in order to retain capital within the REIT operating structure. Thus the taxable investor may want to consider the implications of a high current dividend yield component of REITs. However, the high yield should be considered in light of the fact that REIT dividends are often characterized by the REIT to the shareholder as return of capital or long-term capital gains. To some extent, this provides a modest tax advantage to the individual investor who may invest directly in REITs as opposed to other high-dividend-yielding equity securities.

The Net Asset Value Cycle

It can be seen historically that capital markets that include stocks, bonds, or real estate–related securities go through periods in which they attract considerable marginal new capital. This results in valuations rising to high levels. Such examples of this can be seen in the Internet stock bubble of the late 1990s or the nifty-50 stock market bubble of the early 1970s. Conversely, there are other periods when asset classes go out of favor, thereby creating very low valuations, such as in the real estate markets of the early 1990s. Real estate is a cyclical industry, and these valuation extremes may be considered cycles or mean-reversion situations. In either case, investors are often looking for the opportunity to buy low and sell high by shifting their portfolios among various asset classes to take advantage of valuation disparities. When considering REITs for investment, it may be useful to look at the aggregate value of REITs as an asset class relative to the net asset value of their underlying properties. Historically, the performance of REITs after periods when they traded at a significant discount to net asset value has often been superior.

The opportunity to buy REITs at a discount to their net asset value is said to be an opportunity to buy real estate cheaper on Wall Street than it can be purchased on Main Street. In addition, when REITs trade at a substantial discount to net asset value, dividend yields are often higher than average for the real estate group. This offers the opportunity to be "paid to wait." As expected, real estate values eventually recover to private market level valuation prices or revert back to mean valuation levels. Thus, from a timing point of view, repositioning money into the REIT asset class at a time when REITs trade at a large discount to net asset value and migrating money out of the REIT asset class when a significant premium to net asset value becomes apparent may simply be good timing indicators within the REIT market. It should be noted however, that real estate as an asset class should be considered a long-term investment, and that, for the average investor, the concept of dollar cost averaging into the REIT sector has some appeal.

Conclusion

There are numerous ways to gain portfolio exposure in REITs. Investors may choose to invest directly in REITs or to use separate accounts that are professionally managed by portfolio managers specializing in the real estate sector. Real estate mutual funds and real estate UITs offer the opportunity for smaller investors to invest in REITs through pooled opportunities. Integration of REITs into an investment portfolio should be considered in light of the current economic environment. The fact that REITs provide a hedge against inflation and have a low correlation to other asset classes can make them particularly attractive in a diversified portfolio. The particularly low correlation to technology, communication, and health care sectors of the large-capitalization market also makes REITs of particular interest to investors who may have excess exposure in those areas. For investors with higher exposure to the bond market, the lower sensitivity to interest rates of REITs, when considered in conjunction with their high current yield, may offer some attractive opportunities to diversify a fixed-income portfolio. Taxable investors may want to consider REITs over other high-dividend-yielding sectors of the equity market because of the potential tax deferral advantages inherent in the REIT dividend structure.

Interview with David Shulman

David Shulman leads the REIT research effort at Lehman Brothers. A Wall Street research veteran with over 25 years of experience, he has a sharp eye toward adding value for his clients and is outspoken and direct in his assessment of REITs and their management. He holds a Ph.D. in finance and an M.B.A. from the UCLA Graduate School of Management.

Richard Imperiale: What fundamental characteristics contribute to the independent, low correlation of REITs as a market sector?

Dave Shulman: There are two main factors. One, for the most part, leases are contractual, so there's a great deal of stability to the revenue line. Two, a high proportion of the total return is derived from dividend payments rather than price appreciation. Dividend payments tend to be much more stable than the appreciation component of return. When you put those two things together, you end up with a lower-volatility asset. Of course, some of that is offset by the degree of financial leverage, so if you have an over-leveraged REIT, what I just said might not hold. By and large, though, REITs are moderately leveraged as opposed to overleveraged right now.

Imperiale: Do you have any observations about why some REITs are more bondlike and provide little growth but a high-dividend yield versus those that provide more growth? Do they behave differently?

Shulman: Yes. The more bondlike REITs will trade much more with the changes in the treasury bonds and yield spreads than with the overall equity market. Some REITs, like triple-net lease assets, are more of a pure yield play rather than an equity.

Imperiale: So investors might want to be careful about looking at those yield plays because they may behave like bonds?

Shulman: They will trade much more like bonds than like stocks. Sometimes that's good.

Imperiale: Why do you think that as a group, REITs have a low sensitivity to changing interest rates?

Shulman: I think that's because of the potential increase in income. Rising interest rates are generally associated with a better economy or higher inflation, and that tends to improve real estate rates of return, so it offsets any decline that would result from the interest rate rising.

Imperiale: How can REITs act as a hedge against inflation?

Shulman: They can act as a hedge against inflation over a long period of time—not necessarily a short period of time—as long as real estate markets are in rough balance. If there's too much excess capacity in the underlying real estate markets, then real estate will not act as a hedge against inflation. That certainly was the case in the late 1980s and the early 1990s.

Imperiale: So even though you may have inflation, if there's too much supply in the real estate markets, there is no inflation hedge?

Shulman: If there is too much supply you will not be able to transmit any kind of inflation through income. In the late

1970s and the early 1980s, when we had very high inflation in the United States and at the same time real estate markets were tight, REIT shares did extraordinarily well.

Imperiale: REITs may offer a modest tax advantage to some taxable investors. How would you compare that to the tax implications of corporate bonds?

Shulman: I think it's small because return of capital dividends may truly be return *of* capital and not return *on* capital. It may be return of capital and not income. So it's a temporary tax advantage, but not necessarily a permanent one.

Imperiale: When attempting to diversify a portfolio, what level of REIT exposure do you recommend to your clients?

Shulman: It really depends on the client and what the client's needs are. Some clients have a high degree of exposure and others have a low degree of exposure. Each client is different.

Imperiale: When you talk to institutional investors that have little or no REIT exposure, how do you suggest to them that they look at REITs in the context of their portfolios?

Shulman: Well, I think they have to look at REITs and compare them with other stocks. I think you've got to compare returns on REITs with returns in any other sector in the stock market, because I view REITs as a sector in the stock market and not as an asset class. It really depends how REITs are priced compared to the rest of the stock market and how much in assets the investor wants to put in equity versus fixed-income instruments.

Imperiale: When you look at the relative valuation of REITs versus the balance of the market, are there a few benchmarks that you prefer?

Shulman: The key we look at is the free cash flow yield of the REIT compared to an overall stock market, which we define as EBITDA [earnings before interest, taxes, depreciation, and amortization] less straight-line rents and normalized capital expenditures divided by the firm value, which is the free cash flow return from a hypothetically unleveraged position in the real estate. The other thing we do is try to evaluate the expected total return of REIT shares over a given time period compared to the overall stock market.

Imperiale: How do you do that when you're trying to look at the total?

Shulman: Typically, it's the dividend yield plus the potential price appreciation due to earnings growth.

Imperiale: And when you do that, do you hold the PE [price/earnings] multiple constant?

Shulman: Yes, you hold the PE multiple constant unless you think the stock is overvalued, in which case you lower the multiple. If you think the stocks are undervalued, you raise the multiple in termination. You're trying to get an estimate of the future return from REITs to compare with your best guess for the overall stock market. I use the word *guess* here because that's what it really is. It may be an educated guess, but it's still a guess.

Imperiale: When you look at the valuation level of the stock market when you're comparing it to REITs, is there some benchmark of value that you use?

Shulman: We believe that REITs are low-beta stock, so REITs do not have to return as much as the overall stock market to be long in a portfolio. For example, if an investor expects 12 percent return from the stock market as a whole and REITs deliver 10 percent, that might be very satisfactory given that the REIT beta is only half that of the stock market. So they have to look at REITs in the context of how volatile the shares are. REITs do not have to return as much as the stock market in order to be in the portfolio. I think that's a critical aspect.

Imperiale: Is there anything else you think is important for people considering REITs for their portfolio?

Shulman: I think the key thing is that REITs may become less of a substitute for real estate than in the past because most of the companies have become large national organizations. That makes it difficult to specialize in West Coast office space, which an investor could do by buying shares in Speaker Properties, or Washington, D.C., apartments, which an investor could do by buying Charles Smith Residential.

Those options were available a year ago but are no longer available today, so it's harder to use real estate market knowledge to help pick stocks and make investment decisions.

Imperiale: The opportunity to play supply and demand at the local level is not as available.

Shulman: The local market is much harder to do today than, say, five years ago.

Imperiale: Would you anticipate that over time we'll see more local sharpshooters take their real estate portfolios public?

Shulman: Yes, more will go public or merge into national companies. This is where the future opportunities will occur.

Part Two

Real Estate Economics and Analysis

Real Estate Market Characteristics

Chapter Summary

- Supply and demand drive value in local real estate markets.
- Business and economic growth within a region drives the demand for real estate.
- Development activity is the principal driver of new real estate supply.
- A local region's regulatory environment will impact real estate development activity in that market.
- The real estate market cycle can be divided into four stages: (1) recovery phase; (2) supply phase; (3) rollover phase; and (4) trough phase.
- Real estate firms have unique institutional characteristics that give them an advantage over non–real estate firms in the local market.
- Real estate investment trust (REIT) management provides a local market knowledge advantage.
- Liquidity gives REITs an advantage when dealing with the local market cycle.
- There are a wide range of sources that document local market supply and demand dynamics.

What marijuana was to the sixties, real estate is to the seventies.

—Ron Koslow

Real Estate Market Dynamics

In a local real estate market, supply can generally be defined as vacant space currently available for lease, plus any space available for sublease, plus new space under construction, plus space that will soon be vacated. The total reflects the available supply of space in a given local real estate market. Demand for space in a local real estate market can generally be derived from new businesses being formed, plus existing businesses expanding, plus new companies moving into the region, plus net new household formations, less closing, moving, and downsizing businesses. The total reflects the aggregate marginal demand for space within a region. In the most simple terms, supply is the total space available and demand is the total space required. In the final analysis, it is supply and demand for a given property type in the local real estate market that drives property valuation.

Local real estate market dynamics are driven by supply and demand for a particular property type. There are a wide range of factors that affect supply and demand in the local market. Values tend to be broadly affected by the general level of business activity and population growth. Interest rate trends, because of their impact on business activity, also have a general impact on real estate market dynamics.

It should be noted that the residential housing market and commercial real estate markets differ somewhat with respect to changes in the overall economy. The housing market has historically tended to lead the overall real estate market into and out of recessions. Conversely, the commercial real estate market has a higher tendency to follow rather than lead the overall economy. Although real estate is impacted by the overall economy, it is highly local in nature, and therefore economic activity at the local level or within the region will have a larger impact on property valuations than general overall economic activity. The health of a regional economy normally depends in part on the diversity of business and the base of employment within the region.

A region's regulatory environment is another factor that will impact real estate activity. Many cities have adopted low-growth or no-growth strategies that have made it difficult to develop new real estate. Restrictions on land use and limited access to city utilities, along with the imposition of development fees, school fees, and related activity fees, have made for difficult and limited development. In addition, some local governments have mandated rent control or targeted particular set-asides for low-income housing that are coupled with new development activities. This has had the effect of lowering general expected returns on real estate development and therefore has slowed the growth of development within certain geographic regions. So, in addition to the broad economic factors that impact real estate, many very specific local factors can affect the performance of a real estate market. Thus, the supply and demand characteristics of the local market have the greatest impact on real estate valuations at the local level.

Any local real estate market can be viewed as a quadrant chart (see Figure 6.1). At the intersection of the four quadrants is the point at which demand for and supply of real estate in the local market are at a perfect equilibrium. That intersection can be expanded to create an *equilibrium zone*. This zone reflects a market dynamic where, in general terms, the visible supply of real estate available and the current and forecasted demand for real estate are approximately equal. When supply and demand characteristics for a particular property category within a particular local market fall within the equilibrium zone, property and rental prices tend to be relatively stable at a market level.

As we go on to examine each of the four quadrants of the quadrant chart, we can see a particular series of characteristics that can be attributed to each quadrant. Quadrant 1 (Figure 6.2) represents the beginning of the real estate cycle in a given market or property type. This is the phase where demand begins to exceed available supply. It is sometimes termed the *recovery* phase. In this phase, rents begin to rise as demand begins to exceed supply available in the local market. Rents will continue to increase to a level where yields on new property development will become sufficiently attractive to cause developers to begin to consider adding property to the market. In addition, prices on individual properties begin to rise as occupancy levels increase and the available supply of new space decreases. As vacancy rates fall and available supply tightens, rents may begin to rise rapidly.

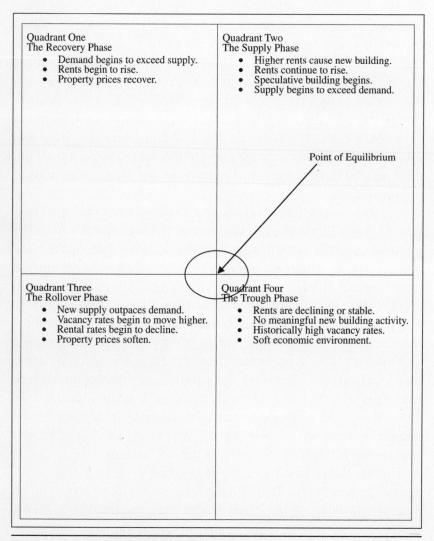

FIGURE 6.1 The Real Estate Market Cycle

Quadrant One The Recovery Phase • Demand begins to exceed supply. • Rents begin to rise. • Property prices recover.	

FIGURE 6.2 The Recovery Phase

At some point, higher rents precipitate new construction activity that leads to the phase depicted in quadrant 2 (Figure 6.3). This is the *development* or *supply* phase in the local market. If financing is available, speculative developers may begin construction in anticipation of continued rising rents, allowing for new building activity to begin, initially on a largely speculative basis. As supply continues to increase, the local market moves

	Quadrant Two The Supply Phase • Higher rents cause new building. • Rents continue to rise. • Speculative building begins. • Supply begins to exceed demand.

FIGURE 6.3 The Supply Phase

through the zone of equilibrium and into a pattern where current space available begins to exceed current demand for space. As this occurs, the growth rate in rent levels begins to subside, and vacancy rates, which had been decreasing, begin to increase slowly. As more incremental space is delivered into the market, rental growth begins to slow more dramatically and vacancy rates begin to rise more quickly.

The local market now moves into quadrant 3 of the real estate cycle (Figure 6.4). This is the *rollover* phase or *down cycle* of the market. New supply arrives more quickly than it can be absorbed, and begins to push rents downward. Vacancy rates begin to move higher than average for the market, causing property values to begin to soften and move lower. As the market continues to soften, property owners understand that they will quickly lose tenants or market share if their rental rates are not competitive. Thus, they begin to lower rents in an attempt to retain or attract tenants as well as to help cover the fixed expenses of operating a given property. This phase is also characterized by little or no activity with regard to transactions in commercial properties. The disconnect between what buyers are willing to pay for properties due to the uncertain outlook and what sellers feel properties are worth becomes wider.

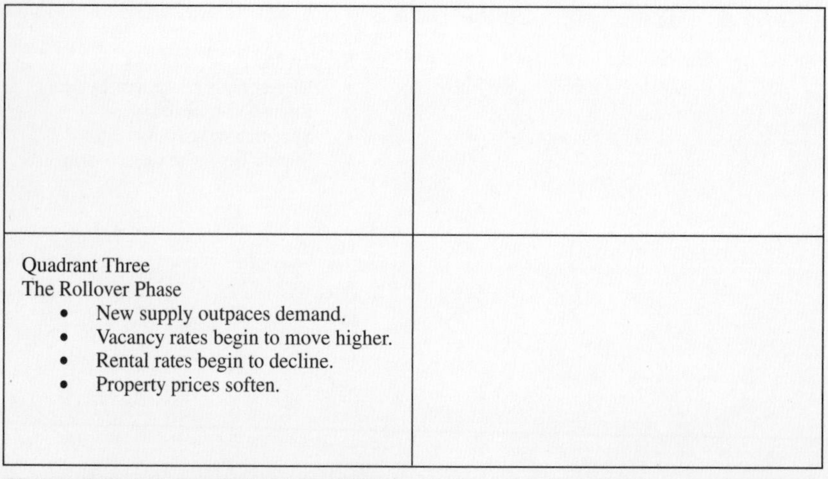

Quadrant Three
The Rollover Phase
- New supply outpaces demand.
- Vacancy rates begin to move higher.
- Rental rates begin to decline.
- Property prices soften.

FIGURE 6.4 The Rollover Phase

This leads the market into quadrant 4 of the real estate cycle, or the *trough* (Figure 6.5). In this phase, rents are generally flat to lower, there is no new supply activity, and there is likely to be a large amount of excess space available in the local market. This might be coupled with lower economic activity or weak demand for space in the local market, which tends to prolong the trough stage and make it deeper and more severe. The market cycle eventually reaches a bottom as new construction dissipates and demand increases and begins to absorb existing supply, moving the cycle back into quadrant 1.

In a theoretical perfect market, supply and demand would remain in the equilibrium zone and real estate returns would remain stable over the long term. However, in the real world, a combination of local market supply and demand factors can have an impact on the real estate cycle in a local market. Local markets that are less inclined to give entitlements to build or to create variances for building purposes will tend to remain in supply and demand equilibrium for a longer period than markets that are prone to rapid and uncontrolled development activity. Local real estate markets may not move through the quadrants in a 1 through 4 sequence. Demand and supply at the local level will likely ebb and flow, causing the local market dynamic to move in and out of the equilibrium zone. From an analysis

	Quadrant Four The Trough Phase • Rents are declining or stable. • No meaningful new building activity. • Historically high vacancy rates. • Soft economic environment.

FIGURE 6.5 The Trough Phase

standpoint, it is normally possible to determine which quadrants a given real estate property category occupies within a local market and to determine in which direction the supply and demand fundamentals are moving. One of the primary functions of management professionals in the real estate community is knowing and understanding which phase of the real estate cycle a local market is in.

Trends in Market Dynamics

One general fact is apparent with regard to the real estate cycle: Over the last decade, the cycle has become less severe than it was in the past. As mentioned in Chapter 2, higher underwriting standards on the part of real estate lenders coupled with the public market discipline that has resulted from the commercial mortgage–backed securities market have led to real estate cycles that are far more subdued than in the distant past. This market discipline has helped most local real estate markets avoid the severe boom and bust cycles that were evident prior to the 1990s. In addition, local economic factors that drive the local real estate economy often create a series of local markets that at any given time may be in any quadrant of the real estate cycle. If a local market is in quadrant 1 or 2 or in the equilibrium zone, the real estate environment is generally considered to be positive. When markets are in quadrant 3 or 4, the real estate environment is considered to be negative.

Although real estate markets in general are driven by growth of the overall U.S. domestic economy, any particular local market might be in any phase at any time. As this dynamic plays itself out in local markets and within each property group, it can be difficult to generalize about where in the cycle the overall real estate market is at a given time. For example, there may be a shortage of industrial space in Houston and a shortage of apartments in Denver, while at the same time there is an excess supply of hotel rooms in San Francisco and too much office space in Atlanta. This suggests that there are generally local market opportunities available for the real estate investor in some markets and in some property categories at any particular time. Local market knowledge is the key to making these specific market determinations. That market knowledge and skill is what a high-quality real estate investment trust (REIT) management team will bring to the real estate investment equation. In addition, a REIT portfolio that is diversified across property types and geographic regions will allow its owner to moderate risk that may result from changing local market dynamics.

Here is where the liquidity available to the shareholder of a REIT is a key advantage over the direct property owner. If, as in our earlier example, the office space market in Atlanta were deteriorating rapidly and supply looked as if it might outstrip demand for a long period, REIT shareholders could liquidate their shares in the REIT that holds property in Atlanta and reinvest the proceeds in a local office market that seems to have a better supply and demand profile. For a direct owner of office buildings in Atlanta, the option to liquidate is available but normally not practical. Due to the time and expense involved in the direct sale of a real estate portfolio, practical consideration dictates that the owner stay in place for the downward duration of the local market cycle. Direct real estate owners usually attempt to mitigate local market cycles by diversifying their property holdings across a number of different geographic regions. In addition, a local owner might diversify across different property types within the local market to help manage local market risk.

Local Market Information Dynamics

Real estate firms have unique institutional characteristics that generally distinguish them from non–real estate firms and give them a comparative advantage when dealing in a local market. These institutional characteristics also give local real estate firms an advantage over real estate firms that may not be present in the local real estate markets. These advantages are normally referred to as *market locality* and *market segmentation* advantages.

The market locality advantage suggests that there is a certain information advantage for participants in a local real estate market, which results from the local nature of the real estate market itself. There are a series of factors that contribute to the market locality advantage, such as a lack of standardized product, the absence of a centralized exchange for clearing information, and the increased research costs for nonlocal firms to develop data about a local market. In addition, a general understanding of the local political process also creates a local market advantage that a real estate firm from outside the area might not enjoy. Under these conditions and in local markets where information can be costly and not generally be available to all participants, local real estate firms are likely to be familiar with and have an information advantage.

Market segmentation suggests that different market segments require different types of expertise and management skills that may be very expensive and not easily transferred from other market segments. Management skills help to reduce the uncertainty associated with business risks resulting from physical operation of real property. This suggests that a firm specializing in a specific real estate segment may gain a competitive advantage as a result of superior managerial expertise acquired through time and experience. This market segmentation knowledge directly addresses the old adage that says: "If I had known how difficult it was, I wouldn't have tried to do it in the first place." Thus the ability to develop superior local market knowledge or the access to those who possess that knowledge can create a significant advantage in real estate investment.

Consider, for example, the local real estate developer who normally attends city planning commission meetings as well as city development and urban planning meetings given by local and state municipalities. Formally or informally, this developer may, through intimate knowledge of the planning process, understand that certain projects such as road extensions or the expansion of municipal services are part of a long-range plan. This same developer may use that information to contact a landowner that may not be in the local market or have similar local knowledge and make an offer to purchase a given parcel of land at prevailing market rates. The transaction could likely be consummated without any of the unknowing parties ever learning of the knowledge that the real estate developer possessed. The subsequent extension of a road or the development of an area could then turn into a highly profitable transaction for the developer, who was armed with deep local market knowledge that an uninformed observer may not have been able to obtain. It is this specific information advantage that local real estate operators bring to the table.

Geographic diversification can increase the efficiency of structuring a real estate portfolio. In fact, research indicates that regional diversification provides more portfolio benefits than diversification by property type. Geographic diversification within a portfolio provides a certain level of economic diversification as well. This economic diversification results from economic specific industry exposure as it relates to a geographic region. For example, San Jose, California, and the San Francisco Bay area are widely considered to be the center of geographic activity for Internet-based companies. Contrast San Jose with Detroit, Michigan, which is the center of economic activity as it relates to the U.S. automotive industry. Compare that to New York City, which has a diverse economy but is also considered to be the center of activity for the financial community. Now compare that to Washington, D.C., which is the center of activity for the federal government. Each of these geographic locations will respond differently to changes in the general economic environment. Therefore, diversifying across geographic regions can provide a certain level of economic diversification within the real estate portfolio. This type of geographic diversification is not normally possible for direct real estate investors unless they are of very significant size. However, an investor in a portfolio of REITs can accomplish geographic diversification as well as diversification by property with a modest investment, while enjoying a level of liquidity not available to the direct real estate investor.

Real Estate Data Resources

There is a wide range of data available for researching local market real estate activity. Most data takes the form of secondary data, which is data that has been gathered for some other purpose and is generally available for review. Secondary data is generally less costly and less time consuming to obtain than primary data. In general, secondary data is widely available at a low cost through libraries or firms that specialize in generating such data.

Primary data may be gathered by communication or observation and is designed to answer specific research questions. Real estate operators within a local market often gather primary data. Primary data may take the form of rent surveys or market surveys done by local brokerage firms. This first-hand data is valuable in assessing the primary supply and demand fundamentals of the local market. There are a number of primary and secondary data sources that compile local market statistics that are worthy of reviewing.

In the end, all data is subjective. The quality and purity of the data is generally considered a function of the source of the data. In the final analysis, the data must be analyzed and interpreted within the context of the local market dynamic. This requires making assumptions about the market and the data to end up with a forecast of local market activity for both supply and demand within a particular property category. This type of forecasting and analysis is embodied in the development process that will be discussed at length in Chapter 7.

Interview with Glen Mueller

Glen Mueller is professor of real estate at Johns Hopkins University in Baltimore, Maryland, where he established the Real Estate Capital Markets Research Program. He is the author of over 60 academic papers and articles on the real estate cycle and supply and demand factors in the local real estate market. His 1995 textbook, entitled *Real Estate Finance*, is widely used as the standard text on real estate finance at the graduate level. Mueller has a B.S.B.A. from the University of Denver, an M.B.A. from Babson College, and a Ph.D. in real estate finance from Georgia State University.

Richard Imperiale: Can you describe how you view the supply and demand cycle in the local real estate market?

Glen Mueller: Sure. I started with this kind of research at the time of the big crash in 1990, when I first went to Prudential Real Estate Investors. I was trying to figure out how we could monitor and look at this over time. I realized there were two processes in motion. First was supply and demand.

Supply of and demand for real estate is very local in nature, and it drives the rental rates in real estate markets. This also occurs at the metropolitan level. I called that the physical real estate market cycle. The second cycle, which I called the financial cycle, involves capital flow. The capital that flows to real estate can come from public or private markets, from debt or equity, and that capital flow affects prices. To get to a final value for a property, you have to figure out the confluence of both cycles—both rental growth and prices—and obviously the connecting point between those is the cap rate.

I actually break the physical cycle into four phases. One is a recovery phase. Then comes a growth phase, where a lot of new properties are being built that are in demand. The peak of the cycle occurs in this phase and is identified by the peak of the occupancy level and the lowest vacancy rate. It's easy to identify using historical data. For instance, the peak of the previous cycle was in 1979, when we had an average vacancy rate of 4.4 percent across the United States. Coming down from the peak is the hypersupply phase, where vacancy rates are still very low, but now all of a sudden supply is rising faster than demand. Rents typically are still going up during this phase. Then you go into a recessionary phase where you really aren't starting any new construction, but you're finishing off a lot of buildings. You may also have a demand-driven recession, where people are putting properties back on the market for subletting, which starts to force rents down.

Supply and demand affect rental growth and therefore the rents in a local marketplace; however, the financial cycle is really national—or even international—in scope where capital decides to flow to real estate or to some other investment alternative. In 1998, the real estate market was in excellent condition, prices were going up, but everybody that was investing in stocks decided that instead of REITs, they liked the idea of high-tech stocks. So even though the average REIT had earnings growth during that year, which meant prices should have been going up, prices actually went down. The stock market seemed to lose the Gordon growth model it's always worked with, which says if dividends are going to grow, prices should go up in expectation. We had dividends growing and prices going down because everybody decided to go to tech stocks, a speculative bubble formed, and people were after potential speculative growth. This was not unlike what happened to real estate prices in the late 1980s. Rents were going down, occupancies were going down, and yet prices were going up, because everybody wanted to buy real estate.

We look very carefully at the amount of supply, and we get our information on that from companies that monitor construction, planning, permits, starts, and completions. We check with a number of different economic sources to look at demand for each individual property type. If both supply and demand are growing at the same rate, then the market is in equilibrium. Vacancy levels are going to stay about the same, and rental growth will vary depending on where the market is in the cycle. In the recovery phase, typically rents are negative because landlords drop rents trying to attract tenants. In the growth phase, rents are usually positive, because landlords are constantly raising rents since there is more demand than supply.

Imperiale: You talked about the dislocation in the public real estate market in 1998. We saw the dislocation in the price of real estate securities, but it seemed that the private valuations held up under that scenario. Is that correct?

Mueller: Yes, because the capital flowing to the private markets builds real estate. People were looking at the fact that there was positive demand, the economy was growing, and the supply wasn't coming on too strong. And once the tech bubble burst and public investors started to say, "Let's go back to fundamental analysis and look at earnings growth and dividend growth," they saw that the real estate market was still doing well. In 2000, REITs had a phenomenal return as the market capital flowed back in and their prices rose back to where they should have been.

Imperiale: Would you agree that there may be some risks for people who focus on investing in REITs that are a bit unlike risks in the direct real estate market, because to some degree REIT investors are at the mercy of capital flowing in and out of the sector?

Mueller: Absolutely. Whenever you make a real estate investment, there are three decisions you need to make. It doesn't matter whether the investment is in mortgage, direct purchase of a property in a REIT, or CMBS [commercial mortgage–backed securities]. First, you need to know the real estate markets and analyze them. You need to know who the tenants are and what the cash flow is. If you have a decent idea of where the market's going, you know whether or not you're going to be able to get higher or lower rent than the last time you leased the space. Number two, if you buy an office building, you have to decide how much debt or equity you're going to put in it, what type, and what duration. Third is the management—who's going to manage the building, lease it out to tenants, take care of the building, decide what leases to sign and how long they're going to be, and so on.

Any time you make any real estate investment, you need to analyze the real estate, the capital structure, and the management. When you do this with a REIT, you do it in a package deal. You can figure out fairly accurately what's going on with the current and future earnings of a REIT. The price of that REIT is going to depend on the emotions of public market. In the long term, I believe that public markets are fairly efficient. In the short-term, they are very emotional. So if you can buy when the emotions are bad, even though the long-term fundamentals are good—as they were in 1998 and 1999—eventually that will all come back into balance.

Imperiale: When you look at the local market, do you believe in the general concept of local market knowledge advantage, or are markets becoming so transparent now that local market advantage is dissipating?

Mueller: To me, real estate has always been a local market phenomenon. You have to know that what people are looking for in Chicago is going to be very different than in Boston.

That applies not only for two markets in the same region, but in the same state. Look at Boston, Massachusetts versus Worcester, Massachusetts. Boston originally grew as a manufacturing town, turned into a high-technology town with mainframe computers back in the 1970s, then went to the financial services industries, and just recently has been back to being driven by computer software. Worcester was a manufacturing town throughout most of that period. Even though they're only 60 miles apart, the fundamentals that drive them are very different. It is very difficult to be successful if you take a cookie-cutter strategy that's done well for you in one state and move it to another one. You need people on the ground who really know a city.

Imperiale: We've seen a trend toward REITs that have exposure to multiple local markets. Some people have argued that that makes it harder to take advantage of the local market cycles because it moves the REIT into a general, overall market performance mode at all times. How do you address that issue, and how do you analyze a REIT that has exposure to multiple markets?

Mueller: As an investor, the perfect situation would be to have one REIT of each property type in each market. At the same time, a company that is focused on one property type and one market takes all of the cycle risk itself by going to additional markets. This diversifies the company's risk in different marketplaces. What we do is look at the markets that a particular REIT is in, run an analysis of what markets and what percentages that company has in each of those markets, and look at that so we can see what cycle the markets are in. Then we can look at the leases and their expirations to determine when we're going to see high risk in this particular company. Say we have a company that has concentrations in four or five markets. We look at the main ones, and for the smaller markets where we may not have information we use the U.S. average to try and model the vacancy and growth levels. It's a little more difficult and more complex, but it works. The REITs are doing the right thing for themselves by diversifying their investments in more markets so that they will have more stable, less cyclical earnings.

Imperiale: A number of people have said the real estate cycle has become less severe than it was historically. Do you think that's true, and what are the factors that are driving it?

Mueller: I certainly think the cycle is less severe. I don't think we'll have an oversupply like we had in the 1980s, where we continue to build buildings when there's no demand for them. That would be very difficult because today the capital sources have much better information than they did. The cycle report that I do today wasn't even possible in 1990. Today we get good information through a number of different sources, and everyone has it. We have more analysts looking at public companies, and we have more people providing information, so we won't have oversupply like we did. However, the variability of demand is something we can't control. For instance, in December 2000, the vacancy level across the U.S. office market was down in the 9 percent range. Then the technology bubble burst, people moved out of their space, and the vacancy level rose to 12.5 percent within one year. It didn't happen because we oversupplied anything, but because demand dropped off, obviously exacerbated by September 11—a unique event that no one could have predicted. That's a fairly quick move through the hypersupply phase and right into the recession phase. Obviously it went very quickly for hotels, because they've got the shortest leases—night to night. Will we reach the 22 percent vacancy rates we had in 1990? I don't believe so. We've seen the economy go through a longer expansion, so therefore real estate cycles might be longer and less volatile. It's a question of just how much less volatile, depending on how volatile the economy is.

Imperiale: So what's happened is that the vacancy rate has started to exceed the long-term average in a property sector, and that's really the signal that supply is exceeding demand.

Mueller: Right. There's still some supply growth because we started some construction on properties. When supply is growing at a low rate, but demand growth drops off to zero or goes negative, then looking at the relative change between the two, you can foresee a downward trend.

Imperiale: And when supply shrinks to below the long-term vacancy rate, would you say that's a market that's moving back into equilibrium?

Mueller: Well, you always have to look at both sides of the equation. But if supply goes to zero, that means no one's starting any new construction, there's just completion. We are coming close to that now. If it happens, and demand continues to be negative, we will continue to push ourselves further into a recession. If demand turns positive and supply is zero, it immediately starts us in a recovery and then eventually a growth phase.

Imperiale: How do you handle sublease space in your analysis? Do you think that you should use a different metric when you're comparing how much of the market is a result of a major firm putting out a lot of sublease space versus how much is actual vacancy that derives from lack of demand?

Mueller: First, if a REIT's tenant decides to sublease space, that REIT still gets revenues. So sublease space gets added into the potential available space that's going to drive short-term rental rates in a market. As soon as that sublease space gets absorbed, typically rents immediately start to move back up, because in sublease space, it's not the landlord but the tenant who is negotiating. Once sublease space is gone, when the economy turns and things get positive, rents will immediately jump back to where they should be, so sublease space is a much more temporary phenomenon.

Imperiale: Are there any other things investors in REITs should be thinking about when they're looking at local market dynamics?

Mueller: Well, one of the advantages of REITs is that they have multiple capital sources. Local developers have to deal with local banks, and if the local bank thinks the market's bad, it just doesn't give the developers any more money. But REITs have the option to use many more capital sources. Private companies have two sources of capital: private equity and private debt. They can get CMBS, but only with debt. REITs can use those sources, but they also can use public equity and public debt. They have more capital sources and they can spread them over multiple markets, which allows them to allocate and maybe pick up a good deal in a bad market at a time when no one else in that market can buy things. That's their real advantage from an investment standpoint.

Imperiale: As far as REIT management teams, should they function more like direct investment portfolio real estate managers or should they be more like operating company management teams?

Mueller: I think they're probably a combination of both. They both operate the company, operate the properties to the best of their ability, manage a portfolio, decide when it's time to sell out of a building, and so on. REITs have had better long-term returns averages over the past 28 years, about 12.5 percent versus 9.5 percent for direct individual properties using the NACREIF [National Council of Real Estate Investment Fiduciaries] Index. How can that be? Well, obviously, when you buy the direct piece of real estate, all you're buying is the real estate. When you buy into the REIT, you also get some sort of value out of capital structure and management. Maybe management was able to buy low at a high cap rate, reestablish a property, put it in good perspective, or sell it to someone at a lower cap rate or higher price. That appreciation is captured in the REIT's value to the investor. And obviously when I take a 9.5 percent unleveraged return and leverage it by 50 percent with some 7 percent money, I immediately increase the return to equity. So, looking at it from that perspective, there is value in management and capital structure through real estate investment.

Imperiale: Do you have an opinion on how you would quantify that value, maybe in terms of NAV [net asset value]?

Mueller: Well, let's look at REITs in terms of stock multiples. We'll use FFO [funds from operations] as our multiple. If you look at the long-term average, REITs have had multiples of around 12 to 12.5. Now let's convert that into direct real estate. Take the long-term cap rate for institutional-quality properties, about 9, and turn it into a multiple of 1. That comes to 11.1. So if REITs are trading at what everybody calls their NAV, they'd have to trade at multiples of around 11.1. But their long-term average has been more like 12.5.

Now let's take an unleveraged property at 9 percent and leverage it very conservatively at 50 percent, and we get about 10 percent increase in our return to equity. That turns our 11.1 multiple into a 12. Then management, through good operations, adds another 5 percent, so now we're up to 12.5. So, over the long term, REITs should trade in a premium to their NAV because of good capital structure and good management. Both add some value; the question is how much. If you look back over time, in 1996 and 1997 we were trading at multiples like 15. These were over the long-term trading value, but at or close to NAV. That means they're trading slightly below the long-term average and there's a good chance they will move up as the market realizes the value that's there.

Imperiale: When you look at the constituency of that excess value, do you consider the frictional cost of putting together a large, high-quality portfolio of real estate? Would you agree that the frictional cost and the opportunity cost of doing that deserves some kind of premium?

Mueller: Sure. I started working with institutional investors in 1990, and they constantly had allocation targets they could never meet because they couldn't buy enough properties. When times were good, they ended up paying premium prices to get them. The one thing that I think really made the REIT market grow and still has great potential in the future is the UPREIT structure. As an individual owner, you don't have to take that tax hit from capital gains from purchasing a property—you have the option of timing your tax when you convert to UPREIT shares. You can take individual buildings that have very high risk and drop them into a diversified pool, so you now have a better investment that's more diversified. Then you decide when you want to convert to publicly traded shares and time the tax event. And if you never do, when you die, the basis gets left to your heirs and they get to skip that. Also, they don't have to worry about breaking up private real estate, because they all have publicly traded shares that they can handle any way they want. It's probably the best planning vehicle to come along in the last three decades.

Imperiale: Do you see that as a potential engine for growth of the public REIT sector in the future?

Mueller: Yes. It eliminates a lot of problems deciding what to do as far as liquidating an investment.

Real Estate Development

Chapter Summary

- Real estate development is the riskiest area in real estate.
- The high risk level is rewarded with high potential returns on successful development activities.
- Development activity is a central part of the business strategy for some real estate investment trusts (REITs).
- Understanding the development process is critical to analyzing local real estate markets.
- Because of long lead times, project timing is critical in real estate development.
- Managing the entitlement process is crucial to the ultimate success of a development.
- The design and construction process requires a high level of risk management skill.
- Successful development activity can add value and earnings for REIT shareholders.

The trick is to make sure you don't die waiting for prosperity to come.

—Lee Iacocca, 1973

Real estate development is the high-stakes poker of the real estate industry. Most people associate real estate development with the whole concept of real estate. Such well-known names as Donald Trump and John Zeckendorf are widely known as real estate developers. And it seems that every regional real estate marketplace has a local Donald Trump who is always proposing a bigger and better project with his name firmly attached. There's a certain blend of entrepreneurship and ego that goes into the development of real estate. The key to success is to make sure that your real estate development activities involve more of the entrepreneurship and less of the ego.

Real estate development is at the high end of the risk scale, but when successfully implemented it is also on the high end of the return scale. The development process is worth understanding if you want to get involved in real estate investments. Development is essentially the supply side of the local real estate market. Understanding the development process also leads to additional insights into the local market supply and demand dynamics. In order to make an accurate assessment of the local market, you need to have an assessment of current development activity as well as of the impact of potential competitive building activity that may not be apparent in the local market. A thorough understanding of the development process allows for a better and more complete assessment of the local market economics.

Historically, real estate investment trusts (REITs) with the best earnings performance have often made development activity an important part of their business strategy. The incremental yield available in a development project over the comparable market yields for existing properties makes development a high-value-added proposition for REITs. For example, the unleveraged cash-on-cash return for an existing industrial warehouse in a particular local market might be 11.5 percent. A developer may see the opportunity in that same market to build a similar industrial warehouse with a projected unleveraged cash-on-cash return of 16 percent. Thus the opportunity to deploy capital is available at 11.5 percent with minimal risk, or at a potential return of 16 percent for a riskier development project. Here is where the real estate expertise of the REIT's management will either add value and earn a higher overall return for the shareholder, or overreach for return and put the shareholder's capital at risk.

The development of real estate is very entrepreneurial in nature. Different types of development activities have distinct differences: Developing warehouses is different from developing offices and developing apartments is different from developing hotels. It is worth noting that the substantial redevelopment of an existing property can be as difficult as, if not more difficult than, a ground-up new development project. Development is the aspect of real estate in which the greatest number of risk variables must be simultaneously managed. It encompasses the challenge of managing a myriad of legal, financial, market-related, and construction risks, as well as managing the many people-related risks related to the project. The challenges can be daunting. In many ways, developing real estate is like creating a new product for retail distribution. Not only does the real estate developer have to envision the "product" from concept through completion, but the product must also be positioned among competing products within the local real estate market.

Timing is critical when it comes to the development process in real estate. The development process has a very long cycle. In some instances, it can take as long as five years to go from concept through completion of a large real estate project (see Table 7.1). The project might start out with a market analysis and location analysis to determine the viability of the project. This can in turn lead to negotiations to control a particular parcel of land. That initial phase of development activity can easily take 12 to 18 months. Following the site analysis and acquisition is likely to be the entitlement process. As discussed in Chapter 2, various communities have different appetites and varying standards for the creation of new real estate projects. It is not unusual for the entitlement process to run 12 to 18 months or longer. Once the project is entitled for building, design through construction and completion can take another 12 to 18 months. Finally leasing activities can take 6 to 24 months, depending on the property type. When it's all said and done, a project can easily take three to five years to complete.

The real estate cycle plays a significant role in the timing of development activities. Because of the long lead time involved in the typical real estate project, it is critical for the developer to know where the local market stands at each phase of the project.

TABLE 7.1 Timetable of Development Stages

Activity	Expected Time
Market analysis	1–3 months
Location analysis	3–6 months
Site acquisition	6–9 months
Entitlement and zoning	12–18 months
Design and construction	12–18 months
Leasing	6–18 months
Total development time	**40–72 months**

The ideal outcome is for the developer to deliver the project at a time when the market is very tight and there is little available supply. The least desirable outcome is when bad timing results in delivering new supply into a soft market with increasing vacancy and declining demand. The ultimate timing of delivery can make the difference between the financial success or failure of a project.

In addition to ground-up real estate activities, a developer may achieve high rates of return through projects that involve major redevelopment of properties. This type of redevelopment can encompass upgrading an underutilized property or a property that may be involved in a lower use. For example, converting a large urban warehouse to office space or residential lofts might be a redevelopment project with high potential. The real estate may be acquired at a very low cost and the redevelopment may provide for substantially increased earnings after capital expenses. The risks associated with redevelopment activities are similar to those of ground-up development except that redevelopment sometimes includes an additional layer of design and construction risk. The developer never knows what will be found until the actual demolition process begins. A redevelopment building might contain hazardous materials such as asbestos that must be properly abated, or unforeseen structural problems might be found. These types of construction-related issues can lead to increased costs and delays.

In nearly all instances, development or redevelopment activity requires overcoming political and local inertia with regard to a project. Overcoming inertia or dealing with opposition to a project requires a high level of skill on the part of the developer. In terms of diplomacy, the developer must be adept at obtaining the best outcome from all participants in the process. He or she must also be an effective champion of the project, continually selling and promoting it throughout the development process. In any given situation, the developer must know what the desired outcome is and how much room is available for compromise. In addition to using diplomacy, the developer need to know when to resort to hardball tactics such as litigation. These factors must all be measured in the context of project timing, financial impact, and project feasibility. For example, adding landscaping might increase the overall cost of a project but have little impact on the overall timetable. However, requiring a higher ratio of parking to building area might substantially alter the financial feasibility of the project. A good developer will know when a project is not going to be feasible and will terminate the entire project rather than create a situation that provides an inadequate return on invested capital. In the final analysis, the numbers have to work.

Overcoming the inertia of the entitlement process allows the developer to begin managing the dynamic process of development and its associated risks. These risks take many forms and may include preleasing activities, maintenance of adequate financial resources, and the general management of the development or redevelopment process. The developer must control an extremely dynamic process while managing financial and business risks.

The Development Process

The development process generally begins with the acquisition or control of land that is targeted for the intended use. In the case of a REIT, this may mean the acquisition of a parcel of real estate or land, or it may result from redevelopment opportunities on land or buildings already owned by the REIT. If acquisition of land is required as a part of the process, it is vital to acquire the land quickly and quietly in order to avoid the possibility of what are termed *holdouts*. Holdouts occur when property owners refuse to sell at any price or demand prices that are so far out of line that they make the financial feasibility of the project unacceptable. Quickly and quietly assembling a land package and avoiding holdouts is key to the development process.

Alternatively, real estate developers and REITs may own land inventories. These land inventories are typically parcels of land adjoining existing real estate projects owned by the developer or REIT. These lands have usually been entitled to build and are held in inventory awaiting market conditions that will support development activities. This pre-entitlement allows the developer to substantially shorten the cycle time of a project because the site analysis, acquisition, and entitlement process is substantially complete. Often this land is perpetually for sale, offered as a build-to-suit site where an interested buyer can acquire the land and the developer will build a building or complex to suit the buyer. There is some debate among analysts who follow REITs over the merits of land inventory. There are those who argue that land inventories are costly to maintain and come at the expense of the overall performance of the REIT's existing property portfolio. The other side of the argument suggests that land inventory provides the opportunity for build-to-suit developments as well as speculative building by the REIT when market conditions will support such activity, and therefore the higher potential returns are generally worth the risks to the shareholder. In most cases, the value added is a function of how skillfully the real estate management team handles the land inventory.

In many circumstances, land is acquired under a conditional purchase agreement or contingent purchase agreement. This is usually prefaced upon a series of conditions being met in order to facilitate the eventual land transaction. In most instances, the developer pays a fee to the landowner to obtain an option on the land subject to certain conditions. The option has a limited term and the developer must complete the conditional process by the end of the option term or risk losing the ability to control the land. In some instances, the landowner may participate by contributing the land to a joint venture with the developer. Large development projects may also be undertaken using staged payments to the landowner, meaning the landowner is paid as each phase of the development is completed. In many instances, the seller receives a monthly option fee to compensate for staging of payments over time as well as an overall higher price for the land.

In some circumstances land is acquired through a process known as *eminent domain.* This is a legal term referring to the right of a public entity, such as a state or local municipality, to seize a property for public purposes in exchange for compensation to the property owner. In some instances, this occurs when a holdout is threatening the viability of a large-scale project that has been embraced by a community. If the holdout controls a key parcel, the local municipality may use its power of eminent domain to acquire that parcel, thus allowing the project to move forward.

Sometimes land acquisition is not really an acquisition at all. There are cases where the land on which a building is built is leased on a long-term basis. This is particularly true in areas where there is a scarcity of buildable land. In such situations a landowner may, rather than sell a parcel, be inclined to engage in a long-term lease. The lease is normally structured in a way that allows the property owner to participate in the success of the real estate project. In many land leases, annual lease payments are supplemented by the landowner's participation in the upside rental growth of the underlying property.

Entitlement

Overcoming inertia to allow a property to be developed for its highest and best use is normally the beginning of the entitlement process. Local governments often perceive development activities to be a threat to the status quo and are generally reluctant to support new development projects. In addition, many local residents view development activity as a "not in my backyard" proposition. Well-organized citizen groups often turn up en masse to oppose development projects. In many instances, circumstances dictate that the local governmental authorities must weigh the gain in tax revenue against the community standard to determine whether a project will proceed and in what form. This is because almost all projects involve some type of variances from local building codes. A real estate project built in complete conformance with all local zoning standards and building codes is normally the exception. Generally speaking, in order to make a project work, the developer needs some changes in regulation or some compromise to allow the project to proceed. This may be an adjustment to the required number of parking spaces, an exception to the required maximum height standards, or a specific variance to route storm or drainage water in a particular manner. In any case, most projects require variances of one form or another.

When it comes to zoning exceptions in many communities, some items tend to be more negotiable than others. In general terms, the larger the scale of the variance that is required, the more difficult it is to obtain from a political standpoint. In order to overcome all these entitlement issues, most developers must attempt to form a political coalition with the local government. Again, the diplomatic and political skills of the developer are required to be at their best during the entitlement process.

Normally time is of the essence during the entitlement phase. By this stage of the development process, the developer needs to keep negotiations moving along in order to sustain the project. In most cases, compromises are struck in order to save time and move the project forward. A good developer will know in advance what compromises may need to be made and what compromises he or she is willing to make in order to move the project forward.

In many instances, REITs and large landowners focus on creating improvements in their land inventory to add value. Management may obtain for option a parcel of real estate and facilitate necessary zoning variances. In addition, some level of infrastructure, such as sewer and water, may be installed to go along with zoning changes. This land is then considered ready for development and staged as a potential project when market conditions dictate the opportunity.

The entitlement process is as much an art as it is a science. Overcoming inertia and opposition, and obtaining variances and building political support for a project, require developers to have political and diplomatic skills. In addition, moving the project along a time line and understanding the financial risks involved require a high level of risk management skills.

Feasibility Planning and Production

Planning and design are the most important aspects after entitlement. Early in the planning process, the developer needs to position the project within the broader context of the community at large. This means the developer needs to work with the community to understand which groups have an interest in a project and what those interests are. This dialogue with the community helps to position the project and build political coalitions.

Once a master plan has been developed, the design process can begin. This process is often difficult to understand, particularly for people who are not involved in the real estate business. It is complicated and involves a high level of input by a large number of parties at interest. The architect goes through a discovery process aimed at determining needs and solutions, then takes this discovery through several different stages using input from the parties at interest in order to formulate a specific solution.

The first stage of the process, known as *programming,* defines the purposes the facility will be designed to serve. Depending on the size and scale of the project, the programming stage may be very formalized or more relaxed. The programming process attempts to gather input from all the local users of the end product and incorporate that input into the design.

The next stage of the process is known as the *layout phase.* Information from the programming stage is used to lay out a preliminary plan for the project. The architect attempts to determine what goes where, how traffic will flow through and around the building, what materials are suitable for the project, and the allowable size of the project.

In the next phase, known as *design development,* the architect uses feedback from the programming and preliminary design phases to formulate a more definite plan. In many ways, there is a cost-benefit approach to the design development phase. From a financial point of view, project costs begin to materialize in this development phase. Trade-offs are made as less expensive materials are substituted for more expensive materials and amenities are added or deleted based on budget considerations. At the end of this phase, there is a set of drawings for the development that are fairly complete and encompass a level of detail that illustrates how the facility will function.

Design drawings are then translated into construction documents, which are also known as *working drawings*. These documents enable building contractors to see a level of detail that allows them to make a construction cost estimate and to begin to determine pricing estimates for the project. The working drawings are the most complicated portion of the architectural process. Many other experts, such as site engineers, structural engineers, and mechanical contractors, have some level of input into the working drawings. In addition, all these subcontractors will be paid by the architect for their work. This is the phase in which most of the design costs are incurred. In many instances, REITs have developed pools of in-house talent that can facilitate to a large extent the design and cost-estimating portion of the feasibility and planning for a new project. This is a valuable resource for REITs.

At the end of the design process, the developer will have a detailed set of working drawings. These drawings will include specifications and a sufficiently high level of detail to allow building contractors to put a firm price estimate on the cost of building the project. In the development process, it is important that the developer understand the construction process sufficiently to manage these negotiations. Most REITs that are active in the development arena have the in-house talent to manage the construction process.

At this point, the bidding begins. The developer circulates documents requesting bids from subcontractors. These subcontractors in turn try to develop a bid that is low enough to get the job, yet high enough to allow for a fair return on their work. Again, this is an area that requires a high level of knowledge about the construction process in order to understand the bids as well as the ability to negotiate effectively in order to create an atmosphere to obtain the fairest level of bids. Once the bidding process is complete, financing for the project needs to be put in place. (We will deal more with financing issues in Chapter 9.) Finally, the construction process must be managed from planning through production in order to bring the real estate development online and available for market use.

Within the world of REITs, there is an ongoing debate over development activity. The question is: Does development activity add value for the REIT shareholder? In general, REIT management attempts to create value through management activity at the property level, but can it create value at the development level? In a stable real estate market environment, there are very few ways to create additional value. Value creation lies in the skill set of management personnel and their ability to properly develop or redevelop new product. It all comes down to a risk profile. Lower-risk development activities include building to suit and development projects with a high level of preleasing activity. Also, there is less risk in short-cycle building activities such as industrial warehouses, which by their nature can be designed and developed very quickly. This allows the developer to end development activity at the first signs of market weakness. Speculative construction is the highest-risk development activity. However, risk assessment really needs to be done on a project-by-project basis.

Each sector of the real estate market generally has specific problems with regard to development risk. Offices that may be built on spec are definitely impacted on changes in the economic outlook and also have a higher level of risk because of the long development time frame. Retail malls have many of the same problems as office space. There is a long time frame with regard to development and construction, and inline retail tenants typically will not sign a lease until the project is within six months of opening. Industrial REITs suffer from low barriers to entry. Generally industrial buildings are simple to build and therefore often are characterized by higher levels of speculative activity. Apartments, because of the short duration of the tenants' leases—typically two years or less—have the opportunity to quickly capture tenants from other projects. Unfortunately, new apartment supply tends to be felt across the local apartment market very quickly. And if apartments spread the pain quickly, hotels spread the pain instantaneously. New hotels have a very fast impact on other hotel properties in the local market. Self-storage has a short building period; however, there is a long lease-up that has the effect of leaving the developer exposed to any potential economic downturn over a fairly long period. Manufactured home communities also suffer from a long initial lease-up period. But, unlike self-storage, manufactured home communities are generally in more limited supply, and the political implications of "not in my backyard" also make entitlement increasingly difficult for manufactured housing communities.

Assessing Development Activity

When it comes to REITs, the best way to assess development activity is as follows:

- Study the history of development activity as a firm and how it integrates into the REIT's overall business strategy

- Study the level of development activity as it relates to the size of the REIT

- Conduct sensitivity analysis to examine the outcome or exposure created by development activity

- Assess the risk exposure for the REIT on a project-by-project basis

The risk assessment should extend to the property category, the supply and demand for that property in the local market, the preleasing activity of the REIT, the expected cycle time for the development, and the pro forma return expectations on the project. These issues are discussed in more detail in Chapter 9.

Merchant Building Activities

Recently, some development-oriented REITs have become *merchant builders*. Merchant builders develop properties and then sell them immediately upon completion in order to make a profit. Merchant building can be viewed as a way for REITs to enhance their earnings while continuously recycling capital on the balance sheet. Merchant building activity will have a positive impact on a REIT's funds from operation; however, a high level of merchant building activity makes it difficult to assess the ongoing performance of the REIT's underlying real estate port-folio. It can be argued that there is an intrinsic value through the merchant development activities, although it is hard to assess the level of value this might add to a REIT's market valuation. Merchant building activities add risk but also add return, and the question remains whether the return is sufficient to justify the risk.

Development activity takes a high level of skill and also requires financial resources. In many instances, developers may have the skills but lack the required financing to put a project in place. Joining together a skill set and capital can be viewed as the quintessential element necessary to formulate a real estate development deal. In chapter 8 we will discuss the many potential deal structures available in the real estate world.

Partnerships and Joint Ventures

Chapter Summary

- The high level of skill required to participate successfully in the real estate market inhibits many financial investors from directly owning or developing property.
- In the real estate world, joint ventures are the preferred methods for marrying financial capital and real estate expertise.
- The terms and conditions of joint ventures are detailed in joint venture agreements.
- The basic provisions of joint venture agreements outline the responsibilities and expectations of the parties involved.
- The agreements address the treatment of cash flow, debt structure, operating objectives, lifetime of the venture, and distribution of profits.
- Joint ventures allow real estate investment trusts (REITs) to expand their business model while preserving the flexibility of their balance sheet.
- Academic studies report positive and statistically significant increases in shareholder value as a result of joint ventures in the real estate community.
- Joint ventures are interpreted as positive by shareholders of the participating firm because of their perceived resulting financial, management, and information synergies.

- Because of their market knowledge, REITs are in a unique position to participate in joint venture activities.

Mr. Morgan buys his partners; I grow my own.

—Andrew Carnegie, 1906

In the last two chapters we discussed at length the methodology in the real estate community related to the analysis of local markets and the creation of new product or new real estate in those markets. It is apparent that a high level of local market knowledge is required when estimating the supply and demand dynamics of a given property type in a local market. In addition, it is apparent that development activity requires a high level of skill on the part of the local real estate developer. The great amount of skill required and effort necessary to participate successfully in the real estate market place inhibits many investors from directly owning, operating, and developing real estate.

The good news is that there are other ways for large institutional investors to participate in the real estate investment process. These are more passive approaches that allow institutions that do not have the skill set to to place capital directly in the real estate sector. The heart of this passive approach involves the concept of joining together the skill set and knowledge of the local market experts with the capital resources of major institutions to formulate a joint venture in real estate.

Joint ventures or partnerships in the real estate world are the preferred methods for marrying financial capital and real estate expertise. There is a spectrum of real estate opportunities available for investment purposes that are designed specifically to create capital and efficiently allocate that capital through joint ventures and partnerships. These ventures range from direct investment partnerships formed between institutional capital sources and real estate experts all the way to syndications and pooled funds with a number of investors participating in a group format. Whatever the legal format—whether it be a partnership, a limited liability corporation, a joint venture or a syndication of some type, either public or private—the basic theory is always the same. Essentially the project identifies the expertise of a real estate investor that possesses market knowledge and experience and aligns that expertise with a pool of capital in the form of equity, and possibly debt, to create a common real estate venture.

The venture will invest the resources in a variety of properties or developments that are initially agreed upon in a statement of intent or general purpose for the partnership or joint venture. The second half of the equation, which is often subject to a higher level of negotiation and analysis, determines who will get paid as a result of the financial operation of the partnership, but more importantly it determines how much each participant will get paid and when those payments will occur. The basic provisions of the agreement will outline the responsibilities and expectations of the parties involved. The agreement will define the concept of project cash flow, which will be defined and analyzed. The notion of a preferred rate of return will be detailed. Debt structure and the limitations of the use of debt will be outlined. The potential tax benefits and their distribution will be agreed upon. In addition, the term of the agreement will be memorialized and the provisions for termination of the venture activity will be outlined. Finally, a discussion of fees, acceptable expenses, and third-party management arrangements will be detailed, agreed upon, and disclosed in the basic partnership or joint venture document.

Cash flow is at the heart of any real estate deal. In addition, the real estate partner in a given deal often has limited personal and financial exposure in a project. Therefore, it is important for all parties to understand the deal structure and to create a structure that aligns the interests of the various parties to the transaction. Aligning interests allows everybody within the investment to have the same motivation and to be in general agreement as to the direction of a given project. Cash flow is normally defined as revenues on the project less expenses of the project, which yields net operating income. By adding back depreciation and amortization expenses, it is possible to arrive at cash flow.

Cash flow is the actual net cash generated from the real estate activities. In a normal joint venture structure, the financial participants receive an annual cash preference with regard to the cash flow. A financial participant that commits $1 million of capital to the project may be entitled to a preferential return of 10 percent per year on its invested capital; thus the first $100,000 of cash flow would be paid to the financial partner to satisfy the preferential return requirements. After the preferential rate of return has been met, the remaining cash flow is divided on a formula basis between the financial investor and the real estate partner. This excess distribution structure might have several different levels to provide for a higher percentage participation in the cash flow as the financial investors receive a higher net return on their investment. In many partnership structures, after a preferential return of 20 percent has been achieved, the balance of the cash flow might possibly inure to the real estate partner. This cash flow arrangement will typically remain in place until such time as the original financial investors have fully recovered their initial investment through cash flow. At that time, the cash flow sharing arrangement might shift to a structure such as 50/50 or may allow for a preferential return to flow to the real estate partner. Again, it is important to note that deals are often negotiated on an individual basis and there is no standard format for structuring who will get paid how much and when. These elements are generally reflective of the level of risk and the profile of the particular deal at hand.

Beyond allocating current cash flow, the partnership agreement must also determine how the final profits of the project are ultimately divided. In most instances, these back-end-sharing arrangements reflect the percentage of capital each partner has committed to the deal. For example, if the financial partner has committed 90 percent of the net capital and the real estate partner has committed 10 percent, then typically the profits on the project are divided similarly, with 90 percent going to the financial partner and 10 percent going to the real estate partner. However, it should be noted that in most instances the real estate partner will receive no final distributions until all the initial capital of the financial partners has been recovered in total. This creates an incentive for the real estate partner to provide for a high preferential rate of return for the financial partners as well as providing for the complete return of the financial partner's capital. This type of structure aligns the financial interests of all participants involved in the project.

Most deals use some form of debt in addition to the equity provided by the financial partners to fund the total capital amount required to complete the real estate deal. Debt structure is often defined at the initial phases of the deal, and the ability of the real estate operating partner to change the debt level or modify the debt terms of the partnership is often subject to the approval of the financial partner. Debt structure is an important aspect of the overall agreement. A higher level of debt can provide for higher potential total returns; however, higher debt also creates a higher risk level for the project. More conservative financial partners may require lower leverage debt structures. Lower debt levels are normally reflected in the hurdle rates and annual cash preferences for the financial partners.

Tax benefits are also identified and distributed in most joint venture situations. As discussed earlier, a major part of the structural problems within the real estate community in the 1970s and 1980s resulted from a tax policy that created an excess supply of real estate. The Tax Reform Act of 1986 lengthened depreciation schedules and increased the useful life over which properties could be depreciated. In addition, it prevented investors from deducting real estate losses against non–real estate income. These changes substantially decreased many of the favorable tax aspects of investing in real estate. However, there are still tax-related issues surrounding joint ventures and tax benefits available to certain participants. In the case of tax-exempt investors such as Employee Retirement Income Security Act of 1974 (ERISA) plans, the tax benefits have little value. Thus it is not unusual to see the tax benefits, if any, being delivered to the real estate operating partners in exchange for higher cash flow benefits being delivered to the tax-exempt financial partners.

The implications of the tax adjustments in the Tax Reform Act of 1986 are quite substantial. Prior to 1986, typical commercial investment properties would be depreciated over a 15-year useful life. Under the Tax Reform Act and subsequent revisions in 1993, a 39-year useful life was enacted. This change in depreciation made a substantial difference in the noncash portion of the depreciation expense, effectively lowering the net cash generating ability of most real estate properties. In essence, depreciation allowances defer taxation until the time the property is sold. At the time of sale, the gain is calculated using the depreciated property value and the taxes are calculated using a capital gains rate that is currently 20 percent rather than 25 percent or 28 percent in effect prior to the 1986 act.

The tax disadvantage resulting from the change in depreciation can be partially mitigated by using higher leverage. If higher loan-to-value ratios are used or higher leverage is employed, the added mortgage interest expense becomes deductible and the amount of equity capital required to finance the property decreases. This in effect creates a higher return on invested capital and a higher cash flow return on capital. The relative advantage of higher leverage depends entirely on the cost and availability of mortgage financing. It should be noted that higher leverage may look attractive from a return on capital standpoint when the property is operating in a positive mode, but leverage also magnifies the potential downside in a property that is not operating well. Thus, debt should be analyzed not just on the upside but also on the downside when considering capital structure.

Beyond operating provisions, the partnership or joint venture agreement must address termination provisions. Termination provisions are usually created to facilitate the financial investor's recovery of capital within a certain time horizon. Because real estate is a long-term investment, most partnerships or joint ventures have relatively long time horizons. Because of its nature, real estate is a long-term asset class. Therefore, real estate joint ventures tend to have a longer term. Most develop-and-hold or buy-and-hold venture strategies have a minimum life span of 10 years. The idea of a predetermined time horizon has a particular appeal for financial investors because it means that real estate partners cannot tie up capital and extract management fees over an indefinite period of time.

The finite time horizon also presents certain disadvantages, which are generally related to the cyclical nature of the real estate industry. Financial partners might find that real estate partners are not inclined to dispose of real estate at any time prior to the termination period of the partnership. Thus, looking at a 10-year partnership, 7 or 8 years into the partnership might be the ideal time to dispose of real estate held in the partnership. However, the real estate partner may not want to dispose of the property at that point and lose two or three years of partnership fees. Also, because it is impossible to predict where the real estate cycle will be at the end of a partnership term, almost any reasonably long period of time might find a partnership ending in an unfavorable real estate market. Because of this, it is not unusual for partnership agreements to have optional extension periods that can increase the life of the fund for one to three years. These extension options are designed to provide an additional holding period that allows real estate market fundamentals to recover. In most instances, these extension periods require the agreement of the financial partner in order to be implemented.

It is apparent that no predetermined financial structure can readily be applied to partnerships and joint ventures in the real estate arena. Each joint venture must take into consideration the properties for the development and the local market factors in determining the general structure of the partnership agreement. More conservative financial partners such as pension plans will tend to have more conservative deal structures that provide for lower leverage and more uniform predictable cash flow to the financial partner. Conversely, opportunity funds that reflect a more aggressive pool of investors might prefer higher levels of debt and require a more aggressive initial sharing of cash flow benefits. Again, each joint venture deal is structured to reflect the general posture of all the deal participants. At the end of the process, the union of money and expertise should enable the participants to negotiate an agreement that substantially aligns the interests of all parties involved.

REITs and Joint Ventures

Joint ventures allow real estate investment trusts (REITs) to expand their business model and employ their substantial real estate expertise while preserving the flexibility of capital on the balance sheet. A REIT operates a direct investment portfolio

(DIP) of real estate. By participating in joint ventures and partnerships, the REIT management team can increase the return on
capital invested in the DIP. In increasing numbers, REITs are
marrying their broad real estate expertise with ever larger pools
of investment capital. Partnerships and joint ventures allow
REIT management teams to extend the use of balance sheet
capital, increase potential returns to investors, and create a
greater level of diversification, thereby reducing risk in the DIP.

Real estate markets have unique institutional characteristics
that differentiate them from non–real estate markets and accord-
ingly are expected to produce results that diverge from results
observed in the non–real estate sector. These characteristics
include local market knowledge and market segmentation, development knowledge that may give real estate firms an information
advantage regarding local real estate markets, and better management and technical expertise regarding real estate ventures.

A number of academic studies have examined the effect of
joint venture programs and their impact on the shareholder
value of REITs. In general, these studies report positive and statistically significant increases in shareholder value as a result of
joint ventures in the real estate community. The research concludes that there are several factors that make the real estate
joint venture successful. The first is the synergies that result from
combining the resources of two or more enterprises. Under the
assumption that the capital market is efficient, real estate joint
ventures are normally interpreted as positive by shareholders of
the participating firm because of their perceived financial synergies resulting from the joint venture. The operating synergies can
be attributed to economies of scale, better competitive position
in local markets, higher levels of primary research, and more efficient use of managerial and human resources as well as reduction of business risk through diversification. In addition, the
ability of the joint venture to increase the overall debt capacity
of the participants is perceived as a financial synergy that is positive for the shareholder.

The other unique institutional characteristics that can be
attributed to the joint venture in the real estate market are the
characteristics of market locality and market segmentation. In
the local real estate market, the lack of standard real estate

product and the absence of a central market exchange require a higher level of research knowledge for nonlocal firms competing in a local real estate market. In local markets where information can be difficult and costly to obtain and may not be available to all participants, real estate firms are likely to be more familiar with and have an informal advantage. The theory is the higher value attributed to joint ventures reflects the comparative information advantage that local real estate firms have within the local marketplace.

Taking the knowledge advantage a step further, it also seems logical that different market segments require different skill sets and managerial talent that may not be easily transferable. A high level of management skill can help to reduce the uncertainty associated with business risks that may result from operation of real estate properties. It is also assumed that that knowledge may be efficiently leveraged over a larger DIP, which can be produced through the joint venture structure. Therefore it is not unreasonable to expect that the real estate joint venture, when properly structured, can produce a comparative local market advantage for the participants of the venture. The following list details the areas where local market knowledge and management expertise can add value in the management of the DIP of a REIT that is involved in a joint venture program.

- *Acquisitions.* Area local market knowledge and a long-term market strategy may allow the local real estate partner to complete due diligence and acquisition negotiations at a lower cost than a nonlocal competitor.

- *Local market strategy.* The local market partner may be better able to define local market niches, thereby understanding local market opportunities at a higher level than the nonlocal participant.

- *Adjustment in strategy.* The local market participant may be more sensitive to changing local market conditions and therefore able to react more quickly to changes in the local market dynamic.

- *Primary research.* The local market participant may have a better institutional knowledge of the local market history, which translates into better and lower-cost direct research in the local market.

- *Dispositions.* The local market participant may have an advantage in completing negotiated transactions with other local market participants as a result of superior local market knowledge.

The net result has been that through local market knowledge and management expertise, REITs have historically availed themselves of the opportunity to participate in joint ventures with capital partners in order to add shareholder value and extend balance sheet leverage and portfolio diversification for shareholders.

Analyzing REITs

Chapter Summary

- Analyzing and valuing a real estate investment trust (REIT) is a blend of conventional real estate valuation and securities analysis.

- Conventional real estate valuation considers replacement cost, local market comparable sales, and capitalization of net income as the primary valuations methods.

- Valuing a REIT applies similar valuation methods to the underlying portfolio of properties owned by the REIT along with public market approaches to REIT valuation.

- The calculation of a net asset value for a REIT portfolio is similar to the replacement cost and capitalization methods in private real estate.

- REIT valuation that uses a multiple of earnings before interest, taxes, depreciation, and amortization (EBITDA) helps compare value across differing REIT capital structures.

- More conventional stock market–type valuation approaches apply multiple-to-earnings growth analysis, return on capital, and weighted cash yield methods to estimate REIT valuations.

- No single valuation method is the definitive answer, but all are very useful when applied in combination to estimate a range of value.

- Looking at the relative public valuations of other REITs is also a method for estimating a REIT's current value.

ualitative value added by the REIT management team
an important factor to consider when estimating REIT
ions.

- Ultimately REIT valuation, like private real estate appraisal,
  is as much an art as a science and requires a thorough
  understanding of all valuation methodologies.

---

*The only dependable foundation of personal liberty is
the economic security of private property.*

—Walter Lippmann, 1934

In the direct real estate investment market there are three basic
methodologies for arriving at the value of a given piece of real
estate. First is the *replacement cost* method. This form of valuation
contemplates what it would cost in the current market environment to replicate a building of similar size and quality in a similar
location. This analysis includes the value of the land on which the
building sits, along with site improvements and general neighborhood amenities. It is relatively simple to discover the general
replacement cost of a building; however, because each property is
so unique, there is no exact substitute for any given property per
se. This makes replacement cost a useful tool for obtaining broad
generalizations about a property's value, but further analysis is
normally required to make a definite conclusion about value.

The second approach to real estate valuation is the *market comparable* approach. This method attempts to estimate a property's
current market value by analyzing recent sales of similar properties in the general area of the property being valued. Again,
because each property is unique, it is difficult to draw a definite
conclusion about market value using the comparable approach
alone. The data on reported sales is based on recent historical sales
activity and thus may not reflect recent changes in the local real
estate market. Although a price agreed on by a buyer and seller in
an arm's-length transaction is typically the best indicator of value,
other issues come into play. Is the seller under some financial or
personal pressure to sell a property? Is the buyer willing to pay a
premium because of specific aspects of the property that may only

be of use to that buyer? These transaction-related dynamics are difficult to determine when studying comparable sales. The solution is to study a range of recent transactions and draw conclusions from a larger sample of data. This is effective in a local market where there is a reasonable level of real estate activity. However, some markets produce a limited volume of comparable real estate transactions, which makes the comparable method less precise.

Finally, real estate value can be derived by the capitalization of net income approach. This *cap rate* approach considers the net income after expenses of a property as a current return required or generated on the price of the property. For example, a property with net operating income (NOI) of $120,000 and an asking price of $1.0 million would have a cap rate of 12 percent ($120,000/$1.0 million = 12 percent). The cap rate approach generally allows for an independent estimate of value that is somewhat more precise than either the replacement cost or market comparable approaches. The cap rate of any property that trades hands as an investment vehicle reflects the competitive real estate investment alternatives in a given local market, giving the appraiser a larger pool of candidates to examine when making a comparable cap rate analysis. In addition, slight adjustments in cap rate allow for a more precise valuation when considering the merits or flaws of a particular property. For example, in a local market it might be simple to conclude from the available data that community shopping centers trade in a cap range of 10 to 12 percent. The newer, bigger, better located properties are in the 10 to 11 percent range, and the older, smaller, less favorably located properties are in the 11 to 12 percent range. This allows the appraiser to apply a more precise cap rate once it is determined where the subject property falls on the quality spectrum.

Each of the standard appraisal methodologies has its advantages and drawbacks. Therefore, in normal valuation analysis, the subject property is examined using each methodology. More or less consideration is ascribed to each approach based on the relevant facts and circumstances about the property. At the end of the process, a synthesis of all the methods rather than one single approach usually determines a value. The valuation methodology is as much an art as a science, and most appraisers will say that the actual market sale price may be higher or lower based on many subjective factors that are difficult if not impossible to quantify.

The valuation methodologies applied to publicly traded real estate investment trusts (REITs) are roughly comparable to those used in the private real estate markets. In addition, there are a number of public-market-based valuation approaches that can also be applied to the financial analysis of REITs. These approaches are all loosely categorized into a group of valuation methodologies that can be called *quantitative analysis*. Like the direct valuation approaches used in private real estate, the quantitative approaches used in public real estate each have certain positive and negative attributes. In addition, just as in private valuation methodologies, a conclusion of value is more accurate when it is considered in light of multiple valuation approaches rather than a single evaluation method. In addition to quantitative methods, there are a range of qualitative factors that must be considered when valuing public real estate. These quantitative and qualitative approaches are examined in the following sections.

NAV Analysis

Net asset value (NAV) analysis is the public real estate version of the replacement cost approach. There are two schools of thought among REIT analysts: those who believe that this approach provides the least accurate measure of the value of an equity REIT and those who believe this is primarily the best method for valuing REITs. At its essence, the NAV approach involves estimating whether a stock trades at a discount or premium in comparison to an estimate of the private market value of the company's real estate assets.

The first step in estimating the NAV of a REIT requires capitalizing the NOI of the properties. This can be done either before or after making a reserve for expected capital expenditures. The key to this process is estimating NOI, because many REITs own interests in dozens of properties located in many different local markets. Although local market conditions may vary widely, REITs often do not disclose the NOI for each building and therefore an overall capitalization rate must be applied to the entire real estate portfolio. The cap rate selected will consider a component for expected real return, an inflation premium, a risk premium, and an amount to compensate for the expected decline in property value due to depreciation or obsolescence, often called the *recapture value.* There is the potential for a large error factor that may result from estimating a portfolio-wide capitalization rate. In addition, a significant difference can result depending on whether the analysis is made using current or estimated forward NOI. Generally, using a blend of past and future estimated NOI helps to moderate the error of an estimate.

To capitalize a future income stream to estimate the total private market value of a company, the next step is to deduct the debt associated with the estimated NAV and adjust the number of shares outstanding if any equity issuance is assumed as part of the analysis. Generally NOI earnings models assume that future acquisitions and development costs are funded by debt, and thus projected average future liabilities (as opposed to current liabilities) are deducted. One of the better factors of public real estate company analysis is that a relatively efficient private transaction market coexists for income-producing investment-grade property. Other private companies may change ownership on a regular basis, but the selling prices are seldom known. Privately negotiated investment-grade commercial real estate transactions total an estimated $250 billion annually, and most are a matter of public record. Thus, a cap rate for an individual property can be estimated with a relatively high degree of accuracy. However, a small error factor for a single asset will compound when applied to an entire portfolio, so great care is required when making these estimates.

In addition, REITs often have other nonrent income that must be considered in the valuation of NOI. Most analysts apply a high capitalization rate on the net property management fees to reflect the fact that management contracts normally can be canceled on short notice, usually 30 to 90 days. Thus a relatively high cap rate of 20 to 30 percent is applied to this income to reflect the possible variability. Adding other REIT assets, normally cash and marketable securities, results in an estimate of total private market value of the entity. Then the total liabilities are deducted, including the aggregate debt, preferred stock, and pro rata share of any unconsolidated joint ventures. This results in an estimate of a REIT's NAV. Finally, the results must be divided by the total diluted shares or operating partnership units outstanding that would result from a conversion to common shares.

From an NAV perspective, the REIT universe has traded at a discount of as much as 31 percent to a premium of 39 percent over the last 10 years based on estimates made by Uniplan Real Estate Adivsors. The average has been about 104 percent of NAV or a 4 percent premium. The discount or premium is often partly accounted for by the fact that the equity market is forward-looking and views REITs as ongoing business enterprises rather than direct portfolios of real estate assets.

Drawbacks of NAV Analysis

The principal drawback of NAV analysis is that NAV calculation involves a temporal analysis of the cash flow on a static collection of real estate assets. The approach can be very helpful in a situation where a REIT owns a few properties that account for a significant proportion of a portfolio's overall value. The other key weakness of the NAV approach is its inability to accurately value a rapidly changing local market or a quickly growing REIT. For a fast-growing REIT, NOI may increase rapidly as the company acquires and/or develops new properties, and the REIT shares may appear very over- or undervalued depending on whether an analyst chooses to capitalize trailing or forecasted NOI.

NAV analysis can also be criticized as a successful stand-alone REIT stock selection mechanism because it fails to acknowledge the different risk profiles of various REIT capital structures. For instance, two companies with a $40 per share NAV might appear equally attractive from an NAV-only perspective. But, unsecured debt may comprise 10 percent of one company's capital structure and 90 percent of the other's, placing the latter in much greater risk category.

Enterprise Value/EBITDA Multiple Analysis

Another method of valuing a REIT that addresses part of the flaw in NAV analysis involves looking at cash flow generated by the REIT. In this approach, a measure of cash flow composed of earnings before interest, taxes, depreciation, and amortization

(EBITDA) is used. The methodology involves dividing the total market capitalization of equity and the nominal value of company debt of the REIT by the total EBITDA or cash flow to the company. One advantage of this approach is that it normalizes the ratio across most normal capital structures and may be used to compare firms with differing amounts of balance sheet leverage. As was the case with the NAV calculations, the enterprise value/EBITDA multiple is normally calculated using an estimated forward capital structure. The enterprise value/EBITDA ratio usually reflects the market's sentiment regarding the expected near-term and long-term growth rate of a sustainability of growth and quality of cash flow. The multiple may also reflect the amount of anticipated or budgeted capital expenditures and future obsolescence of the property. Some analysts prefer to use EBITDA less capital expenditure reserve as a measure of operating cash flow.

Multiple-to-Growth Ratio Analysis

Multiple-to-growth ratio analysis helps to answer two REIT-specific valuation issues: (1) How much is the market willing to pay for each unit of growth? (2) Can value and growth be available in the same REIT? It is important to understand that profitability and growth are not the same. Growth of earnings or funds from operations (FFO) growth alone cannot provide a valid single measure for assessing investment value. However, some investors implicitly assume that this is a valid single measure when they apply the current period's price/FFO multiple to some terminal year's earning rate. Growth only adds value to a REIT when the return on investment exceeds the cost of capital. However, some REITs may be focused on growing the portfolio simply to expand in size. That business strategy depends on a company's ability to sell shares at frequent intervals at higher and higher prices. As the enterprise continues to expand in size, the amount of acquisitions necessary to sustain the per-share FFO growth rate also expands in size and often becomes unsustainable. Thus, the growth rate falls, and with it the premium multiple the stock may have commanded. The opposite of an upward growth spiral is the collapsing death spiral discussed earlier.

In a traditional growth industry, a company's P/E ratio is often compared with its long-term expected growth rate; firms with P/E ratios less than their growth rate are often considered to be undervalued. The multiple-to-growth ratio forms a relative perspective when used to rank a universe of REITs on the ratio of price/FFO multiple versus sustainable growth rate.

The central problem confronting a REIT analyst is the sustainability of a high-growth period for a given REIT. Because REITs must distribute at least 90 percent of their taxable income, in most instances there is only modest free cash flow and almost all acquisition and development growth must be financed from external sources. Typically, this has been accomplished through the repeated sale of primary shares along with the expansion of balance sheet leverage. Most REITs fund incremental acquisitions and developments via debt and then turn to the capital markets to deleverage with equity.

The sustainable, internally generated operating cash flow growth rate for most equity REITs is realistically 3 to 5 percent, based on the constraints of the REIT structure. Adding an appropriate level of balance sheet leverage may increase cash flow growth to an average of 5 to 8 percent. REIT FFO growth rates in excess of 10 percent are thus not sustainable over an extended period without the use of higher than average leverage.

REIT EPS

Operating earnings per share (EPS) has relevance in the valuation of REIT equity securities. It is incorrect to dismiss the EPS measure as simply not appropriate for real estate companies because accounting depreciation overstates physical depreciation of the real property asset.

The EPS measure is widely used across many industries. Analysts covering other sectors often supplement EPS results with alternative valuation metrics. In general it is important not to overemphasize the importance of, or place too much focus on, any one figure. Thus the very popular Wall Street focus on EPS figures—or any other single statistics—can be misleading. In using the EPS figure, an analyst should always be alert to the components of the net income figure and how that figure is used for comparative purposes.

Using operating EPS as a measure of REIT earnings power has drawbacks. Calculations for some companies involve predecessor entities with different tax bases requiring step-up depreciation adjustments and adjustments for distributions to minority partners in excess of net income that dramatically lower EPS. Other companies make acquisitions for cash and have componentized depreciation, lowering reported net income and allowing the REIT to retain more capital to fund development activity. In conclusion, despite various drawbacks, EPS can be a useful device in assessing the valuation of REIT securities.

Positive Earnings Revision Analysis

REIT valuation by positive earnings revisions involves identifying and valuing REIT shares based on owning companies where Wall Street earnings estimates are being revised upward. The basic application of this method involves choosing stocks with earnings revisions that are rising, thus creating unexpected positive earnings. Another form involves buying stocks in companies whose sequential earnings growth rates are accelerating. This is often known as an *earnings momentum* strategy. These two approaches are less classic real estate valuation approaches and more Wall Street–based valuation approaches. The idea is that public market investors are more willing to pay a premium on any company when it delivers sequential earnings growth at a level higher than expected by the consensus of analysts covering a stock.

Return on Capital versus Cost of Capital Analysis

The earnings life cycle for a REIT that continually issues new common equity is inextricably linked to its price/FFO multiple. From 1998 through 2001, average REIT price/FFO multiples ranged between 7 and 14.5 times forward four-quarter FFO, reflecting a nominal cost of 14.3 to 6.9 percent for raising new common equity, before factoring in the cost of underwriting. On a purely mathematical basis, a REIT that sells new shares at such multiples and invests the proceeds in properties with initial capitalization rates of at least 14.3 percent (7 × projected first-year NOI) will have completed a transaction that is additive to earnings. The more equity issued and the more properties acquired, the higher the year-by-year FFO growth, provided that increasingly large amounts of stock can be sold at equal or higher multiples.

A company that buys a business trading at a lower multiple than the buying company itself will by definition enhance its EPS growth rate. After the purchase, the low cash flow multiple attributable to the operations of the acquired company is often revalued at or close to the original firm's higher multiple. This is the accounting definition of accretion. However, although such a transaction may be additive to earnings from an accounting perspective, it may be dilutive to true shareholder value in the economic sense. A review of a variety of valuation parameters is needed when analyzing real estate stocks. Such items include property type and geographic portfolio characteristics; growth rates in net income, FFO, funds available for distribution (FAD) and dividends; earnings momentum; relative price multiples for an individual company versus peer companies and sector averages; current and anticipated dividend yield and dividend safety; leverage; trading volume; and management track record and capability.

Measures of corporate performance based on return on capital are often cited as means of distinguishing among REITs. When evaluating REIT performance, it is important to include return on capital and cost of capital analysis. The specific value of comparing weighted average cost of capital (WACC) with cash yield on cost (CYC) for a real estate company is that it relates a firm's capital structure decisions to its operating business results as measured by true economic (as distinguished from accounting) profitability.

CYC

A company's CYC is equal to NOI from the property portfolio (essentially operating property revenues less operating property expenses) divided by gross (undepreciated) investment in real estate. This is a measure of a company's unit profitability as distinguished from its sales growth. Simply put, it is a measure of return on assets or return on invested capital.

WACC

The WACC is the weighted average of the costs of debt and equity. The WACC represents the rate at which projected cash flows may be discounted to determine net present value (NPV). If the present value of the expected future cash flows, using WACC as the discount rate, is positive, then a potential investment should be pursued. Similarly, if the NPV of an investment is negative, then the investment should be rejected. In other words, a positive NPV is equivalent to a project's total return on internal rate of return exceeding WACC. Alternatively, WACC may be considered a hurdle rate for evaluating the minimum acceptable rate of return for a potential investment. From an equity investor's perspective, companies that consistently pursue business opportunities with positive NPVs will increase firm value by boosting the growth rate and hence share value. Investors will buy REITs with positive and rising investment spreads between CYC and WACC. All REIT acquisitions may not be immediately accretive to shareholder value (exceed a company's WACC). However, a property investment should be able to generate a sustainable cash yield above the REIT's WACC within some reasonable time period, perhaps 24 to 36 months.

Spread Investing

What is the value of comparing WACC with CYC? First, until recently, REITs rarely sold properties. Although capital appreciation in assets may occur, it is often not realized, and therefore the focus is on current and future cash flow from real estate investments. Second, a REIT that operates with low leverage will have a higher WACC and thereby implicitly raise the hurdle rate it must achieve on new real estate investments.

There are many potential attributes of a successful REIT investment, some of which we have just discussed. Nevertheless, because of the primacy of income generation in a REIT's total return, comparing CYC to WACC is a useful method of evaluating potential or existing REIT investments. However, some REITs derive significant value from potential capital appreciation on assets. In such cases, the usefulness of the investment spread methodology may be limited. In these instances, this analytical tool should be used in conjunction with other, more traditional measures of equity valuation such as operating cash flow growth, relative earnings multiples, and NAV.

Drawbacks of the Methodology

There are several potential drawbacks to this methodology. First, current-period cash yields may not remain static; sustainability or growth in NOI is key. The individual company cost of capital reflects a dynamic process that incorporates growth in revenues and expenses from existing properties, acquisitions, development of new buildings, and management expertise.

Second, the length of time between the original investment and the current period may have an impact on the reported CYC. This is particularly true in the case of umbrella partnership REITs (UPREITs), where the original investment may have taken place years previously. In fact, research has shown that the CYC-less-WACC investment spread is larger in the case of UPREITs than for traditional REITs or real estate operating companies. However, the difference is almost entirely a function of UPREITs having greater leverage—and thus a lower WACC—since the CYC is similar for UPREITs and non-UPREITs.

Third, fast-growing REITs that may have low leverage today and have a negative or marginally positive spread between WACC and CYC may add debt in the future, lowering their WACC, and may boost NOI over time, eventually reversing the investment spread. Depending on a firm's capitalization policy for new construction, some heavily development-oriented REITs may have below-average current cash yields on invested assets. However, given that property development generally entails greater risk than acquisitions, investors should expect such developer REITs to obtain above-average return on assets within some reasonable period following completion of a project.

Thus, just as in the private market, there is no single method in the public market that can be used as a stand-alone valuation tool. Rather, REIT values should be considered in light of all the various methods to determine a range of possible outcomes when valuing public REIT shares.

Advanced Financial REIT Topics

Chapter Summary

- Real estate investment trust (REIT) accounting requires an understanding of generally accepted accounting principles (GAAP) between earnings and funds from operations (FFO).

- The industry is moving toward a more standardized form of earnings reporting.

- Dividend distributions paid to shareholders by REITs may consist of ordinary income, return of capital, and long-term capital gains. Thus it is generally not possible to calculate in advance the portion of the dividend distribution from a REIT that will be taxed as ordinary income.

- Real estate investment trusts provide a modest tax shelter for taxable investors by allowing the deferral of tax on current cash receipts and taxing them at a lower rate upon the disposal of the REIT shares.

- There are several alternative REIT corporate structures that help REITs operate more efficiently for tax purposes.

- The paired-share REIT has been eliminated by legislative action but is worth examining.

- The paper clip REIT structure can effectively create the benefits of a paired-share structure.

- Taxable REIT subsidiaries allow REITs to engage in certain revenue-generating activities and still be in compliance with the REIT tax rules.

Figures don't lie, but liars do figure.

—Old accounting saying

REIT Accounting Issues

There are a number of advanced accounting issues that should be understood with regard to real estate investment trusts (REITs). Historically, the steady and predictable earnings and consistent dividends generated by REITs have created a high level of interest. However, investors who are not familiar with the sector may find it confusing to compare earnings because many REITs report quarterly results using funds from operations (FFO), as opposed to earnings per share (EPS), which is the typical measure of profitability used in almost all other industries. Recently, several Wall Street brokerage firms have announced that they will create EPS estimates for REITs rather than FFO estimates. This move has touched off a debate over the best way to measure the earnings capacity and financial performance of REITs.

Currently most REITs report quarterly results using FFO numbers. Calculating FFO begins with earnings calculated in accordance with generally accepted accounting principles (GAAP), also known as *GAAP earnings*. These earnings are then adjusted to exclude gains or losses resulting from the sale of portfolio properties or from debt or financing activities. Then depreciation and amortization charges are added back to the resulting number to come up with FFO. Funds from operations actually reflects operating cash flow generated as a result of portfolio activities of a REIT. In one sense, FFO reflects the cash-generating ability of a REIT portfolio, but on the other hand it at times overstates the economic performance of most REITs. Because FFO does not reflect reccurring capital expense items, and because it allows the adding back of a wide range of expense items that management might deem to be nonrecurring, for practical purposes—it often overstates the cash-generating ability of a real estate portfolio. Observers of and participants in the REIT industry have been engaged in a long debate over the correct metrics and methodologies that should be used to value REIT earnings.

In 1995 and 1999, the National Association of Real Estate Investment Trusts (NAREIT) published a white paper commenting on potential changes to the definition of FFO. In general, the industry's trade association seeks to move FFO into a more structured form that would more closely resemble GAAP net income. Originally created in the early 1990s, FFO was intended to be a supplemental performance-measuring device available to the management of REITs. It was promoted by NAREIT in order to help investors better understand and measure the performance of REIT earnings.

NAREIT has recommended that the industry adopt standard accounting practices with regard to a number of broad areas. The first area of recommended change is nonrecurring items. NAREIT suggests ending the practice of allowing REIT management to add back a variety of one-time expenses as an adjustment to the calculation of FFO. Historically, REIT management has been able to add back any items deemed nonrecurring. As would be expected, some REIT management teams are far more aggressive than others about adjusting for nonrecurring items. Studying real estate financial statements, it can be noted that a broad range of items are often added back as nonrecurring expenses. These typically include losses on interest rate hedging transactions, costs related to failed acquisitions, employee severance packages, and advertising and public relations costs related to building brand identities. Under GAAP, most of these items would not be considered nonrecurring or extraordinary. In addition, some REIT management teams routinely add these items back as nonrecurring, whereas other management teams reflect them as ongoing business expenses. This adds to the confusion when attempting to compare FFO across a universe of REITs.

The second broad area that NAREIT has targeted for modification is gains and losses from property sales and debt restructurings. While gains and losses as well as debt restructuring expenses are included in net income under GAAP, gains on sale are often included in FFO by aggressive REIT management teams. To the extent that gains on sale are not related to merchant building activities or build-to-suit transactions, it could be argued that they are not usual and customary in the context of direct real estate portfolio operations and therefore should be excluded. In 1999, some industry observers suggested the inclusion of gains and losses on property sales in the new FFO calculation. It is safe to say that gains and losses from property sales are a part of GAAP net income and are an issue in industries other than real estate. Critics of the practice suggest that including gains and losses on property sales will allow REITs to manipulate FFO by manipulating the timing on property sales. Because many REIT portfolios contain a large number of easily salable properties, the criticism is that REITs may engage in such sales in order to enhance FFO.

In an attempt to calculate the actual financial performance of REITs, several other common measures of operating earnings have been promulgated in addition to FFO. Adjusted funds from operations (AFFO) is calculated by beginning with FFO and making an adjustment for the straight-lining of rents. In addition, AFFO typically reflects a reserve expense that accounts for costs that may not necessarily be recurring or routine but that are typically not recoverable directly from tenants. In most instances, this includes non-recurring maintenance costs and costs related to leasing activities. When adjusted for these expenses, the resulting figure is AFFO, at times referred to as *cash available for distribution* (CAD). This is the actual cash flow created by a REIT.

It should be noted that in any activity that adjusts REIT earnings, gains created by the sale of portfolio properties are typically not added back to reflect operating cash flows. This is because gains on property sales are not generally considered reccurring cash flows. Gains and losses on debt restructuring, however, are generally added back to calculate FFO or funds available for distribution. Debt restructurings are extraordinary events, and, to the extent they are not regular activities, there should be adjustments in FFO or items considered extraordinary when calculating GAAP earnings.

It could be concluded that gains from the sale of residential land development activities should be included in AFFO reporting. The rationale suggests that AFFO numbers are used in conjunction with capitalization estimates by investors when estimating share values of REITs as discussed in Chapter 9. Operating properties produce income that is reflected in AFFO and therefore in capitalized valuations. The argument can be made that adding gains on the sale of income-producing properties would mix reccurring rental operating income with capital gains from underlying real estate properties, making it more difficult to use AFFO in capitalized valuation methodologies. It could further be argued that, when using the capitalized earnings approach to valuing real estate, a real estate appraiser would not include gains and losses when valuing an overall property portfolio. However, residential land sales generate no reccurring income stream. If the gains resulting from the sale of land are not included in AFFO, then value created through raw land activities would not be reflected in REIT valuation when using a capitalized earnings approach.

Recently 15 major Wall Street firms including Merrill Lynch, Morgan Stanley, and Solomon Smith Barney announced that they would forecast REIT financial performance using GAAP earnings in addition to FFO. These firms uniformly suggested that GAAP earnings are calculated through a standardized set of rules and therefore are most helpful in comparing operating performance. In addition, the use of GAAP earnings makes it easier to compare REIT operating performance to the earnings performance of stocks and other industry sectors. It seems clear that the industry is slowly moving toward a more uniform GAAP EPS calculation. It is simply a matter of time until the industry participants debate and agree upon a methodology that all participants can embrace.

The final area addressed by NAREIT is changes in depreciation rules. It is generally agreed that typical GAAP depreciation overstates the correct charge for the true economic depreciation of real estate. It could also be argued that adding back all depreciation to arrive at FFO understates the actual economic expense of property depreciation. The underlying issue is how best to calculate the actual economic depreciation experienced by the property owner. Although NAREIT suggests a number of different methods to adjust depreciation, each has positive and negative aspects. Estimating the useful life of real estate assets is difficult, and many industry participants would argue for the least costly adjustments with regard to impact on earnings. Real estate investment trusts that engage in a high level of ground-up development activities generally have less flexibility in categorizing depreciable items as compared to acquisition-oriented REITs. In addition, many companies have differing definitions of what might fall into shorter-term categories, such as tenant improvements, and what items might be classified as long-term building improvements. These factors will make the standardization of the depreciation calculation a more complex issue for the REIT industry.

It is expected that revised depreciation standards will put a heavier burden on certain REIT sectors. Office properties and hotels, which typically have higher ongoing capital expenses, will likely suffer more than the industrial or manufactured home sectors, which have fewer capital expenses. Beyond that, it is hard to predict what if any impact depreciation changes will have on the public market's level of valuation of REITs.

Real Estate Dividend Accounting Issues

For income tax purposes, dividend distributions paid to shareholders by REITs may consist of ordinary income, return of capital, and long-term capital gains. Because REIT management teams are becoming more active in managing their direct investment portfolios, REITs are more frequently realizing long-term capital gains in their underlying property portfolios. A REIT may designate a portion of the dividend paid during the fiscal year as a long-term capital gain distribution that may have resulted from property portfolio transactions. The advantage to shareholders is that they will pay taxes on that portion of the dividend at the current lower capital gains rate. The return of capital portion of the dividend is not declared as current income or capital gain on an investor's tax return, but rather is used to lower investors' original cost basis in their shares of the distributing REIT.

It is generally not possible to calculate the amounts of dividends that will be tax deferred by examining the GAAP accounting statements of a REIT. The return of capital portion of the dividend distribution is based on distributions that are in excess of the REIT's taxable income as reported for federal income tax purposes. The differences between net income available to common shareholders for financial reporting purposes and taxable income for income tax purposes relate primarily to timing differences between taxable depreciation (which is usually some form of accelerated depreciation) and straight-line depreciation (which is generally used for book accounting purposes). Accruals on preferred stock dividends can also create differences between taxable and book net income. In addition, realized gains and losses on the sale of investment properties that are deferred through the use of tax deferral trusts and methodologies also create differences in book financial income as related to taxable financial income. These capital gains and losses are typically distributed to shareholders if they are recognized for income tax purposes; otherwise they are considered return of capital. Thus it is generally not possible to calculate in advance the portion of the dividend distribution from a REIT that will be taxed as ordinary income. As noted, the principal problem revolves around differences between financial income as defined by GAAP and taxable income as defined by the federal tax statutes. It would require extensive tax disclosure by a REIT for shareholders to be able to calculate the return of capital portion of the dividend distribution.

Interestingly enough, the notion of return of capital dividend allocation creates a situation where a REIT shareholder could conceivably avoid the income tax that is payable with respect to the portion of dividends from a REIT holding that were classified as a return of capital. Upon the death of the shareholder, federal income tax laws currently allow for a step-up in basis to the current market value of the REIT share. Under this scenario, the death of a long-term shareholder could result in elimination of income taxation on a significant portion of a REIT's return of capital dividends that had been paid out to the deceased shareholder, while the estate takes a step up in basis to the current market value of the shares. This may be of interest to income investors who might consider REITs as an integral part of a long-term income investment portfolio. If a shareholder sells REIT shares prior to his or her death, the difference between the tax basis and the net sales price is recognizable as a capital gain. To the extent that the final capital gains rate is lower than the ordinary income tax rate, REITs provide a modest tax shelter for taxable investors by allowing the deferral of tax on current cash receipts as dividends and taxing it at a potentially lower rate on the disposal of the REIT shares.

Alternative Corporate Structures for REITs

The REIT structure comes with some requirements. In order to avoid corporate income tax, REITs must operate within the tax code. The ownership of apartment buildings, shopping centers, and office buildings allows REITs to enjoy the full economic benefit of those property categories. As the real estate industry becomes more operations intensive, such as in hotels and nursing homes, REITs are limited with regard to the income they can generate from certain restricted assets. These restrictions apply as a result of the management-intensive nature of restricted assets. Generally speaking, the net operating income from these real estate investments does not qualify under REIT rules as rent. While leases based on revenues generated from these restricted assets are not uncommon, these leases create certain practical difficulties. For example, because of the high operating leverage, many hotel properties might experience increases in net operating revenues that outpace revenue growth. Shareholders of hotel REITs with leases based on hotel revenues would not enjoy the full benefit of the upsurge in the cash flows. In addition, these more complex lease structures make it difficult for REITs to fully control properties and therefore add value at the property level.

Given their desire to make investments in the restricted asset class, REITs have sought to craft solutions that comply with REIT rules but allow the ability to invest in restricted assets while maintaining control over those assets and participating in a greater share of the economic benefit generated by those assets. The taxable REIT subsidiary (TRS) is the most common method of investing in a small number of restricted assets. In order to facilitate larger investments that represent a higher percentage of the operating income of REITs, REIT managements created several different investment alternatives that complied with the REIT operating rules. These investments are known as *paired-share* and *paper clip* REITs.

Both paired-share and paper clip REITs involve two separate companies, a REIT and a C corporation. The REIT operates within the limitations of the REIT rules and thus structures leases that are generally based on gross revenues rather than net income. The corporate side of the structure is free to engage in the management and operation of the real estate asset with an eye toward maximizing the total return and economic value of the asset. In addition, the C corporation structure allows property management and franchising to be in-house activities and allows the REIT, through its corporate affiliate, to invest in businesses unrelated to real estate. In the paired-share structure, investors may not own a share in the REIT without owning a correlating share in the C corporation. This creates an economic situation where whatever operating benefits are lost by the REIT due to the revenue-based lease structure are returned to shareholders through their ownership interest in the C corporation. Historically, there were five paired-share REITs. These were grandfathered in as an exception in the REIT laws, but in 1998, Congress eliminated them unless they were willing not to acquire new assets or engage in a new line of business.

The paper clip structure, however, does continue to exist. Unlike the paired-share structure, the paper clip structure does not require that the REIT shareholder own a correlating share of the C corporation affiliated with the REIT. Therefore an investor in the REIT side of the paper clip structure would be subject to all the operating negatives that result from the REIT structure. However, the investor could voluntarily create a paper clip structure by simply buying shares in the publicly traded C corporation that represents the paper clip side of the REIT structure. Hotels, because of their management-intensive operations, are often prime examples when discussing the paper clip structure. During the 1980s and early 1990s, hotel management companies were paid on a percentage of hotel revenues. As a result, non-owner managers had an incentive to generate high revenues without regard to the net income or profits of a property. Rules require that hotel REITs structure leases in which the lessee pays rent based on revenue rather than net profit. These requirements create conflict of interest problems because there is an incentive for the lessee to increase net income as opposed to increasing revenues. While focusing on net income is normally a desirable corporate activity, it may result in REIT shareholders not participating in the total economic benefit that can be created by a particular property. If net income were to increase rapidly while revenues increased at a slower rate, shareholders in the REIT would receive only modest increases in cash flows from the property.

The paper clip structure uses the same executive management team at both the REIT and the C corporation affiliate. Executive management can operate the real estate in a manner that maximizes the overall economic benefit. The only caveat is that, because of the decoupled nature of the REIT and the C corporation, the REIT side of the structure may not have the same shareholders as the C corporation. Thus the officers and directors of each company have a fiduciary obligation to ensure that deals between the two sides of the structure are equitable. Unlike the paired-share structure, under the paper clip structure, shareholders of each entity do care and are concerned with the operating outcomes of each independent company.

Because REITs do not pay taxes at the corporate level and C corporations do, the common management of the paper clip REIT has some incentive to transfer expenses to the C corporation in an attempt to minimize taxes paid by the overall entity. Investors can deal with this situation by owning both REIT shares and C corporation shares. In this way, they effectively create a synthetic paired-share REIT. The loss of investment returns to a REIT that is caused by expenses paid to a service provider or lessee is known in the real estate industry as *leakage* or *profit leakage*. Profit leakage occurs when revenues leak out to a service provider based on management contracts or service arrangements. They often result from lease structures that do not allow the REIT to fully participate in the cash flow growth of a restricted investment. It should be understood that leakage is a true economic loss if the property owner could provide a similar service at or below the cost of the outside service provider. Leakage is avoided in a paper clip structure because a C corporation is able to bring property management and franchising in house if the economics suggest these would be profitable for the C corporation. While the REIT continues to suffer from leakage under the paper clip structure, the leakage inures to the benefit of a sister company with the same management and the ability for the REIT shareholder to own shares in the affiliated company. A possible risk of the paper clip structure is that, over time, the business pursuits of the REIT may diverge from those of the C corporation to such an extent that the two are no longer effectively operated as one entity with a combined management team. This is typical of what happened to the paper clip structure in the health care REIT area. A number of health care REITs were spun out of large health care companies in the 1980s. Over time, these health care REITs became less dependent on the parent companies and more independent in terms of their real estate activities. A number of these companies now operate independently of their original sponsors. The paper clip REIT structure begins to lose its effectiveness as this change begins to happen. Without an ongoing synergy between the REIT and the C corporation, investors in either receive no special benefit from the relationship.

TRSs

Real estate investment trusts utilize taxable subsidiaries that are typically C corporations to conduct business activities that may not be allowed under the REIT operating rules. By migrating non-REIT activities such as property management into taxable subsidiaries, REITs are able to continue to engage in these businesses and still be in compliance with the tax code.

The REIT Modernization Act that became effective on January 1, 2001, created the TRS. The new rules allow a REIT to own 100 percent of the common stock of a TRS. The TRS allows the REIT to provide services to the REIT's tenants that might otherwise be considered nonqualifying income under the REIT structure. Dividends from the TRS do not qualify under the 75 percent income test, and TRS securities may not exceed 20 percent of a REIT's total assets. However, within these guidelines, the TRS allows the REIT to participate in property-related service opportunities that would not be possible under the former REIT structure. The following areas of nonrent revenues are thought to be of most interest to REITs:

- Real estate brokerage fees
- Construction management fees
- Joint venture development fees
- Merchant building sales
- Property management fees

Although REITs may enjoy the benefit of some of these fees, which may currently flow into the REIT through other allowable structures, the TRS is expected to make these arrangements simpler in structure and easier to administer for REIT management.

Interview with Bill Camp

William T. Camp, vice president, joined the securities research effort at A.G. Edwards in 1999 after seven years as an investment banker at A.G. Edwards. He is a member of the NAREIT. Prior to joining A.G. Edwards, Camp spent seven years as a senior engineer in private industry. He received his M.B.A. from Washington University and M.S. and B.S. degrees in engineering and a B.S. in mathematics from the University of Wisconsin. Since joining Securities Research, Camp has assumed primary coverage responsibility for industrial and office/industrial REITs.

Richard Imperiale: Let's talk about how you analyze REITs from an investment perspective. In real estate appraisal, property value is usually based on three major methods— the cost approach, the income approach, and the market value or comparative approach. How do you consider each of these when valuing a REIT?

Bill Camp: If we look at the cost approach, we're not fundamentally driven. Some of us are bigger believers in NAV than others. Personally, NAV is a nice benchmark if it's used on a property-by-property basis. I use it more as if one of the REITs that we follow is buying a building. What are they paying for that building, and is it reasonable? It's more of a test of management than it is necessarily a value for the stock, because it's very hard to determine NAV accurately without going through a property-by-property, cap rate–by–cap rate analysis of a portfolio. So what we typically do is take a range of cap rates and come up with a range of valuation. We look at one year forward NOI and cap that at some level of cap rates that we determine to be realistic through our discussion with real estate brokers or the companies themselves. We also use quarterly reports on where they're selling and buying buildings.

Imperiale: Is that where buildings are changing hands in that local market or where the REIT is buying and selling buildings?

Camp: That's typically where the REIT is buying and selling buildings, but we also use market estimates. That's why we talk to the brokers too, to find out where buildings in those markets are generally trading hands. It also depends a little bit on the condition of the building itself. For example, take a REIT that only owns one building and is going to buy the building next door. They should be the buyer that pays the most for that building if it's adjacent to their existing holdings. There's more synergy there than you can really put a dollar amount on. There are a variety of things that they can build into the cost. It also depends on how the portfolio is shaped. Does the REIT own a lot of assets in one market but maybe only one or two in other markets? That's a very expensive way to go, and it may actually hurt their valuation.

Imperiale: So if they have just a few properties widely spread out over different markets, it hurts rather than helps the value of the REIT?

Camp: Correct. If you want geographic diversification, you have to have geographic diversification and concentration. You can't have a little bit everywhere. While that is a good strategy, it's very cumbersome to manage in my opinion. Especially if you're getting into properties that need on-site management. For example, with office or retail properties, you probably need a site manager for just about everything you do. Then, as soon as you have a site manager, you have regional managers, you have managers of the regional managers, and all of a sudden you've got an infrastructure that you can't really justify if you only own one or two assets in a particular market.

Imperiale: So there's a scale issue here?

Camp: Exactly. The other thing about using a cost approach or income approach is that we definitely believe in market value in terms of looking at NAV. We use the income approach to get to a market value. Twelve-month forward NOI caps back at some reasonable level, but you have to take into consideration certain other things. Look back to two years ago, on the West Coast when the embedded rent value was huge. The gap between market rents and current rents in the portfolio was so high that there were buyers willing to pay more than just capping a 12-month forward NOI, because they thought they could capture that rent increase.

Imperiale: In other words, the rents in a lot of their buildings were substantially below what the current market rents were, and so a new owner had an opportunity over the upcoming two years to mark those rents way up just to be at market rates?

Camp: Yes.

Imperiale: And built-in growth?

Camp: Yeah. They built in growth. When you're putting a market value on a stock or on a REIT stock, there's some component that if they're in a hot market, there's going to be more embedded value, even though you probably are taking the more traditional methods of cost per square foot or any kind of cap rate on forward cash flow. If there's embedded value, you're going to negotiate somewhere in the middle of that, between the buyer and the seller.

Imperiale: When you make your analysis of those properties and those markets, do you consider the mark-to-market rents before you apply a cap rate?

Camp: Typically not. What I was doing was giving them a partial benefit. So if I knew that rents were going to roll up, I might actually give them credit for the next year's rollovers, and I'd build that back in. I would give them some credit for rents that were going to be raised by a certain percentage or that were expiring in the following year. But it was very subjective, because it becomes a negotiation process, and I don't know if you can pinpoint where the buyers and the sellers are in terms of price. The spread began to widen dramatically, and I think that spread still exists because the market reversed so quickly. Now it's just the same thing for the opposite reason.

Imperiale: Let's talk about that a little bit. The spread occurs because a buyer feels the property is worth X and a seller feels it's worth Y, and the difference between those two numbers is the range of disagreement between what a buyer is willing to accept and a seller is willing to pay. At times you get a disconnect there and that spread gets really wide. Can you explain in a little more detail why that is?

Camp: I think the biggest reason is perception between the buyer and the seller. The seller always thinks that a property is worth more than it really is. The seller is trying to extract value from a property. In a hot market, like northern California in 1999 and 2000, people thought that if their rents were $100 per square foot, they could cap that back and get a huge dollar price. That's where I think the cost per square foot comes in—when things get way out of whack with rent versus what the space might actually be worth.

Imperiale: So that's an economic justification.

Camp: It's checks and balances. When we look at REITs in general and they're buying an asset, we'll ask what kind of cap rate they paid and whether that is reasonable versus market cap rates at that point in time. The other thing we'll look for is whether the REIT is buying the property at or near, or even hopefully below, replacement cost. That's the hot market scenario. When you look at that weaker market scenario, you come back to cost per square foot as a benchmark. For example, in Northern California, rents are falling, so sellers are trying to get last year's rents rather than the current market rents capped out. The buyer wants current market rents capped out and in some of these cases the building's empty. This goes back to pure price per square foot. Because there's so little activity in the market-place, people are saying, "We know what it costs to build it, we know what the land cost is, so if we can get it for below that total, we'll take it. If not, that's okay, you can sit on it for another month and carry it and we'll talk to you again a month from now."

Imperiale: So the deteriorating market becomes a motivating factor?

Camp: The motivator is, "Can we get this cheaper than we can build it? Because if we can't get it cheaper than we can build it, why don't we just buy land and build it?"

Imperiale: And perhaps avoid the cost of carrying the property until we know with greater certainty that somebody will occupy the building and pay the rent?

Camp: Right. When you're building a property, you're going to have the newest property rather than a used property. You can improve on what's sitting right next door that's empty when you're building your own property. That's not to say there's not more risk in building a new building, because it takes a while and you don't know what the market will be like when you get done.

Imperiale: So in some ways, you're really taking the cost, income, and market value approaches and reinterpreting them for purposes of REITs?

Camp: Yes. It's not rocket science. These are mathematical for-mulas, but they're not the ultimate metric.

Imperiale: Are there other methods for valuing REIT shares?

Camp: Yes, there's a variety of things, none of which stand out over and above the others. In general, we look for all the different parameters and try to align them so that nothing seems way out of line. Basically we look at price multiples. We look at a growth multiple or a price FFO versus the growth rate in FFO. In this environment we look at a divi-dend discounts model more closely now that the real estate markets are softer, thinking that in the end, what the investor really gets is the dividend. If there's not growth, you have a dividend.

While we think valuation is always important, we are cautious to not overweigh one versus the other. As a rule of thumb, REITs typically will trade with a multiple somewhere near their long-term sustainable growth rate. So if you think XYZ REIT is a long-term grower of 8 percent a year, then that REIT probably should trade somewhere around an eight multiple.

Imperiale: Do you base that long-term growth rate on historic growth rate?

Camp: Yes, but it can be derived in a number of ways. One would be historical, and another would be the business format. If you look at long-term triple-net lease companies, their growth rates tend to be closer to inflation, and they're typically not quite as leveraged, so their growth rate may be lower. Then you add something for acquisitions, because that's typically the only way they grow. In simple terms, we believe that REITs are inflationary growers, just in core growth. Maybe a little better than inflation because management does add some value and they should grow. There should be a reason people want to pay a higher price to be with a solid management team. You should want to pay a little bit higher rent if they're managing your property well.

Imperiale: If the quality of what you get is a little bit better, the value deserves a premium?

Camp: Yes. And so, if you assume that inflation is 2 to 3 percent on average and if you assume that REITs do a little bit better than that—say, 3 to 4 percent—then what you should do is run that growth rate through the balance sheet. Assuming you're probably somewhere around 50 percent leveraged, just to make the math work easy, you get something that is in the 6 to 8 percent growth range. Then you tack on any kind of external growth, whether it's acquisitions or developments, and that typically will add 100 to 200 basis points. On average, we think REITs should have growth rates in the upper single digits.

Imperiale: On a long-term basis?

Camp: Yes. Good REITs will be a little bit better than that, others will be on the lower end of that range. We think management teams play an important role in the multiple. We also believe that statistical studies show that actual credit rating has something to do with multiple. On average, the higher the rating, the higher the multiple. That gets a little muddy when you get into the lower triple Bs and the nonrated credits. But certainly the REITs that carry the A credits are trading at higher multiples on average.

Imperiale: How do you estimate a REIT's cost of capital and why is this an important number?

Camp: Well, if I can acquire my capital for a lower cost than another competing REIT, the outcome is I can afford to pay more for a building yet still make a higher return on it.

Imperiale: When you can win more often, how is that reflected in your analysis of a REIT?

Camp: It's more of a subjective thing for us. Obviously REITs are all competing against each other, but in reality, I don't know if there are really that many REITs that necessarily go head to head on a daily basis bidding on properties. I think the competition in the REIT industry is more among private investors rather than REIT versus REIT. The reason I say that is that really only about 10 percent of all commercial real estate is in REIT ownership. Therefore, to run across another REIT when you're bidding is probably more rare than it is for investors to be in competition in the other 90 percent of the market. Keep in mind that a large majority of that 90 percent is owner occupied and may not ever bid on a property that's on the market. So let's say 50 percent is completely removed. You still have a 40 percent private market versus a 10 percent REIT market.

Imperiale: And that 40 percent of potential bidders that you're working against would be institutional real estate buyers for large funds? And who else?

Camp: It could be pension funds. It could be mom-and-pops.

Imperiale: Sometimes called local sharpshooters.

Camp: You know, in every market, there's certainly at least a handful of private developers that are local sharpshooters.

Then there's another whole sector of high-net-worth individuals who need a portion of their assets in real estate and decide that direct ownership is better than an alternative. They have brokers working for them, bidding on things. They will typically be higher bidders because they're looking for bondlike returns. Whether it's 10 percent or 9 percent, if it's only one asset, that return is almost immeasurable to them. They can't tell the difference on an annual income basis. But for a more organized group, it's more of a big deal. It comes down to basis points rather than hundreds of basis points. Of course, you'll still get the crazy individual investor that doesn't know the market as well, wants to get into the market, and has a hungry broker that wants a commission.

Imperiale: And therefore maybe pays too much?

Camp: Correct. But it takes it away from even the strongest REIT. It doesn't matter what they're borrowing at. And the other side of the coin is that those private investors can lever up much higher than a REIT can, so they can pay more because they're going to borrow all of it anyway.

Imperiale: Private buyers aren't subject to the public capital market discipline that REITs feel.

Camp: Correct. The best way to put it is that they don't have to answer to anybody. And as you know, the capital markets have been a powerful policing agent of public real estate. As an aside, we do see REITs going into JV [joint venture] structures just to quietly increase their leverage.

Imperiale: In your analysis of REITs, how do you deal with the joint venture structure creating leverage off the balance sheet? We understand the REIT management's position that they're trying to maximize the impact of their equity for the shareholder, but how do you account for that?

Camp: I think there's a trade-off between what's right for the shareholder and what's right for the marketplace. While I view the sell-side analyst's job as protecting the investor in some respects, I don't necessarily see the rationale that the capital markets get tight and that in the past, everyone's been really hurt because they've been overleveraged. If you look at some of these companies and say they're 30 percent leveraged on their property, and you really start to think about that, you say, "This is crazy. Why isn't 50 percent acceptable? Why isn't 60 percent?" Obviously 80 percent and 90 percent is not acceptable. But to be down in the 30 to 50 percent range, which is where most REITs fall, is too low a leverage. It's unfortunate that the market has policed REITs into a situation where they feel they have to go the JV route to theoretically increase their leverage because it's off the balance sheet. I think that's an unfortunate situation, but I don't think it's an excessive amount of leverage.

Imperiale: Do you think that's why some REITs have gone the JV route?

Camp: I don't know if it's necessarily that manipulative. I think it's more of a situation where if you can strike the right partnerships, and your partners are very agreeable, it's a great way to enhance your return on equity. With the higher leverage, you'll get higher returns. So the things that they're doing on the off-balance-sheet structure are all things to help the shareholder, and if it's structured the right way, the shareholder should be protected from the downside. It's hard to know about each one because they're such private deals that you can't find out much about them.

Imperiale: Is it fair to say the management of most REITs really doesn't give you a lot of transparency on joint venture deals?

Camp: Certainly not on the downside. You don't ever know if the REIT is ultimately responsible for having to sell the assets under the breakup. Or if occupancy falls and the partner says, "I'm out of here," what happens? Most of the REITs are JVing with very strong entities, so it's not like the partner's going to go belly-up. If anything, the marriage of the two creates a situation where the REIT can derive extra capital. I look at JV structures as just another arrow in the quiver. It's another way to tap the market to get more capital. The fundamental thing about REITs that everyone needs to understand is that they must have capital to grow. This is a very simple model, but if inflation is lower, that dramatically affects the internal growth of the REIT. So in order to get adequate return on a REIT, if you're only getting growth in the 4 to 5 percent range, you need capital to grow. You need to make your portfolio bigger, and the problem with that is it works under a lot of small numbers. For a small REIT, adding one building to a portfolio makes a huge difference. But when you get to a large REIT, adding one building doesn't even hit the radar screen.

Imperiale: Let's talk about some other ways you might generally value REITs, for example, looking at AFFO [adjusted funds from operations] yield relative to the 10-year treasury and the S&P utility index. What do you think about those valuation methods?

Camp: I think they're all important to look at. Comparing industry to industry is a great way to look at REITs because it makes it look as if REITs are better cash flow vehicles. The better you look relative to other industries, the better your multiple will eventually get. After all, REITs are only a 10-year industry, really.

Imperiale: What do you anticipate for the REIT industry in the future?

Camp: I think the big swings in valuation will narrow. The cycle will become less severe. In the 1990s, when every REIT was acquiring every building under the sun and the growth rates were way north of 15 percent, people thought this was normal. So they put a huge multiple on REITs. We got up to near 20 times multiples, and then in 1997, when we were at peak multiples and growth rates were high but falling, we thought the world was coming to an end. In reality, the real estate cycle was just kicking into gear, but everybody thought that REITs were way overvalued, so they started selling them off. When you look back at the valuation and growth rates then, you realize how unsustainable those growth rates were and that maybe the market was pretty smart.

I believe the market will become more stable as the industry grows. In the early stages, it's always more volatile, and I think we're at a period now where instead of saying it's normal to have 15 percent growth, people are now looking at long-term sustainable growth rates. Some years we're going to be less than that, some years more, but the valuation should always gravitate toward the mean. As people get that perception of gravitating toward the mean, in bad times we won't see people fall off to a three times multiple, which would be representative of the growth rate. We're seeing them falling to six to eight times multiples, and maybe that's what people really think are the sustainable growth rates. So, while some of the yield parameters are good measures, I don't know if they're going to be the ones driving the multiple or the valuation. I think they all need to be looked at collectively.

Imperiale: So your methodology is to look at all these factors to get a general valuation.

Camp: You know, nothing is going to give you *the* right answer. It's not that simple. And in fact, valuation is not at the top of our list of things we really care about. We think valuation is extremely important, but we have a much more fundamental long-term view, and real estate is a long-term-hold asset. Because of that, we tend to weigh more heavily toward the management team.

Imperiale: In your opinion, what's the best way to assess the management team?

Camp: Obviously experience and track record mean a lot, and we're gaining more experience and more track record as we move forward. The thing that we don't have is a given REIT's history as a private company. But really, we only have 10 years of public history as an industry, and that was 10 years of a very good real estate cycle. There are companies out there that have been around forever, and you can get cycle history for them, but their market caps were so small back then that it's a completely different industry. So, in addition to experience and track record, we look at the depth of the team, who's got control, who's making the decisions, and how those decisions are being made—whether it's a committee process or the CEO directs everything because it was his company when it was a private company and you better do it his way. We put more credence in a broader management team that has group decision-making power. We also look at the board involvement—is the board independent or not, are they involved, do they care, are they showing up to meetings? Those are the important things. Is there a way to police the activity in the REIT either at the board level, or by internal controls, or ways that we as analysts can watch some of this stuff? If there's no way, then it's very difficult to get positive on a story. We're more skeptical about names that don't have a lot of coverage in the public markets. We look for people that are accessible, management teams that are accessible. You've got to be able to talk to them and you've got to believe that they're telling you things the way they are. There are also external ways to look at things, like what kind of unit deals they're doing, how they went public. Some were bailouts or highly leveraged private companies that needed recapitalization.

Imperiale: In the form of equity?

Camp: Yes. There were no real other alternatives; the banks were calling in loans because their buildings were sitting empty and they couldn't carry them anymore. You have to look at how those deals were structured. Obviously management teams, when they go public, make personal money, and you want to make sure that they didn't just get a big pot of gold at the end of the rainbow for almost having a bankrupt company before the market bailed them out. There's also ongoing surveillance—for deals with a relative or an affiliated company. There have been companies that have buried fees under the table and things like that on these deals. You have to watch out for these things, but I think they're becoming fewer and farther between. I think that's where the policing of the capital markets has come in.

Imperiale: In the 1970s and 1980s real estate was seen as being like a high-stakes poker game with a lot of big egos around the table. You point out management is becoming more professional now. So although we know there will always be big egos in real estate, are those big egos being more disciplined about how they carry on business?

Camp: I think they are. The other thing you have to watch for is, Are they all real estate people? There are two ways to look at a management team. One is a collective group of buddies that ran their private company and now all have a position in upper management. Whatever their titles are, they're all real estate people. That can work, it's just maybe not the optimal way to look at it. The other side of the coin is a management team that has people with varying backgrounds. The CEO or the COO are probably real estate people. The chief financial officer is either from the finance community or from the accounting community. The leasing person might be a broker. There's real synergy there in that the members play off their strengths, rather than just figuring that since they were all doing this before, they can figure it out as a public company. We've seen some disasters when that has happened. The more professional you get in the management ranks and the more seasoned you get in the public world, the more you build creditability, and therefore multiple.

Imperiale: How important is it for a REIT to have a very clear and well-articulated business strategy?

Camp: It's very important that they be focused on whatever their strategy may be. Even if it's fuzzy, that's OK. If it changes, that's where I have a hard time. It indicates that management really doesn't know what they want to be when they grow up. Obviously the good orators who can articulate their story in a very user-friendly way carry a premium multiple, whether they deserve it or not. The ones who can articulate their story convince people to buy their stock. You can argue that some of them don't deserve it, but they can tell their story better than anybody and win. They can win the hearts of the shareholders, and those are long-term relationships, so it shows up in their valuation.

I think it's important that they have that, but in strategy, we look for two things: geographic diversification and product diversification. These two strategies are probably equal in protecting the investor, just very different. There are different risks associated with them. Geographic diversity protects you from local economy downturns, but who's to say the entire market won't decline?

Imperiale: You really can't insulate yourself from a general downturn that goes across the entire economy.

Camp: Right. Of course, you can find pitfalls in any strategy. Unless you're a triple-net company, it's very difficult to have a single asset here and there, but I do think the triple-net people can carry it off because there's no management involved.

Imperiale: You remove the management layer and essentially the occupant of the property is going to be responsible for basically everything on a long-term basis, so you don't need to manage the property.

Camp: Right. So we do look at those. We look at the diversification of the portfolio, whether it's product or geographic. We look at the real estate market conditions. Obviously, there's more inherent business risk in the Silicon Valley than there is in Chicago, by virtue of a less diverse economy and also because there are more peaks and valleys in the real estate cycles. The real estate cycles on the West Coast tend to have very high peaks and very low valleys. This creates more inherent risk in both stock prices and company survival in those markets because of the huge volatility. The Midwest markets tend to be a little more slow. You don't get the peaks and valleys that you do on the West Coast. And the Midwest loses manufacturing, but it never really loses that many professional workers, and those are the people that are making the economy go in some respects.

Then we look at competition. Markets that have huge competition obviously create more problems for the REIT. If they're strong, private competition that can get 80 or 90 percent loans, that's a huge competition for REITs.

We also look for whether the markets are dynamic or static. We tend to put more value or less business risk on dynamic markets. If there's activity in those markets, then even though there may be slow periods and down periods, as long as buildings are trading hands, REITs can make money. As long as there are acquisition or build-to-suit opportunities, even if the economy is weak, REITs will be typically the dominant player and therefore should win more deals. So there's less risk in general.

Imperiale: When a REIT is in multiple markets, do you try to aggregate all of that and balance the good and the bad markets?

Camp: Yes. Obviously you want more good markets than bad markets, but I think just by its nature, geographic diversification is probably more powerful than product diversification. There are certain regions of the country that are somewhat insulated from economic downturns. I am a firm believer that Washington, D.C., because of the government, is more protected from an economic downturn than the West Coast, or even the Midwest. When the government starts spending in an economic downturn or creates stimulus to get the economy going, that stimulus will start in its home territory. So there are some areas where you could be geographically concentrated and win all the time. Washington, D.C., is never the top market, but I bet it's always in the top five. And there are other areas that are that way. I think Manhattan is pretty close to that now. They've suffered through some big boom and bust areas, but they are so land constrained now that it is very difficult to overbuild the market place. It's not going to be a developer getting caught hanging out, although rebuilding the World Trade Center might be a classic example of it. If 15 million square feet are added, that's a lot of incremental absorption that has to happen.

I actually argue that the only reason the Northern California market has the peaks and valleys it does is because companies are doing some crazy things. They think there's no space left, so they bid up the prices. The demand-driven economy that is out there is so volatile because when times are good, they're really good. Then some overenthusiastic user starts a bidding war, and that part of the economy can't handle that. For example, one California user recently bought their buildings for $775 a foot. That doesn't work. I mean, replacement cost is $250. Because of things like that, you're going to have bigger peaks and valleys. You want stable markets and you want a stabilizing factor in the markets. There is no stabilizing factor in the California market other than land constraints. That could ultimately be a stabilizing factor, but the economic cycle of technology right now is still big boom and bust periods. That is a very young industry, and peaks and valleys are usually higher in the early part of existence.

Imperiale: So you consider those kind of economic risks.

Camp: You have to. You have to look at what's happening in the economy. REITs are so thinly traded that you have to look at the external drivers of the REIT industry. That gets back to my fundamental thesis, that valuation doesn't necessarily matter all that much to us because we hope that most investors in real estate are looking for a longer-term investment.

Imperiale: When you're thinking about the valuation of a REIT and the business risk, how do you factor in development activities and merchant building activities? Some people in the industry argue those deserve a premium value, and some say they really hurt your value because you don't get paid for the risk you take on.

Camp: Factors like these all come from external things besides just pure rent growth. They all provide diversification to the business model of a REIT, so I think that in that sense they are good things and if you are successful at them throughout good and bad periods in the real estate cycle, then you deserve a premium multiple for it, because you have more ways of deriving revenue throughout a business cycle. However, if you can't sustain that success, then they become one-time events, which means you can't deserve the same type of multiple as pure internal organic rent growth.

Because this is our first really down cycle in real estate since REITs have been public, it is yet to be proven whether or not these external factors can work throughout a business cycle. The only one that seems to be working now is the JV structure in some respects. In fact, we're actually seeing more demand for certain companies that do third-party money management, because people are tired of the volatility of the stock market, so they are looking for private money managers. And as long as you're looking for a private money manager in real estate, why not bury your money with one of the REITs? They know what they're doing. They'll charge a fee, but they'll invest it in really good assets.

Imperiale: So the institutional investor that's looking for a real estate opportunity is more likely to undertake or invest in a joint venture with a REIT?

Camp: Potentially, yes. There are two different correlations between the private and the public market. In theory, the private market, whether you're investing alongside a public REIT or directly in your own real estate, correlates to the real estate market. The REIT stock market tends to not correlate with much of anything. It rides waves that sometimes are unexplainable, as we saw in 1998 when real estate markets were really good. Throughout 1998 and 1999, REIT stock prices suffered dramatically and there was really no rhyme or reason for it other than that other areas in the market were doing very well and investor sentiment was against us. I think there's a portion of the REIT investor community that would want to correlate to pure real estate rather than to the REIT public market. And I think that proves out in slow times because during the slow times, while individual retail investors are looking at the yield of the REIT as an alternate investment vehicle, they are not buying that REIT because of fundamental reasons of the real estate markets. They're yield buyers. And because of that, the institutional investor, the pension fund, and the various other avenues want to be correlated to the real estate market. Right now, REIT valuations are actually increasing at a time when they should be falling. I think there's a portion of investors that don't trade like the public REITs do, they trade like real estate does.

Imperiale: There's a give-up for being in the private real estate, and that is that you don't have the liquidity that you have in the public sector of real estate.

Camp: One thing we haven't touched on is the external factors in the marketplace that drive REITs. Several different types of correlation studies have found that REITs aren't necessarily correlated to much of anything in the broader markets. But the one driver in REIT share price return that we continuously find over a long period is an inverse correlation to spot interest rates. There are two schools of thought—actually, I think they both combine to get you to the same place. One is the yield-driven investor. As bond yields go low, REIT yields look pretty attractive, so you bid up the price. It's an alternate investment tool as that spread between interest rates and REIT yields widens, and right now we're at a very wide point, so maybe that's what's holding up share prices. The other side deals more with the fundamental business strategy side of REITs—as interest rates go lower, their WACC comes down dramatically, and I am not convinced that in the past year of lowering rates, the returns still are not high and going higher because of the weakness in the economy. The more long-term stabilized returns are probably going a little bit higher, but not much. They're probably pretty stable, actually. But yet, cost to capital is way lower. When you look at it from that perspective, REIT returns should fundamentally accelerate coming out of this thing, because interest rates are so low. So there are two drivers on the external side, all having to do with interest rates, one internal to the REIT and one external to the investor, that could drive valuations higher in the future. Even in a prolonged down cycle, it could drive REIT returns higher.

Imperiale: In a rising interest rate environment, what would you argue?

Camp: In that case I actually argue the opposite. In a rising interest rate environment, you have bond yields coming up so investors can trade off the risk of owning a stock to improve credit quality, flock to safety, and still get a fair return. So as interest rates come up, they would trade out of REITs into bonds as that spread narrows. It depends what the reason for the increase in interest rates is. If it's an inflationary environment and everything's going up, that spread probably doesn't change. But if it's a more normal economic growth, I don't think REIT yields will be 10 or 12 percent in that situation. I think they may be in the 6.5 to 7 range. So we bid those prices up and the yields come down, the spread narrows, and then interest rates start picking up and that spread narrows even more because we've already come down. Then it's almost an even-up trade to come out of REITs. You've got a gain locked in because the price went up, you got a lower yield, you can get out of it and into a bond that yields basically the same thing, and there's a lot less business risk. At that time, while yields on REITs will probably go back up because the prices are coming back down, the spread difference will probably still be narrower.

On the other side of the coin is that as those interest rates come up, while a lot of REITs have fixed-rate debt, incrementally they would have to tap those markets because you always need capital to grow. That capital would become more expensive, and your cost of equity capital is rising also because investors are going to expect a bigger return. While that all fundamentally looks like a disaster scenario, I don't know how big a disaster it really is, because returns go up when interest rates rise. They have to. People bid the prices lower to get a bigger return because there are bigger hurdles out there.

Imperiale: Could you also say that the rental revenue stream may grow at a faster rate in a healthier business environment?

Camp: Absolutely. And cap rates come down. When the economy is good and rents are rising, people will bid down the cap rates so the prices go up on properties. So the returns are not necessarily as high on buildings as they were in a slow economy, because you'd have a long-term tenant in there with 4 percent rent bumps. You would pay up for that rather than a 10 cap today that only has two years left with rents coming down.

Imperiale: Let's touch on the stability of cap rates, because it's remarkable that people in various sectors of the REIT world say, "Cap rates on community shopping centers have been 9 to 10.5 and they always are, that's just the range they trade in."

Camp: And high-end apartments have always had cap rates of 7 to 8. I think that's true, but even a 100-basis-point fluctuation in cap rates is a big fluctuation.

Imperiale: That converts into a big change in price?

Camp: Correct. And when you're a large-scale buyer, it's big. You know, if I move my cap rate 25 basis points on one of my companies, they have heart failure when I report their new NAV. That cap rate change more than offsets any kind of increased NOI. You can have the greatest gains in occupancy, and your markets might be terrible, and your cap rate goes up. You've got bigger NOI but you've got a higher cap rate and your valuation is actually low. There's nothing that's more frustrating to a management team than that. That's why I don't put a lot of credence on it, because it is fluctuating and it does vary.

Imperiale: The cap rate valuations do change over time and you get trends up and down.

Camp: I think that's true in the sense that in aggregate, it doesn't look like cap rates all change that much. I mean, there were office buildings in Northern California a couple years ago going sub-8 cap rates that now are probably trading above or darn close to 9. It's the kind of thing people don't really think about very often, but 100 basis points and a 7 cap is a bigger difference than 100 basis points and a 10 cap. It's kind of like refinancing your mortgage. If you're at a 7 going to a 6, that's a bigger difference than if you're at 8 going to 7. And you don't need as big a move in those interest rates as you get down lower and lower, because on a percentage basis, you're making bigger moves with a smaller change. The magnitude of the change as a percentage becomes greater.

Part Three

Dynamic Trends and REITs

Residential REITs

Chapter Summary

- The total value of all apartments in the United States is estimated to be $1.6 trillion.
- Apartments are approximately 25 percent of the aggregate commercial real estate market.
- Real estate investment trusts (REITs) own an estimated 8 percent of all apartment units.
- Apartment REITs represent 19 percent of the National Association of Real Estate Investment Trusts (NAREIT) Equity Index.
- The demand for apartments is driven by population growth and household formation.
- Current demographic trends have created a favorable outlook for apartment demand.
- Returns on apartment REITs are among the most stable for all REIT sectors.

Rent—a waste of money. It's so much cheaper to buy.

—Fran Lebowitz, 1981

Apartment or Multifamily Properties

For official purposes, apartment buildings or multifamily properties are defined as residential dwellings consisting of five or units in a single building or complex of buildings. The terms *nent* and *multifamily* are often used interchangeably, igh *multifamily* is more commonly used when describing buildings of four or fewer units.

The total value of all apartments in the United States is estimated to be $1.6 trillion or approximately 25 percent of the aggregate commercial real estate market. Real estate investment trusts (REITs) own an estimated 8 percent of all apartment units. As a group, apartment REITs represent 19 percent of the total capitalization of the National Association of Real Estate Investment Trusts (NAREIT) Equity Index (see Figure 11.1).

Quality Classifications

For investment purposes, apartment buildings, like most other commercial structures, are often classified by quality level. Individual properties are judged in terms of quality and are classified as class A, class B, or class C. There is often a very strong correlation between the age of a given property and its classification.

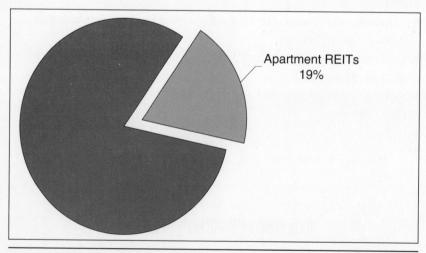

FIGURE 11.1 Apartment REITs as a Percentage of NAREIT Equity Index December 31, 2001

The construction quality of a property, the location within the local market, and the level of amenities are all factored into a property classification. Local standards also have a bearing on quality ratings. For example, a newer suburban garden apartment complex in Milwaukee might be considered a class A project based on prevailing local market standards. But replicate that exact complex in suburban Phoenix or Palm Springs and it might be considered a class B project because it lacks amenities that are part of a higher local market standard in Phoenix. There are no hard and fast criteria for grading properties or defining the distinctions between class A, class B, and class C. The classifications are partially subjective and leave room for some degree of interpretation.

Class A apartment buildings are the newest structures built of high-quality materials and are in the best locations by local market standards. Class A buildings normally also offer amenities over and above those of average or typical apartment buildings. Luxury lobbies, doormen, concierge services, party facilities, health club facilities, and other lifestyle amenities are typical of class A properties. The rents at class A properties tend to reflect the level of amenities and service that a tenant could expect.

Class B buildings tend to be slightly older. In many instances class B properties are between 10 and 20 years in age. The new building luster has faded, and they typically offer a more limited range of the lifestyle amenities than those found in class A buildings. The location of a class B building might be in an average or even less desirable local market. And, the building materials and improvements found in class B properties tend to be average relative to community standards, whereas class A properties often have above-average construction features when compared to local community standards.

Class C buildings tend to be the oldest buildings in a given community. These buildings are often "recycled" properties that were originally built for a given use and then rehabilitated and adapted for another use. Old multistory urban warehouse buildings that are renovated into loft apartments are typical of class C properties. These buildings are often located in less desirable neighborhoods that might have a mix of low- and middle-income families. Class C buildings have few amenities and are often functionally obsolete for the current use. Class C buildings are seldom owned by publicly traded REITs unless they are purchased for renovation or redevelopment to class B or better levels.

These classifications are subjective at best. They attempt to broadly group properties into groups or general categories that are easily recognized by knowledgeable observers. Buildings are often classified as class B by a potential buyer and class A by the seller for purposes of negotiations. To further complicate matters, real estate professionals often create categories within a class. For example, better-quality class B properties are often called "high-B" buildings, or lesser class A buildings are termed "low-A" buildings. These distinctions are helpful to real estate professionals but often confusing to the uninitiated. However, in general, REITs tend to invest in class B or better apartment buildings, and the majority of apartment REITs focus on class A properties.

Physical Structure Classifications

Apartment buildings are often classified in broad terms by their size and style:

- *Low-rise.* Normally under three stories, often in attached townhouse style.

- *Mid-rise.* Over three stories, but subject to relative local standards. For example, a 10-story building in Cleveland is a high-rise, but in Chicago or New York it is a mid-rise.

- *High-rise.* Normally 10 stories or over in most local real estate markets.

- *Infill.* Often termed *urban infill,* these properties are normally built on smaller parcels of land in higher-density urban locations.

- *Garden.* Sprawling suburban complexes with low- to mid-rise buildings on a campuslike setting. These often have higher levels of amenities such as swimming pools, tennis courts, and clubhouses.

The number of stories is a simple way to classify because it is an easily identified building feature. The height of a building also has an impact on the building's operation cost. Generally, the taller the building, the higher the cost of operation due to the more complex building systems and the higher initial cost of development. High-rise and mid-rise properties are most often found in higher-density urban locations where land value is high and availability is scarce. Low-rise and garden projects tend to be located in suburban locations where density and land cost are less of an issue. Submarket dynamics also have an impact on building type. Land use restrictions and other zoning laws such as maximum densities and height restrictions ultimately affect the type and style of project that is built. These limitations are more apparent in some markets and have an impact on what gets built and where it is located.

Apartment Demand and Residential Market Dynamics

The demand for residential housing, and more particularly apartments, is driven by population growth and household formation. Increases in the population of a geographic area tend to drive the demand for housing in that locale. According to the U.S. Census Bureau, population growth averages 2.1 percent annually. This steady and stable growth in population drives the demand for housing. Demand for housing from population growth is further affected by household formation, which is a result of people moving into their own residence. These formations usually occur due to newly married couples starting new households or people moving out on their own, normally young adults leaving existing households or the breakup of existing households due to divorce. In any case, it is highly likely that people forming new households will initially rent for some length of time. This drives the need for multifamily units.

Relocation of existing households to a new area also drives the demand for housing in a local market. Relocation may benefit the growth statistics of a given market while having a negative affect on another locale. The classic paradigm of this relocation trend is the movement of households out of rural Midwestern communities. Some of the older population in many of these communities chooses to migrate to warmer retirement destinations such as Florida and Arizona. Many of the younger people in these same places often leave to look for better employment opportunities in larger urban centers. The net result is population migrations that create shifting regional demand trends for residential real estate.

Shifting regional demand patterns tend to drive the general real estate cycle as discussed in Chapter 5. In the case of residential real estate, the cycle is relatively smooth and stable when compared to other real estate sectors. Household formation and population migration stimulates demand in a local market. The existing supply of available residential options becomes absorbed causing a general tightness. Demand exceeds available supply and prices begin to rise. Prices rise to the point that it stimulates building activity to meet the increased demand, thus creating a growth trend in the local market. This pattern often creates expanding demand in other sectors of the local real estate market as the increasing population requires places to work, eat, and shop, which stimulates additional demand for all the private and public services that support the growing economic base. At this stage of the growth pattern, local market dynamics begin to have a large bearing on the supply and demand outcomes in a given local market.

Affordability is a key component of the local housing market dynamic. If you need a place to live, the options are to own or to rent. Certain factors such as consumer confidence, mortgage interest rates, economic growth, and employment trends all have an affect on the decision to own or rent. But the ultimate rent-versus-buy decision in a local market is largely driven by affordability. The affordability factor then impacts the tone and outlook for the local multifamily housing market.

An example of how affordability affects the rental market dynamic is the rise of the Internet and the dot-com revolution. The growth of Internet-related businesses in the San Jose and San Francisco Bay area was a large driver of the local economy for the last half of the 1990s. Large flows of capital into the local economy supported the explosive growth of Internet-related businesses. This led to a high level of job formation, which fueled a rapid growth in household formations. The median household incomes generated were the highest in the country, exceeding $83,000 per year in 1999. But a confluence of local market factors including limited amounts of developable land, difficult entitlement requirements, stringent local zoning regulations, and a shortage of skilled construction tradesmen made housing affordability a major issue in the region. This created a large demand for affordable rental housing as the price of local rents rose to very high levels and vacancies declined to near zero. Contrast this with local markets in other parts of the country, where land is available, entitlement is easy, zoning is relaxed, and there is an adequate supply of skilled construction tradesmen, resulting in better housing affordability even when median household incomes are far lower than the national average.

Demographics and Amenity Trends

In the aggregate, current demographic trends have created a favorable outlook for apartment demand. In 1998, the first of a generation known as the Echo Boom began to graduate from college. These are the children of the 78 million post-WWII babies well known as the Baby Boom generation. It is expected that about 4 million of these well-educated, affluent Echo Boom consumers will graduate from college this year and join the workforce. And we can expect to see about 4 million a year for the next 18 years. This dynamic should lead to a strong trend in household formations over the next decade. Couple that with the fact that the parents of the Echo Boom are living a longer and more active life and the trend in demand for residential real estate looks strong. Substantially all of the expected growth in rental unit demand over the next decade will come from the emerging Echo Boom and the over 45-year-old portion of the Baby Boom generation. These two groups have already begun to influence the trends in design and amenities of newly developed apartment communities.

Providing state-of-the-art technology connections is the major trend among most apartment owners. The Echo Boom generation has been raised with computers and comes from educational settings where high-speed Internet service is abundantly available. They want this same amenity, along with cable television and the availability of multiple telephone lines. These amenity categories are consistently among the most requested by Echo Boomers. Business centers and conference rooms are also in demand by the Echo Boomers, who often work from home. In fact, the business center has become a social gathering spot for many hardworking young professionals.

The number one requested amenity among both Baby Boomers and Echo Boomers who rent is fitness centers. With the growing trend toward better fitness, apartment communities are adding fitness centers that are as well equipped as the average freestanding health club. The other most frequently requested amenity is an in-unit washer and dryer. Most new communities now include this feature in every unit. As in any other business, changing consumer preferences will continue to drive the amenities offered by apartment owners. This has given rise to much more segmented marketing strategies among owners and developers of apartments. Lifestyle strategies that target older renters-by-choice, which include gated communities with higher levels of security and larger, more well appointed units and common areas, have experienced a growth in demand. The recent change in capital gains tax laws that has eliminated the first $500,000 in gains on homes sold seems to have encouraged a generation to consider alternatives to home ownership. These tax policies and other legislative attempts to influence housing policy are worth monitoring because this is a favorite area of legislative tinkering at the federal as well as the state level.

When the demographic trends are coupled with the changing consumer attitude toward renting, it is expected that demand for multifamily units will average 570,000 units per year over the next 10 years. This takes into account increasing household formations and the obsolescence of existing apartment stock over the next decade.

Operating Characteristics

The good news about apartment rents is that they are adjusted to market levels about once a year for each unit. This is also the bad news about apartment rents. The most challenging aspect of apartment ownership is the tenant turnover. The average tenure of an apartment tenant is about 18 months. This means apartment owners must find a new tenant for each unit in their portfolio every 18 months. The only operators in the real estate community who experience a shorter rental duration are hotel operators, who are forced to rerent their rooms about every other day.

In most cases, apartment owners require either a six-month or one-year lease, depending on the local market. This short-duration rental cycle allows the apartment owner to reprice rents to market frequently, so loss-to-lease expenses tend to be modest for apartment owners. In addition, most apartment owners have several other smaller rental streams from their tenants. Most owners collect fees from cable television and local telephone operators for allowing them access to their tenants on a preferred basis. Covered parking and concierge services also provide additional income for some owners.

Because most apartment complexes have hundreds of units and most owners hold thousands of units, the relocation changes of a small number of tenants have a minimal affect on the operation of most apartment portfolios. In addition, because most people need a place to live, apartments are considered one of the most defensive of the real estate sectors. And, because the physical interiors of apartment units are permanent in nature, the expense of tenant improvements is not often a material factor when considering the operating performance of a property. Contrast that with an office building, where the owner may be required to spend $15 to $30 per square foot on tenant improvements in order to lease vacant space. In fact, the largest variable expense for most apartment owners is the cost of remarketing vacant units when a tenant leaves.

Summary Data

Returns on residential REITs are among the most stable of those for all REIT sectors (see Table 11.1). Over the last five years the residential sector has produced an average annual return of 11.3 percent, the highest for any REIT sector. The volatility of the residential sector as measured by the standard deviation of returns is 16 percent, second only to that of

TABLE 11.1 Historical Sector Data for Residential REITs

	2001	2000	1999	1998	1997
Total return on sector	7.44%	35.53%	10.73%	–8.77%	16.04%
Dividend yield	6.97%	9.13%	7.85%	5.60%	7.22%
Estimated NAV	105.00%	97.00%	85.00%	98.00%	114.00%
Market cap of sector ($B)	30.2				
Index weight	22.0%				
All other sectors	78.0%				
Volatility	16.0%				
Five-year return	11.29%				

Source: NAREIT; Uniplan Real Estate Advisors, Inc.

manufactured home communities. The stable and defensive nature of residential property, along with positive demographic trends, makes the long-term outlook for the residential sector very positive.

Interview with Paul D. Puryear

Paul D. Puryear is managing director at Raymond James. Specializing in real estate and real estate–related industries, Puryear has more than 20 years of experience in the fields of real estate and financial analysis. He was recently named one of the top 10 analysts of 2000 by Forbes. Puryear began his career with W. R. Grace in New York. He has served as chief financial officer with two real estate companies, including Portman Barry Investments, Inc., an Atlanta-based office developer. Puryear holds a B.S. in industrial engineering from the Georgia Institute of Technology and an M.B.A. in finance from Georgia State University.

Richard Imperiale: What characteristics distinguish residential real estate as a property group within the real estate spectrum and within the REIT world more particularly?

Paul Puryear: First, shorter-term leases, and second, the key word, *residential.* People protect their homes and their lifestyle even when the economy declines. Consequently, the impact of an economic slump is diluted to some extent for residential real estate. There are some people who, for one reason or another, have to change their residential situation, but you have an extra line of defense when you invest in residential real estate. As far as length of lease, you feel the impact faster, so the market adjusts pretty quickly to the downside, but it also adjusts pretty quickly to the upside. So when the market hits bottom and things start to turn up, you'll see it pretty quickly start to work its way through.

Imperiale: Residential real estate is one of the few sectors where you really have some alternatives—apartments, single-family detached homes, manufactured homes, and so on. Can you comment on what's going on with those different groups and how they all fit into the spectrum?

Puryear: Manufactured housing is clearly the lowest-cost housing alternative, and that sector has made great strides in recent years in upgrading the quality of the product. But it got too bullish and the capacity in the industry got way overbuilt, so we had a period for the past couple of years where because the pipeline of new product was so full, it was pushed onto buyers with credit terms that were too loose. There were some problems there, and there's still a correction going on as the market tries to find the right demand-capacity equation. The manufactured sector has been beat up—I'm talking about the manufacturers themselves, not necessarily the REITs. The REIT's have held out pretty well.

Then, of course, you have rental apartments, which historically have catered to an 18- to 35-year-old age category. This is where you start out; nobody buys right off the bat. So that sector caters to single people, young professionals, single-parent families, immigrants, and so forth. More and more we're seeing trends toward empty nesters or established professionals moving into rental units, particularly in business centers. But that's secondary to the 18- to 35-year-old age category that makes up the bulk of renters.

Then there's single-family housing. Once you get into your occupational years, you're married and you start your family, you buy a starter home. Right now, prices in the United States are about $125,000 to $150,000, but you can buy a manufactured house for $60,000. Later you might move up into higher-level markets.

Imperiale: In your opinion, what drives the supply and demand dynamic within the residential segment? Is it demographic?

Puryear: Yes. Of course, supply tries to attract, meet, and anticipate demand in all sectors, but demand is really some combination of demographic and economic factors. Job growth is key in household formation, and when you start losing jobs, ultimately that's going to spell trouble.

Imperiale: Because it slows down household formation?

Puryear: Yes, it detracts from the ability to buy or rent. Particularly in apartments, the number one indicator we've always used has been job growth, and the rule of thumb is that for every 10 jobs you create, you create demand for two apartments, a 20 percent ratio. That's probably not a bad number, but you've got to think in terms of location. If you move into Manhattan, what are you most likely to do? You're most likely to rent. So there the ratio may be 80 percent instead of 20 percent. In other words, for 10 new jobs you might have demand for eight new apartments. But in a market like Little Rock, Arkansas, where single-family housing is a very inexpensive and affordable proposition, percentages of rent are very low.

As far as demographic trends, the live birth rate in the United States really started to accelerate in the 1980s. In a few years those kids will be out of high school and either going to college or in the job market. That age category— 22 to 30—really creates this demographic driver in the apartment sector. The other thing is immigration trends. Immigrant numbers have been running at about 700,000 a year. The events of September 11 are going to impact that, but still, when an immigrant moves into the United States, the propensity to rent is extremely high. After they've been here about five years and are established, the propensity to own escalates pretty dramatically.

Then you have people who have finished college, have been working for five years, have gotten married, plan to have a child in two years, and want a house. Then there are first-move-up buyers, who may have the income to jump into the second move up, which gets you into a $200,000 or $300,000 house, or maybe even a luxury, which is half a million and up.

Imperiale: In terms of the immigrant issue, how dramatically would a change in policy impact the apartment sector?

Puryear: Well, for starters, the immigrant population tends to come in at B- and C-level properties as opposed to the very high-end A properties. And you tend to see most of it in the Sunbelt areas of California, Texas, and Florida, where service fields are heavily dependent upon immigrant populations. To some extent, the impacts are going to be market specific and I don't think it's going to impact the REIT world that dramatically, because the REIT world is focused more on the A unit, which really caters to young professionals.

Imperiale: How big is this Echo Boom segment that's just starting to rent apartments?

Puryear: The estimate for 2000 is 68.4 million. By way of comparison, for 1990, it was 69 million, so it actually went down a little. For 2010, it escalates to 72.7 million, for 2020, 76.7 million, and for 2030, 79.3 million. This trend is really going to take hold in the next two to three years, and it's going to drive the numbers higher. It's going to impact things like colleges. The public schools are jam-packed right now, and the reason is that they didn't anticipate this trend.

Imperiale: What are the thematic trends that are in play within the residential sector in terms of changing lifestyles? You mentioned a little bit about people electing to sell their homes and move into apartments. Are there other lifestyle trends going on that could have an impact?

Puryear: Yes. Especially in urban centers—Chicago, for example—people are opting to move closer to work and get rid of the commutes. And not only are we seeing empty nesters and families opting for an apartment lifestyle, I think the percentage of single people in the United States as opposed to the percentage of married couples is increasing. The standard 2.2 kids, dad works, mom's at home, is the minority today. So there are a lot of people who opt for the apartment lifestyle as a permanent decision. It's not a given anymore that just because you get to 35 and you're successful and you've got the income, you're going to buy a house.

Imperiale: The trend toward renting as a lifestyle is being translated into some trends in the apartment world, isn't it? How have apartment owners and developers changed the mix of services they deliver to cater to that group?

Puryear: They're offering a lot of technology-related services— data ports, high-speed transmission so you can work out of your apartment. Then there are various types of food services, dry cleaning services, day care, and so on.

Imperiale: Some people believe that other sectors of the market, particularly the urban A sectors of office and industrial, are moving toward oligopolistic ownership, where all the best properties are owned by just a few public players. Do you envision apartment communities ever moving in that direction?

Puryear: Well, the apartment market is about 17 million units. As far as I know, the largest single operator has 300,000 apartments. That's pretty small. If you look at the high-end products in Southern California, the percentages go up pretty dramatically. But if you look at it on a national level, it's not going to be as dramatic as what we've seen in the mall sector. Malls are huge properties on a relative basis. An apartment complex costs $8 million, a mall costs $80 million. I think the residential sector will become less fragmented. I think there will be consolidation, and I think the REITs have created a vehicle that will attract more and more dollars when investors figure out how solid and predictable the income can be over different cycles. I think it's going to create the opportunity to have larger and large companies, but I don't think you're going to see a day where 60 percent of the market is controlled by five players.

Imperiale: What type of cap rates are available for developers in the residential section?

Puryear: It varies dramatically from market to market and based on property type. Typically the higher-end properties carry a little bit lower cap rate or just higher valuations. So you can see cap rates in the sevens at the low end, and they can go all the way up into the elevens and the twelves, depending on the property type. If I had to pick one number, I would say that cap rates are generally in the nines.

Imperiale: What benchmarks do you believe are appropriate for measuring the performance of residential REITs?

Puryear: First and foremost is net asset value. The key driver in our investment decision is whether or not the companies are capable of delivering growth in value over a period of time, and earnings are measured in a lot of different ways. I think FFO [funds from operations] is still the key measure, although it certainly has its faults. FAD [funds available for distribution] analysts have just recently agreed on a new EPS [earnings per share] number, which I think is going to help us a lot toward getting to a uniform reporting number. Then you've got EBITDA [earnings before interest, taxes, depreciation, and amortization]. When all is said and done, you really want to comp against the rest of the marketplace. There's a market out there in apartments just like there's a market in stocks. So, there's a value that's set every day, and values are going up and down. To the extent that you can take those cap rates, apply them to these companies, and measure the value creation or diminution, I think you get a sense for how to buy the stocks.

Residential REITs are in an interesting period. Forecasts for household formation predict 1.1 million to 1.3 million formations a year for the next five years. If we have those kinds of numbers, especially knowing what's happening with the Echo Boom, we're heading into a period that could be very good for the apartment sector. If you look back at the 1990s, the performance of apartment REITs was pretty strong during a decade when the demographics really didn't favor the apartment sector. I think that speaks to a couple of things. It speaks to how well the companies are managed, the strength of the management teams, the fact that there's a new discipline in the real estate world, and the fact that we haven't had a big downturn in this cycle. Throw into that a much more favorable demographic picture and I think you have yourself set up for some pretty good performance over the next few years. We're right on the leading edge of it, so it'll be interesting to see how it unfolds.

CHAPTER

12

Manufactured Home Community REITs

Chapter Summary

- There are an estimated 9.3 million manufactured homes in the United States, with an estimated value of $12 billion.

- There are estimated 28,000 manufactured home communities (MHCs) in the United States.

- Real estate investment trusts (REITs) own an estimated 3 percent of all manufactured housing sites.

- Manufactured home community REITs represent 1.5 percent of the National Association of Real Estate Investment Trusts (NAREIT) Equity Index.

- The demand for manufactured housing sites is driven by the growth in sales of manufactured housing.

- The affordability of manufactured housing has created a favorable outlook for unit demand.

- Returns on MHC REITs are among the most stable for all REIT sectors.

A house is a machine to live in.

—Charles Le Corbusier, 1923

MHCs

The manufactured home industry is often misunderstood and has long been maligned by many casual observers. The terms *trailer park,* and *trailer trash,* which are used to refer to manufactured home communities (MHCs) and the people who live in them, certainly suggest less than a positive image. Although the negative perception of the industry is pervasive, the economics of MHC ownership are compelling. In many respects MHCs have most of the positive attributes of multifamily or apartment ownership with fewer of the negative features. In fact, the economics of the sector are so compelling that Sam Zell, the legendary real estate investor, was a founder of the first public MHC real estate investment trust (REIT). The company went public in 1993, offering Zell's portfolio, which he had been accumulating since the early 1980s. In spite of its much maligned reputation, there is some smart money involved in this real estate sector.

It is important to draw a distinction between a manufactured home and an MHC. At an MHC, the owner provides the land and improvements on which manufactured homes are located. As MHC owner, the community provides the streets and utilities as well as the amenities of the common areas along with the location or site where the manufactured home will be located. The MHC owner does not own the actual manufactured homes; the residents of the community own their own homes. These homeowners pay rent to the MHC owner for the use of the site where their manufactured homes are located. Thus, the MHC owner maintains the common area and infrastructure, and the homeowner is responsible for maintenance of the home itself. This is the key distinction between MHC REITs and apartment REITs. It is also the principal economic advantage of MHC ownership over apartment ownership.

A Brief History of Manufactured Homes and MHC REITs

Investors in REITs had one of the first chances to participate in a publicly offered MHC REIT in 1993. One of the first owners to go public was Sam Zell. Three other private MHC owners were quick to follow into the public arena later in the same year. Prior to 1993,

MHC owners included a few syndicators dedicated to MHC properties and some limited partnerships, but the vast majority were and still are small private owners. Little or no ownership of these properties was attributable to institutional real estate investors. The negative reputation of manufactured housing had kept the often skeptical institutional players out of the sector.

The industry of building manufactured housing emerged during the 1940s when mobile homes and camper trailers became widely used as temporary housing and vacation homes. After World War II, the demand for housing exploded as returning veterans flooded the existing housing market. The sudden demand for housing led to the widespread use of mobile homes as permanent housing. The fact that the manufactured home industry has it origins in the recreational vehicle business may account for part of the reason why the industry has not gained wider acceptance within the residential arena. Had the sector been conceived in the home building or multifamily arena, it might be better understood and accepted by consumers and real estate investors.

The manufactured housing industry is regulated by the U.S. Department of Housing and Urban Development (HUD). These regulations, which became effective in June of 1976, preempted any existing state or local construction and safety codes applying to the product defined as manufactured housing. In order to qualify as manufactured housing, HUD requires that a manufactured home have a chassis and undercarriage that support their own wheels, on which they are transported from the factory. The lack of this factory-installed self-transporting feature moves the dwelling into the category of prefabricated homes and removes regulation from HUD into the hands of less predictable local building inspectors. The goal of the federal regulations was to more clearly define mobile homes as buildings rather than vehicles. The Housing Act of 1980 adopted this change officially, mandating the use of the term *manufactured housing* (or *factory-built home*) to replace *mobile home* in all federal law and literature for homes built since 1976. This ushered in a new era for the manufactured housing industry.

It is estimated that there are 9.3 million manufactured homes and 28,000 MHCs in the United States. The vast majority of the million homes are located on sites within MHCs. The National

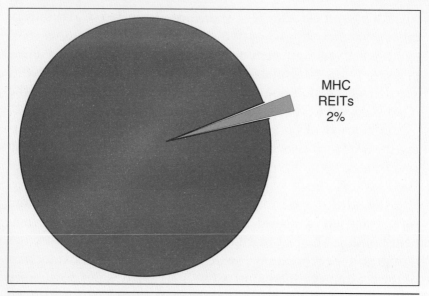

FIGURE 12.1 Manufactured Home Community REITs as a Percentale of the NAREIT Equity Index as of December 31, 2001

Association of Real Estate Investment Trusts (NAREIT) Equity Index includes five publicly traded MHC REITs. These REITs are a subgroup of the residential sector and represent about 2 percent of the total index (see Figure 12.1), or about $2.3 billion in market capitalization, as of September 30, 2001. When combined with the apartment REITs, the residential sector in total represents about 22 percent of the NAREIT Equity Index.

Quality Classifications

For investment purposes, MHCs occupy a very wide quality range. Class A communities have resort-level quality. Amenities similar to and in some cases even exceeding those of class A apartment communities are the norm. Manicured lawns, golf courses, swimming pools, and tennis courts are among the features found in some of the better MHCs. On the low end of the quality spectrum are the class C communities. These are little enclaves of long, thin old mobile homes squeezed tightly together in narrow rows with no amenities. The class C communities are the ones that contribute to the seedy image of MHCs.

As discussed in Chapter 9, there are no hard and fast criteria for grading properties or defining the distinctions between class A, B, and C. The classifications are partially subjective and leave room for some degree of interpretation. They attempt to classify properties broadly into groups or general categories that are easily recognized by knowledgeable observers. In general, MHC REITs tend to invest in class B or better communities, and the majority of these REITs focus on class A communities.

Types of Communities

MHCs fall into two broad categories. The first are general communities that accept residents without restrictions. The second are senior living communities for adults ages 55 and over. Each type of community has its own specific set of advantages and challenges.

Homeowners of more modest means normally populate general communities. The average resident has a median household income of about $27,000, with 65 percent of the households having only one or two members. These residents are more transient than those who reside in the senior communities. The financial demographic requires a higher level of diligence on the part of management when considering new tenants and makes it difficult to raise rents aggressively. The transient nature of these residents can create higher turnover of tenants in general communities.

Senior communities tend to have more stable populations and lower turnover rates than general communities. And, although senior communities have residents who are on fixed incomes, they tend to be more financially affluent than their general community counterparts. Many seniors own homes in class A senior communities that are second homes and are occupied on a seasonal basis. Because the majority of these residents are retired, they have more time on their hands, giving rise to strong homeowner associations that can effectively organize against rent increases as well as increased management costs in the area of maintenance and amenities.

Each type of community has its own specific set of advantages and challenges. However, the most critical element in successful

MHC ownership is diligent, high-quality on-site management. Without a high management standard the character of the community is likely to decline. This results in an increasing number of less desirable residents who displace the quality community–oriented owners. This *death spiral,* as it is often called, is hard to reverse and can take years of intensive management to correct. Thus, good quality of management is particularly important in the MHC arena.

MHC Demand and Residential Market Dynamics

The growth in demand for manufactured housing is driven by its affordability when compared to conventional site-built homes of similar size. The final cost of a manufactured home is about half that of a conventional site-built home. This affordability factor drives demand in two key segments of the residential market: retirees and moderate-income households.

Over the last decade the quality of manufactured housing has made significant strides. Features and amenities such as balconies and patios are common. The new generation of homes are often built in two or more sections that are assembled on site. This *double-wide* feature, when coupled with add-on architectural details such as garages and porches, make these manufactured homes nearly indistinguishable from conventionally built properties.

These product improvements have resulted in growing consumer demand for both new and existing manufactured homes. This has been helped by the availability of a wide array of better financing options. In the past, manufactured homes were often financed as personal property, which made the financing arrangements available only through a specialized lender. Now conventional financial institutions offer a large array of lending programs that are structured much like the terms on a conventional home. Buyers may select loans with terms ranging up to 30 years. The house can be financed as personal property, on leased land, in an MHC, or on a private site. This growth in flexible financing options has also aided the growth of demand in this housing sector.

Demographics and Amenity Trends

In the aggregate, current demographic trends have created a favorable outlook for MHC demand. The 78 million post-WWII babies known as the Baby Boom generation are rapidly approaching retirement. This generation has a more stable financial outlook than their parents' generation. They tend to be more leisure oriented and demand a generally higher level of amenities. This has fueled a rapid growth in class A MHCs in resort and retirement areas. These communities cater to the growing percentage of Baby Boomers who are buying second homes in leisure areas. The affordability of manufactured housing has made this a growth area for MHC owners.

Expanded affordability and increased quality have also made manufactured housing popular among working households earning under $30,000 annually, by providing the opportunity for home ownership at affordable levels. When the demographic trends are coupled with the changing consumer attitude toward manufactured housing, it is expected that demand for manufactured housing units will average 370,000 units per year over the next five years. It is predicted that about 20 percent of this will represent replacement housing, while 80 percent will be additions to the pool of existing manufactured homes.

Operating Characteristics

Lower turnover of tenants is a key differentiation factor when comparing MHCs to apartments. The average annual turnover in MHCs is about 20 percent. This means the owner of a MHC only needs to replace a site renter about every five years, compared to about every 18 months in the apartment sector. And, even if there is tenant turnover in an MHC, it is likely that there will be no interruption of rental income because only 5 percent of manufactured homes are moved between communities each year. It is more likely that the home will be sold to another owner who will begin paying rent on the day the sale closes. Until then, the seller pays rent on the unit that occupies the site.

Very low static vacancy rates are another interesting aspect of

MHCs. Once a community is filled, it normally remains filled. A site is only vacant if an owner moves the manufactured home to another site, which happens less than 5 percent of the time. This creates a very stable occupancy level once the community is full. Also, the likelihood of being impacted by new construction is minimal. Even if a new community were to open nearby, owners are not likely to relocate units due to the high cost (as much as $8,000).

The primary advantage for REITs in the MHC sector is the low rate of capital expenditure. MHCs tend to expend about 5 percent of their net operating income on capital expenses. Because the owner is responsible for only the common area and infrastructure, the capital expenses tend to be minimal. With a trend toward higher levels of amenities among MHCs, the amount of capital expenditure is expected to increase over the next five years. However, rental growth is expected to exceed growth capital expenses by a comfortable margin.

Some of the positives also lead to the negative aspects of the MHC sector. The nature of the residents and the stable occupancy characteristics make it very difficult to grow rent at a rate of much more than one or two percentage points over the consumer price index. The same factors make increasing profitability during a positive market environment less of a possibility. The ability to translate demand into operating leverage is minimal. Expanding an existing community through the addition of more sites is the primary means of achieving operating leverage in the sector.

Real estate investment trusts have also seen their growth in the MHC area constrained by the scarcity of good acquisition possibilities. The lack of any meaningful number of large private owners has made acquisition strategies difficult. It is estimated that there are about 3,500 privately owned class A communities that would be of acquisition interest to the MHC REIT sector. But the high margin associated with stabilized class A portfolios creates very few purchase opportunities for the bigger REITs—there simply are not many sellers at any given time. The large numbers of highly fragmented mom-and-pop owners remain largely unconsolidated and most single communities do not offer the size or scale to be of interest to institutional buyers. This makes development of new communities the primary driver of external growth. This is a lucrative avenue, but it requires a large initial capital expense for land and improvements, and it often takes five years to lease a big community fully.

Summary Data

Although it is a small part of the total residential REIT sector, MHC ownership offers some very positive attributes when compared to apartment ownership and is certainly worth reviewing for inclusion in a diversified REIT portfolio. Returns on MHC REITs have been the most stable of those for all REIT sectors for the past five years (see Table 12.1). During that time, the manufactured housing sector has produced an average annual return of 9.5 percent, the third highest five-year return of any REIT sector. The volatility of the manufactured housing sector as measured by the standard deviation of returns was 11 percent, indicating that this has been the most stable sector. The general growth in the volume of manufactured housing along with the generally constrained availability of home sites makes the long-term outlook for this sector generally favorable.

TABLE 12.1 Historical Sector Data for Manufactured Housing REITs

	2001	2000	1999	1998	1997
Total return on sector	13.60%	20.9%	−2.8%	−0.9%	18.7%
Dividend yield	6.97%	8.32%	5.96%	5.23%	6.98%
Estimated NAV	97.0%	84.0%	86.0%	105.0%	119.0%
Market cap of sector ($B)	2.3				
Index weight	2.0%				
All other sectors	98.0%				
Volatility	11.1%				
Five-year return	9.45%				

Source: NAREIT; Uniplan Real Estate Advisors, Inc.

Interview with Gary McDaniel

Gary McDaniel is chief executive officer of Chateau Communities. He has been involved in the manufactured home industry since 1972 and is active in several state and national manufactured home associations including those of Florida and Colorado. In 1996, he was named Industry Person of the Year by the National Manufactured Housing Institute, where he currently serves as chairman of the board. He is a graduate of the University of Wyoming and served as a captain in the United States Air Force.

Rick Imperiale: What characteristics distinguish MHCs as a property group within the real estate world and within the REIT world more particularly?

Gary McDaniel: There are several things that really distinguish manufactured housing from other kinds of real estate, both generically and in the REIT world. First, we are characterized by very stable and predictable cash flows that grow every year. Because of the nature of our business—we own the land and provide the services, but our residents own their own homes—we have a sort of bifurcated tenancy where tenants have equity in their homes and therefore don't move as often as tenants in typical rental housing. And if they do move, in most cases they will sell the home on site to a new resident, which, from our standpoint as an operator, is a nonevent. There's no tenant improvement or turnover cost, the home is just sold and we have a new resident the next day.

The other distinguishing factor is that we can be more affordable than other rental housing because our rent portion is only about 50 percent of the tenant's housing cost. So we lever our rent growth off the fixed rate they have on the cost of their home, which means that if we increase our rents, which historically are about 1.5 percent higher than inflation, we can get a 4 to 5 percent rental increase. That's the equivalent of twice the increase in an apartment. As a result, we maintain affordability, so people don't turn over nearly as quickly and we can get rental increases on virtually every site, every year. That makes us a very stable and predictable housing class.

Imperiale: And the long-term numbers of the MHC REIT sector reflect that.

McDaniel: They do. Historically, the rental increases are better than inflation and the operating expenses are relatively low because we have no costs associated with the actual home, so we bring a lot of money to the bottom line.

Imperiale: We've read a lot in the press lately about the difficulties some tenants have had with their manufactured homes because the job market's gotten bad and the value of the mortgage is larger than the value of the manufactured home. In that instance, where they're literally giving the keys back to the bank, that's really a nonevent for you as well, isn't it, because somebody's going to pay the rent on the land where the house is sitting?

McDaniel: Under normal circumstances, it is a nonevent, because what typically happens is that the tenant owes us one or two months' rent, which would be bad debt, but the lender really prefers to leave the home in the community on site. The lender takes whatever loss against their financing, then pays us rent from the time they get the house until it's sold to a third party. At that point we receive a commission for selling the house, which offsets any loss of rent we had, and life goes on.

Imperiale: Can you tell us a little about the history of the MHC world and how it developed as a real estate class?

McDaniel: We're a very young industry. The manufactured housing land lease community business actually really only got going in the late 1960s. At the time a lot of people decided to utilize a piece of land temporarily, so the philosophy was, "We'll take this land, we'll build a mobile home park, people will move in here for four or five years and the land will then become more valuable, and then we'll kick everybody out and build a shopping center." The reality is that the economics for the most part never worked that way. People found that the increasing cash flow stream generally would create more value as an ongoing entity than as a conversion. And so in the mid- to late 1970s, people started looking at this more as a business than as a temporary parking place for land, and communities got better. The quality of the construction and the value of the homes increased, and so communities became much more permanent. We focused on the first-time home buyer and the empty nester—the people who are getting into the housing market and the people who are exiting the housing market. It was very affordable and a good-quality way of life. You had the security of a neighborhood and the environment, but you could also leave for an extended vacation knowing that somebody was there looking after your property.

In the past 10 years or so we've continued to see an evolution. Today's communities are mostly multisection with permanent foundations and attached garages, longer-term financing, and a better quality of residents. The industry has evolved to produce a product competitive with built housing, and they're selling about 60 percent of the product to private land.

Imperiale: In your opinion, what drives the supply and demand dynamic within the segment, and is there an MHC cycle at all?

McDaniel: The supply and demand is very much driven by the overall economic conditions. As the demand for housing goes up, so does our supply and demand, and vice versa. We tend to attract a somewhat narrow population of the housing market, but the demand comes and goes in cycles very much as for other forms of housing, with the caveat that we tend to cycle a little bit later.

Imperiale: Some people have suggested that the real growth in this segment has been in leisure communities, where people view manufactured housing as affordable second homes or retirement homes. Do you see that as a key growth driver from a demographic point of view?

McDaniel: Yes. I'm not sure the percentage is as large as people think it is, but with Baby Boomers moving into retirement age, that part of our product is going to continue to grow. On the other hand, one of the things we have seen is that today's Baby Boomers and people that are retiring in their late fifties or early sixties aren't as interested in moving into an all-adult retirement community. We're seeing an increasing percentage of all-age communities with people that are empty nesters. A lot of these people want to buy a home in one of our communities and downsize so they can be free to travel and do whatever they want.

Imperiale: Do you see any emerging thematic trends in the MHC business that would impact the communities?

McDaniel: My concern about the future of our business is that manufacturers are now building product that for the most part is not suitable to go into the existing land lease communities and the larger multisection high-end homes really don't suit our customer in a typical land lease community that's 20 years old. The manufacturers are basically building product that is designed more for placement on private land, and we're competing with stick-built. We're going through a cycle where the manufacturers are building product because that's what they can sell, but my feeling is that there's a huge market out there for a quality, affordable product in existing land lease communities that doesn't necessarily have to be residential product. For the first time in several years, some of the manufacturers are starting to address those issues. As we move this industry forward, there's going to be somewhat of a bifurcation. Residential housing will continue to be a major part of manufacturers' production, but I think we'll see a return to product geared for land lease communities. The reason I say that is because so many of the land lease communities in the country today, particularly in urban areas, have incredibly good locations. People are going to want to live in those locations, and, when the demand picks up, if we can provide the right kind of product, then I think we'll see an ongoing gentrification of some of these older communities.

Imperiale: Is part of that driven by the obsolescence of the existing housing stock in some of the older communities?

McDaniel: That's right. Unfortunately, people do not tend to go through major remodeling projects for manufactured housing, so we find 25-year-old homes that are truly 25-year-old homes. From a value standpoint, it's more economical to move that home out of the community and replace it with a home that's a 2002 model because then you attract a higher caliber of residents who can afford to pay today's rents. That's what really moves along the process of keeping these communities updated.

Imperiale: How much of that is precipitated by the owners of the land lease communities? Are there some communities that say, "We're on an upgrade cycle and we want you to buy a new unit?"

McDaniel: Typically you can't force an existing resident to either move or buy a new unit, but you can say, "When you sell the house, it either needs to be upgraded to these standards or it needs to be removed from the community." But then you get into all the political issues, so it's easier said than done. What happens is that we buy the house and remove it from the community and then we can put a new one on the site. We're not necessarily driven by the profit motive on the sale of a new home, so if we buy a new home and it costs us $4,000 or $5,000 to have it removed from the community, we build the cost of that into the price of the new home. Because we are not looking to make a big profit, and we're looking to continue our rental growth, then we can still be competitive with outside salespeople and be able to sell the house to a new resident.

Imperiale: How would you describe the long-term outlook for the communities and the investors?

McDaniel: My feeling is that it continues to be an excellent investment vehicle. There's always going to be a demand for affordable housing and there are always going to be people who like the environment in our communities. Every year, we take bigger steps to overcome the negative image associated with manufactured housing. We're seeing more and more people who say they've lived in a manufactured home and liked it or have relatives that live in these homes. For years and years, we had to sell the houses multiple times, but today we don't see that nearly as much.

Imperiale: What type of cap rates do you see currently available for developers and buyers in the sector, and what performance benchmarks do you think should be used in measuring the performance of manufactured housing REITs?

McDaniel: For years cap rates were in the 9.5 to 10 range, and then they came down a little as more institutional money became interested in our business and public companies like ours started to emerge. Today cap rates for the highest-quality communities are in the range of 8 to 9, so there are about 100 basis points on property.

As far as performance factors for REITs, typically everybody looks at FFO [funds from operations] per share and how it grows over the years and at growth pattern, and that's valid because that's how REITs are judged. But it's also important to know how the corporate portfolio will operate year in and year out, what are the rental increases, how is net operating income growth, how does occupancy hold up. A larger company can move the numbers a lot with capital transactions, whereas day to day, if you look at that core portfolio, it'll give you the long-term history of the kind of business the REIT has done and should do.

Imperiale: When you are looking to develop a community, what kind of a long-term cap rate do you target on a stabilized community from the development point of view?

McDaniel: We'd like to target about a 15 percent internal rate of return from the time we turn the dirt to the time it's stabilized. That's a much longer stabilization period than other forms of housing. We typically only lease somewhere between six or eight units a month, so a 400-site community can take over five years from start to stabilization.

Imperiale: Are there any developments on the entitlement side that are particularly good or bad?

McDaniel: It's still very difficult and it takes a long time. We still have to battle the "trailer park" stigma, but the other important thing is that to be economically viable, we've got to build 300 to 500 sites. In today's housing climate, it doesn't matter who you are, getting an entitlement for 500 sites is not going to be easy. It would be easier if we were building these things in 50-site blocks.

Imperiale: Are there any other issues you think we should discuss?

McDaniel: Well, I think that until we get realistic financing for our business, things are going to continue to be difficult. And so I think the challenge for our business in the next year or so is to figure out a way to get more people involved in financing the product. We've had a huge exit of major players in the past two-and-a-half years. The financing availability has shrunk down significantly.

CHAPTER

13

Office REITs

Chapter Summary

- Office buildings represent 20 percent of the total commercial real estate market.
- Publicly traded office real estate investment trusts (REITs) represent about 21 percent of the National Association of Real Estate Trusts (NAREIT) Equity Index.
- Real estate investment trusts own approximately 8 percent of the investment-grade office properties in the United States.
- The complex and volatile nature of the office segment make it one of the most analyzed sectors.
- The U.S. economy is expected to create demand for about 225 million square feet of office space per year.
- Communication technology and modern lifestyles have changed the pattern of office demand.
- Office and industrial space is the only space used primarily by businesses.
- Investment returns on offices are among the most volatile for any real estate sector.
- There are 27 publicly traded office REITs in the NAREIT Equity Index.

I yield to no one in my admiration for the office as a social center, but it's no place to actually get any work done.

—Katharine Whitehorn, 1962

The Office Market

The aggregate value of the total U.S. office market building sector is estimated to be $1.05 trillion. This figure includes all owner-occupied corporate office properties, which are estimated at roughly $200 billion. The remaining $850 billion of office properties are investor owned. This overall total, including owner-occupied buildings, is about 20 percent of the total commercial real estate market. Real estate investment trusts (REITs) are estimated to own approximately 8 percent of the non-corporate-owned office sector. Publicly traded office REITs as a group represent about 21 percent of the National Association of Real Estate Investment Trusts (NAREIT) Equity Index (see Figure 13.1).

Although it is not the biggest sector in the REIT universe or in the total real estate pie, a great deal of time and attention is devoted to the office sector. This is due to the fact that this sector offers perhaps the widest array of opportunities and challenges of any real estate category. For owners and investors, the challenge is to forecast economic demand, assess and use the capital markets, and deal with tenants and prospective tenants whose

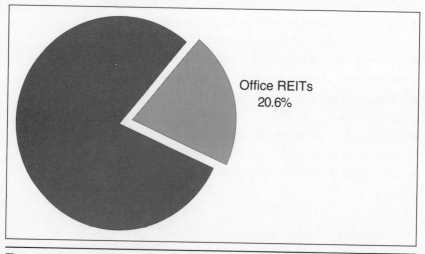

FIGURE 13.1 Office REITs as a Percentage of the NAREIT Equity Index as of December 31, 2001

needs for space and financial conditions change on a continuous basis, all while assessing current and future supply and demand trends. Owners and investors who manage this complex set of challenges well can realize excellent returns and create a high level of value-added return on investment through management and financial leverage.

The myriad of factors that influence the office sector and the number of owners and investors involved make it the most volatile and cyclical of the real estate segments. The primary customers of office building owners are businesses. The only other sector in real estate whose primary users are business tenants is the industrial sector. This is why the office and industrial sectors are often lumped together for purposes of discussion and analysis. In addition, a large number of commercial buildings combine both office and industrial space in a single facility. For purposes of the discussion in this chapter, office and mixed-use office-industrial properties will be considered as a single group. The pure industrial property sector has many of the same issues as the office sector, but it is unique enough in terms of physical and investment attributes to warrant a separate discussion in Chapter 14.

Quality Classifications

For investment purposes, office buildings, like most other commercial structures, are classified by subjective quality level. Individual properties are judged in terms of quality and are classified as class A, B, or C. As in other sectors of the real estate market, there is a very strong correlation between the age of a given property and its classification. The construction quality of a property, the location within the local market, and the level of amenities are all factored into a property classification. Local standards also have a bearing on quality ratings. A newer office building in downtown Minneapolis might be considered a class A project based on its age and prevailing local market standards, but that exact building in downtown Houston might be considered a class B project because it lacks construction materials and amenities that are part of a higher local market standard in

Houston. As discussed in Chapter 9, there are no hard and fast criteria for grading properties or defining the distinctions between class A, B, and C. The classifications are subjective and leave room for some degree of interpretation.

Class A office buildings tend to be the newest structures in a local market. They are generally built of higher-quality materials, such as marble, and are in the best locations by local market standards. Class A buildings normally also offer a higher level of amenities than the average office building. A large luxury lobby with soaring vaulted spaces displaying prominent, well-staffed security stations is an amenity in most class A buildings. Concierge services, meeting facilities, health club facilities, retail and food service offerings, and other lifestyle amenities in demand by the professionals that occupy the building are typical of class A properties. The rents at class A properties similar to those of newly constructed buildings in the same local market.

Class B buildings tend to be a slightly older than class A properties. In many instances class B properties are slightly older than the average property in the local office market. In some markets, where there has been a lot of recent construction, this could mean a building over 10 years old. In other markets it could mean a building over 20 years old. Either way, the class B building is one whose new building luster has faded. Class B buildings offer a more limited range of lifestyle amenities than class A buildings. A class B building might be in a more average location within the local market. And the building materials and improvements found in class B properties tend to be average relative to community standards, whereas class A offices have above-average construction features when compared to local community standards.

Class C buildings tend to be the oldest buildings in a given community. These buildings are often recycled properties that were originally built for a given use and then rehabilitated and adapted for another use. Old multistory urban warehouse buildings that are renovated into loft-style offices or live-work spaces are typical of class C properties. These buildings are often located in less desirable neighborhoods that might have a mix of office and industrial properties. Class C buildings have few amenities and are often functionally obsolete for the current use. Class C buildings are seldom owned by publicly traded REITs unless they are purchased for renovation or redevelopment to class B or better levels.

These classifications are subjective at best. They attempt to divide properties into groups or general categories that are easily recognized by knowledgeable observers. For purposes of negotiations, buildings are often classified as class B by a potential buyer and class A by the seller. To complicate matters further, real estate professionals often create categories within classes. For example, better-quality class B properties are often called "high-B" buildings, or lesser class A buildings are termed "low-A" buildings. These distinctions are helpful to the real estate professional but often confusing to the uninitiated. However, in general, REITs tend to invest in class B or better office properties.

Physical Structure Classifications

In addition to the quality classifications just discussed, office buildings are also classified by size and style. In broad terms, these classifications are as follows:

- *Low-rise.* Normally under three stories, often in attached townhouse style.

- *Mid-rise.* Over three stories but subject to relative local standards. For example, a 15-story office building is a high-rise in Milwaukee, but in Chicago or New York it is a mid-rise.

- *High-rise.* Normally 15 stories or over in most local real estate markets.

- *Flex.* Often termed *R&D*, these properties are normally built on smaller parcels of land in mixed-use areas and combine office and light industrial space in one building.

- *Office park.* Sprawling suburban complexes with low- to mid-rise buildings on a campuslike setting, often with additional land available for expansion of existing facilities.

The number of stories is a simple way to classify a building because it is an easily identified feature. The height of a building also has an impact on the building's operation cost. Generally, taller buildings have a higher cost of operation and are more expensive to build. High-rise and mid-rise properties are most often found in higher-density urban locations where land value is high and availability is scarce. Low-rise office park projects tend to be located in suburban locations where density and land cost are not so much an issue. In many instances, suburban office parks are built in phases to keep the supply and demand equation in balance. The style and design of a given phase of a suburban office project may be the result of a single tenant or of the type of tenant that the developer is seeking for a particular location. Submarket dynamics also have an impact on building type. Land use restrictions and other zoning laws such as maximum densities and height restrictions ultimately affect the type and style of property that is built. These limitations are more apparent in some markets, and they have an impact on what gets built and where it is located.

Market Dynamics

During the tax-motivated era of real estate, the most overbuilt and volatile sector was the office sector. When the era started in 1982, the national office vacancy level stood at about 6 percent. The demand outlook was forecast to be strong as the economy moved away from industrial production and into the information age. Construction started in the mid-1980s and did not stop until the early 1990. To make the problem worse, as the 1990s started, U.S. industry began a long period of corporate downsizing. By the end of that era, the office vacancy rate in some major markets had soared to well above 25 percent. It took over five years for the national office markets to absorb the excess and return to a more normal historic long-term supply and demand balance. Those who bought office property in the early 1990s made spectacular returns as the office markets normalized later in the decade.

The demand for office space is highly correlated to the expected growth in office employment or job growth. This growth is driven by general macroeconomic trends in the local and national economy. In general terms, local economic demand for office space is impacted by:

- The location of suppliers and customers
- The available pool of skilled labor
- Infrastructure such as roads, parking, airports, and public transportation
- Quality of life amenities for employees
- The relative location of areas where executive officers live
- Local government attitude toward business

Supply dynamics begin with the current market and submarket vacancy rates. This is the beginning point in the analysis of any business looking for new or additional space. The mix of available space is also a factor. For example, there may be a large amount of class C space on the market, while at the same time little class A and B space may be available. Or there may be a large number of small spaces containing less than 10,000 square feet available, but no single blocks of space of over 50,000 square feet. The available space mix issues can impact the market dynamic at any given time depending on what the demand side of the equation for a given type and size of space might be.

Sublease space—or, as it is often called, *shadow space*—plays an important role in the supply side dynamic. This is space that a tenant that is legally obligated on a lease is attempting to re-lease or sublease to another tenant. In the worst instances, a property owner may be competing against an existing tenant to lease in the same building. For example, imagine a five-story, 200,000-square-foot suburban office building with a single 40,000-square-foot floor that is vacant and advertised for lease by the building's owner. Imagine a tenant in the same building leasing two floors totaling 80,000 square feet, with five years remaining on the lease. That tenant decides to downsize its suburban operation and consolidate it at another location, thus vacating one of the two floors. The tenant is obligated to continue to pay rent because of the lease, but it will be in the market trying to sublease that 40,000 square feet against the building's owner, who also has a floor to rent. This is not an uncommon problem in large, active office markets.

In addition to vacancy rates and shadow space, another important factor in local market analysis is visible supply of new space. Planned developments, building permits approved, and projects under construction all total to indicate new supply. The good news is that this new supply tends to be very visible because of the size and scale of most new office real estate projects. In addition, it is very visible because it takes a relatively long time to plan and construct an office building. When vacancy rates and sublease space are added to new development, the total is the supply profile for the market.

Forecasting long-term future demand for office space is notoriously difficult. As mentioned, the multitude of changing factors that impact the complex office market dynamic are hard to predict and gyrate wildly in the short term. Over the long term, the U.S. economy is expected to demand an average of about 225 million square feet per year. (Keep in mind, however, that this number can go up or down quickly.) Of that amount, 45 million square feet of annual demand is expected to result from obsolescence of existing office properties.

Trends Impacting the Office Sector

In the early 1980s an interesting event occurred. The aggregate total amount of suburban office space exceeded the aggregate total amount of central business district (CBD) or downtown office space. Since then, suburban space has grown at twice the rate of CBD space. This clearly points up the ever growing trend toward the suburbanization of American cities. The trend started in the 1950s, when people followed large new highways out to new single-family homes. Then we witnessed the malling of America in the 1960s and 1970s, when the shopping amenities followed the population out to the suburbs. Since the early 1980s, growth in suburban office buildings has resulted in jobs moving to the suburbs, creating large metro areas of suburban mass that surround dozens of CBDs. These suburban cities are bigger than many of the major old cities they surround.

The widely accepted explanation for this shift in locational demand is the theory of urban labor markets, which suggests that cities tend to develop outward before they ever develop upward. Once housing is constructed outward, it presents a fixed asset base with an opportunity cost associated with its replacement. This cost delays any eventual replacement for decades and even centuries. The idea is that residential development will normally move outward first. Upward redevelopment only happens after outward movement is constrained by geography or by distance. With outward development, the commuting time of residents into the CBD becomes increasingly burdensome, much more so than if development occurred vertically. As commuting increases, firms begin to consider the prospect of a suburban location. At a suburban location, firms can, in theory, attract workers for a lower wage, because such workers will have less of a commute. This theory predicts that the wages paid for comparable workers in the CBD will be higher than wages in the closer suburbs, and, in turn, higher than wages paid by firms even further out. Studies of wage patterns suggest this is true.

Why is this important? In the real estate world, this trend alarms the multitude of institutional real estate investors, including REITs, that own class A CBD office buildings. This is worrisome because it means most firms will ultimately move to the suburbs and cause decay in value of CBD office properties. However, there are several factors limiting this process. The first is that employers using a diverse labor force cannot always find a wide range of workers in a single suburb. Workers with different skills often are spread across different suburbs because of the historic patterns by which housing developed. Community zoning standards often reinforce these patterns. If executives live on the North Shore while administrative workers live on the South Shore, as is the case in Milwaukee, the location of easiest access may still be the CBD. A second factor is the public transportation system and existing road patterns. In some metropolitan areas the transportation systems were built to move workers between suburbs and the CBD. Rail transit systems often provide strong radial links that help the CBD and slow the development of the suburbs. Thus the historic development of a city's transportation system strongly influences the ability of firms to decentralize.

The other big topic of debate in the office real estate sector is the impact of telecommuting on the demand for office space. The telecommunications and information revolution has correlated closely with the trend of suburban office decentralization. The Internet, computers, mobile phones, e-mail, and faxes all mean that face-to-face interpersonal communication is much less important in the operation of many businesses. It is very easy today for various branches of a company to be situated at widely different locations. Sales, marketing, and other forms of business communication have also become less dependent on direct personal contact. As business contact costs and needs are reduced, firms will be able to take advantage of the lower wage and cost structure that suburban sites offer.

It is not certain that telecommuting has altered the demand structure for office space. However, it has aided in expanding the ability of most businesses to decentralize their operations. It has also affected the type and style of space used by businesses. For example, increased computer usage creates a demand for more complex floor and wiring systems. Employees who travel frequently and use laptop computers as their link to the organization are seldom given permanent offices; rather, they use an office or cubicle designed to accommodate transient employees who happen to be at the office.

These factors and trends have led to a basic change in standard working conditions. Companies are putting employees into open offices, which allows more employees to populate a smaller space. The allocation of space per person in an office setting has dropped from 350 square feet in the mid-1970s to about 225 square feet today. This trend is expected to continue as technology allows more workers to telecommute and remain in smaller decentralized locations.

Summary Data

Returns on office REITs are the most volatile of those for the major REIT sectors (see Table 13.1). Over the last five years the office sector has produced an average annual return of 9.7 percent, the highest five-year return of any REIT sector other than

TABLE 13.1 Historical Sector Data for Office REITs

	2001	2000	1999	1998	1997
Total return on sector	5.50%	35.5%	4.3%	−17.4%	29.0%
Dividend yield	6.97%	8.84%	7.94%	4.58%	6.27%
Estimated NAV	95.0%	93.0%	79.0%	100.0%	122.0%
Market cap of sector ($B)	30.2				
Index weight	20.6%				
All other sectors	79.4%				
Volatility	21.2%				
Five-year return	9.70%				

Source: NAREIT.

residential. However, the volatility of the sector as measured by the standard deviation of returns was 21.2 percent, making it the most volatile of the major sectors. The basic characteristics of the office sector make it more sensitive to economic and business conditions, and the long lead time on office construction makes timing the cycle for offices more difficult than for sectors with shorter cycle times.

Interview with Richard A. May

Richard A. May cofounded Great Lakes REIT and has served as the company's chairman and chief executive officer since its inception. Great Lakes REIT owns and operates 5.2 million square feet of suburban office space in the Midwest. May received his B.S. in mechanical engineering from the University of Illinois and his M.B.A. from the University of Chicago.

Richard Imperiale: In your mind, what characteristics distinguish office real estate as a property group within the real estate community and the REIT world?

Richard May: Well, first of all, the REIT world is a collection of a variety of real estate businesses, a lot of which are barely even remotely related. We all gang together because we have a common interest in tax status. So the idea of office REITs being in the same business with hotels or self-storage or even apartments is pretty far-flung. What makes us different in the office sector is that our typical lease structure is different than most. Our typical leases today are usually for 3 to 5 years, but 3 to 15 years is not atypical. We've got an average lease size of 10,000 square feet, and our average building is 150,000 square feet, so we don't have as many big tenants as equity office properties might. We've calculated that about 75 percent of our tenants have strong credit, as opposed to apartments or self-storage properties, which can have a very weak credit profile. Also, we don't have a lot of multiple-location tenants like retail. If you're in the mall business, you can have tenants that anchor many spaces in many different properties. The lease structure for smaller retail tenants is probably similar to ours, in the 3- to 10-year range. But the big tenants are probably 20 years, maybe even longer. Our rent structure is also different. With hotels, it's daily, and for self-storage it's monthly.

Imperiale: So one thing that distinguishes office real estate is lease duration. As a real estate investor, how does that protect me?

May: It gives you more diversification. Having a lot of tenants of 10,000 square feet with relatively long lease expiration schedules and a lot of credit means the office sector has less risk than some other sectors. Those characteristics bode well for someone who is risk averse.

Imperiale: It is well known that when there's a new supply of hotel space, because of the short lease structure, it impacts other hotels immediately. Would you say that for office REITs, a supply of new space has less impact than it would on properties that have shorter leases?

May: I'd say that's the general rule, but clearly overbuilding impacts us all.

Imperiale: In your opinion, what drives the supply and demand dynamic within the office segment?

May: From the demand side, the economy drives occupancy. Right now is a tough time in the business, because very few people are looking for space. In fact, people are generally looking to contract, especially since they oversubscribed to office space in the past when the economy was so over-heated. On the supply side, the capital markets drive the business. When the lenders need to get money out the door, they'll relax their standards, requiring less equity, and that allows more marginal companies to be attracted to the business. A good market is when there's the right amount of demand to meet the supply of new products. Usually, we've been driven into poor real conditions by an oversup-ply, but that hasn't been the case this time the way it was in 1990.

Imperiale: Let's expand on that. We hear and the data suggests that the real estate cycle may be getting less severe than it has been historically. Do you believe that?

May: Yes, it's a fact, and the reason is directly related to the transparency of the public markets. In the late 1980s, nobody knew who was doing what and where. Even though public real estate owns less than 10 percent of the assets in the United States, it provides people an opportu-nity to see what's going on. Right now there is about 2 to 3 percent supply that's still being developed. Last time around it was 8 to 10 percent, and it was because people didn't know what everybody else was doing. They didn't know the deal structures or how much equity was being put into the transactions. Now there's a much clearer pic-ture for lenders in particular.

Also, it seems to me that the developers learned how to use personal computers earlier than the bankers back in the early to mid-1980s. They could adjust their assumptions to come up with whatever answer they wanted. I'm not joking. I believe that was a factor. Developers are a smart bunch, and they would put together whatever numbers made the deal work to get the loan. Their ability to adopt technology faster kept them ahead of the bankers. Nowadays, there are standard real estate analysis programs. So now nobody can pull the wool over anybody's eyes—they say, "Send me your assumption in such and such a file format." But in the old days, somebody just threw a spreadsheet in front of you and said, "Here's what it looks like," and you had to make a guess whether their assumptions were right. Of course, we had just come into a period of really high inflation. But the developers would use assumptions like 10 or 11 percent rent growth with 3 and 4 percent expense growth. Any numbers for any real estate transaction will work with those sorts of assumptions.

Imperiale: The tax-driven motivation for real estate in the 1970s and 1980s created a lot of excess supply. Now that the tax motivation is different, the visibility of the capital markets puts a discipline on the community. But has the game substantially changed since the Tax Reform Act of 1986?

May: Well, the Tax Reform Act of 1986 is really what created the REIT industry, because it allowed REITs to be self-managed. Before then, you couldn't manage your own properties, but nobody cared because there wasn't a capital problem. Then in 1991, all of a sudden there was no access to capital. You couldn't refinance any existing loans even for properties that were cash loans. That forced a lot of developers to go public or go broke. They really didn't have a choice, so when the 1986 Act allowed REITs to be operating businesses, that suited the developers fine.

Imperiale: They had an avenue of escape because, even though they couldn't refinance conventionally, they could manage their portfolio of properties in the form of a REIT.

May: Yes. They could run their businesses the same way, they just had different capital structure. But they could not have done that without that provision in the 1986 Tax Act.

Imperiale: How did that provision get put into the Act?

May: I couldn't tell you, because REITs were nothing back in those days, and nobody paid any attention until 1991, when REITs had to recapitalize. But it was a very significant piece of legislation.

Imperiale: But at the time nobody seemed to be paying any particular attention?

May: No, nobody cared because they could run their businesses just fine. They were making a lot of money. They were borrowing 100 percent or 110 percent from banks, and why would you want to give it to the public markets? Why would you want to go through all the scrutiny and all the headaches that are attached to being a public company unless you don't have a choice? That's what it came down to—they didn't have a choice. We're different as a REIT, because we started from scratch to be a public company. We were a private company initially, but we had no money and no properties. We just started raising equity and buying properties simultaneously in the face of an unusual market, a buyer's market, which nobody recognized. There was not a single REIT doing deals in Wisconsin, Illinois, Minnesota, or Michigan except for Great Lakes until June of 1996. We've been doing business since 1992.

Imperiale: And that was the hangover era of the office REITs.

May: Right. Our business was to buy REO [real estate owned] from the banks and life companies. REO is property that was foreclosed, and then the regulators for the various states told the lenders they couldn't carry all this real estate on their balance sheets, so they were forced to get rid of it.

Imperiale: That was an era then when there was a lot of excess supply and demand was just beginning to build.

May: Yes, developers were building 8 to 10 percent of existing product every year and demand was still only 2 to 3 percent. That was because the lenders would lend them more than 100 percent of the financing. Today you have to put in 25 to 50 percent or more of equity. Not only that, but most lenders require a certain level of preleasing activity. The thing about developers is if they had any equity, they've already spent it. Once a developer has equity, they put it into the next deal, so a developer never has any equity, by definition. So if no one will give them the equity, that slows everything down. That's why during the recent expansion we were seeing as much as 4 to 4.5 percent of the existing inventory built per year, which is half of what it was during the crazy years of the 1980s.

Imperiale: What are some of the current trends that you see in the office sector?

May: I think the resurgence of the CBD is something that should be noticed. The CBDs were pretty much dead in the water until the mid- to late 1990s. Then people started flocking back to the center city—not only tech people, but young adults as well as empty nesters. Still, irrespective of the renaissance in the CBDs, people want to work near where they live, and most people still live in the suburban markets. So the suburban market can obviously get over-built a lot faster than the CBD, because of the lower barriers to entry. In this industry, everyone seems to think that suburban office is dead, which is baloney as far as I'm concerned. It's just overbuilt right now.

I think we're going to see a lot of companies that wanted to go downtown may change their minds. I don't think that's going to be long-lived. It will probably occur for the next year or two, until we get over this terrorism issue. I think terrorism is going to continue, but I think we'll get used to it and people will go back to a more normal way of life, but everybody in the Sears Tower today wants to get out. I think we'll see that trend for a while. But the suburban market will always be a good market irrespective of disruptions such as that.

Imperiale: Let's talk about the need to understand your sub-markets when you're in the office business.

May: Well, there are supposedly four or five submarkets here in Chicago, depending on whether you want to break up the east-west corridor into two pieces, but actually there are 25 submarkets. Every major intersection is its own submarket of people who want to be within a mile of that corner. And each submarket has its own dynamics. What drives us crazy is when we're looking for a joint venture partner, and these real big shots come in and want to do transactions. So we show them a transaction and they'll say, "Well, I don't think I want to do that one, but if you come up with something else, we'll take a look at it." In the meantime, they go out and do the dumbest real estate transaction you've ever seen in your life. I'm talking about deals we tell them up front are just plain stupid and of course, they always wind up being stupid. We know the tenants, we know the brokers, and we know everything that can go wrong, but they still think they're smarter than we are. The local sharpshooter clearly has a huge competitive edge.

Imperiale: The academic studies bear out that people do better in joint ventures with local real estate operators than when they try to go into a market on their own. So why do big institutions in a joint venture setting tend to shoot themselves in the foot like that?

May: Because they're arrogant. They think they know more than the locals do. Part of our frustration comes from trying to educate people. I think we have easily the best track record of sales in the business by far. We're the only office REIT that provides information to the public—these large pension fund advisors can't even come close to matching us. So we wonder why they don't just partner up with us. We'll put in 20 or 25 percent, so we have a stake in the deal, but they get the bulk of it. And in addition, when we've got our own money in, who's going to be a better manager, us or a commercial property manager who got the assignment, who has no financial interest? That's why local market knowledge is important—It reduces risk. It may not give you that much more of a profit, but it takes the risk out of the deal.

Imperiale: It has been said that the office sector is going to decline because with telecommuting, people aren't going to go to the office. And we have observed that the number of workers of per square foot has been declining somewhat. Can you comment on these trends?

May: We haven't seen these trends in our 5.5 million square feet. And office employment growth typically exceeds general employment growth by a factor of 50 to 100 percent per year, so more people are working in offices on a percentage basis. Telecommuters have never been more than a minuscule percentage of workers, and their numbers have peaked. People get most of their information around the office. They don't get that information working from home. It has not worked, and it's not going to work. Office employment growth is the figure to watch.

Imperiale: In other words, the numbers of people who work in offices are growing faster than for people who work in factories or in the field. So that's a very important driver for office occupancy.

May: Exactly. And the studies suggest it's going to continue, because we're becoming a more service- and information-based economy. Actually, I don't see anything negative out there for the office sector in the long term.

Imperiale: What about immigration trends?

May: Well, the growth in our economy is driven largely by immigration. So there could be immigration issues that could cause the country's growth to slow and also cause office employment growth to slow, but only to the extent that we start closing our borders. If we were to restrict the ability of foreign intellectual capital to come into this country and work here, that might have an impact on the office sector.

Imperiale: In general terms, what in your opinion has been happening in cap rates over the last five to seven years?

May: Cap rates have been moving up, but that could change tomorrow. It really depends on the economy. If the economy gets better, cap rates are moving up, and there's less property available. Cap rates in general have been moving up relative to where they were when all of the public companies were overpaying—all except for us!—in the late 1990s. People were paying more for portfolios on a per-square-foot basis at that time than today. Portfolios were hot. If it was a 10 cap on a one-off deal, you had $500 million worth of stuff to buy.

Imperiale: If you had a portfolio.

May: That was really crazy. But it's totally reversed itself.

Imperiale: So those cap rates were low because people had money to buy properties?

May: What's going on out there is price. The price of the stock was above net asset value, so any deal made sense. People were going out and buying properties because money was being thrown at them from the public equity markets. It didn't make any difference what they bought or what they paid. We didn't participate in that, which is why our return on invested capital isn't far and away the highest in the business.

Imperiale: It's not always easy to figure out what a REIT's return on invested capital is, but that's an important number because it shows how much value the management adds for the shareholder.

May: Yes. And a lot of people bastardized return on invested capital in deference to these development companies.

Imperiale: Could you explain that?

May: Return on invested capital, simply put, is the income divided by the undepreciated book value of the assets that you control in the business. Some analysts divide the income from the portfolio by the undepreciated book value of the operating assets as opposed to land or work in process. Now the assets of the company are the assets of the company, in my opinion. They may not be throwing off any income, but hopefully you're going to get a lot higher return on that work in process by going out and buying something. Therefore, to exclude work in process for the denominator of the calculation is absurd, and yet it is done.

Imperiale: You touched on something important there, which is that that's a higher-risk process and if they're wrong about the outcome, it hurts return on capital. So in an environment like this, where the economy has slowed remarkably and there's a lot of development activity going on, then ultimately that big portfolio of developed or developing real estate in a downward market is going to substantially reduce return on invested capital, because at some point companies are going to have to admit that that money is part of the capital of the company and not performing real estate.

May: Yes, and that was the thing that I wanted to talk about, that educating people about the attributes of public real estate is the most important issue facing the industry today. Especially with bond and money market rates at these lows, it's time that people realize REITs are an attractive alternative, especially on a risk-adjusted basis. We've got good visibility and transparency, so hopefully more people will understand that REITs are a good place to put your income-oriented money for the long term. Looking at my own portfolio, I wish I had invested 100 percent in REITs over the last five years, including the run-up and run-down in technology.

Imperiale: Large institutional investors have known this for a long time, but smaller investors don't really appreciate the fact that you get a lot of incremental return in REITs for just a very small amount of added risk.

May: And that diversification dampens the effect on the rest of your portfolio, too, so you're picking up two benefits. It's a wonderful investment, and more people have to understand that and get comfortable with it.

We're the last industry in the United States to go public. Everything else went public a long time ago. Yet we only control about 10 percent of the real estate out there. But we expect that that's going to grow over time.

Industrial REITs

Chapter Summary

- Industrial buildings represent about 15 percent of the total commercial real estate market.
- Publicly traded industrial real estate investment trusts (REITs) represent about 13 percent of the National Association of Real Estate Investment Trusts (NAREIT) Equity Index.
- Real estate investment trusts own about 8 percent of all U.S. industrial properties.
- There is no uniform system for categorizing industrial space.
- Industrial space, like office space, is primarily used by businesses.
- Industrial properties are among the most stable sectors of the commercial real estate market.
- Final demand for industrial space is expected to be about 270 million square feet per year.
- Changes in industrial patterns affect the final demand for industrial space.
- There are eight purely industrial REITs and eight REITs that own primarily flex properties.

Industry is the soul of business and the keystone of prosperity.

—Charles Dickens, 1841

The estimated aggregate value of industrial buildings in the United States is $2.2 trillion. That total includes owner-occupied industrial real estate valued at $1.2 trillion. The remaining $1.0 trillion of properties are investor owned. Research suggests that about 10 percent of industrial space is classified as flex space, which contains both office and industrial areas and could be considered either office or industrial depending on the criteria employed when classified. Investor-owned industrial buildings represent about 15 percent of the total commercial real estate market. Real estate investment trusts (REITs) are estimated to own about 8 percent of investor-owned industrial properties. Industrial REITs as a group represent about 8 percent of the National Association of Real Estate Investment Trusts (NAREIT) Equity Index (see Figure 14.1). But, keep in mind the fact that within the office segment of the index, about 5 percent is made up of flex properties that have components of both office and industrial space in a single property. These could be categorized as either office or industrial. If they were classified

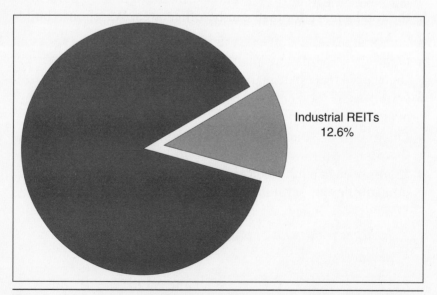

FIGURE 14.1 Industrial REITs as a Percentage of the NAREIT Equity Index as of December 31, 2001

as industrial, the weighting of this category within the NAREIT equity index would approach 14 percent.

Building Classifications

There is no standard classification system for industrial buildings. In many ways the term *industrial property* represents a generic concept that covers a vast array of real estate. It describes buildings that are used for the production or manufacture of products as well as properties whose function is distribution or warehousing. In most instances industrial buildings fall into one of the following categories. Each category services a particular type of industrial tenant by providing a specific type of building functionality.

- *Warehouse.* This is the most common type of industrial property. It is estimated that there are over 6 billion square feet of warehouse space in the United States. Warehouse space is the most commonly tenant occupied, with over 70 percent of all warehouse space being classified as rental space. For a building to classify as a true warehouse, no more than 10 percent of the total square footage can be office area. Warehouse buildings have multiple loading docks to accommodate the rapid loading and unloading of trucks. Some warehouses may also have rail siding for the movement of freight by railroad. In general, modern warehouses have high ceilings to accommodate the vertical loading of content. Ceiling heights are normally in the range of 18 to 40 feet.

- *Manufacturing.* This is the second most common type of industrial building. It is estimated that there are over 3.1 billion square feet of manufacturing space in the United States. Unlike warehouses, manufacturing space is owned more often than rented, with an estimated 60 percent being owner occupied. The highly specialized nature of most manufacturing buildings makes these types of buildings of less interest to the investment community. Also, the larger the manufacturing facility, the more likely it is to be owner occupied. The ever changing, capital-intensive nature of big manufacturing facilities also makes large-scale users unlikely to want to be involved in a leasing situation.

- *Flex and R&D.* These properties are normally built on smaller parcels of land in areas of mixed-use buildings and combine office and light industrial space into one building. They are most often one-story buildings with ceiling heights in the range of 10 to 15 feet. The ratio of office to industrial space is not set and is usually dependent on the end use of the tenant. Buildings of this style usually have a truck loading dock and also have floor-height loading to facilitate the easy use of smaller vehicles. About 40 percent of this type of space is owner occupied and 60 percent is leased. Because it combines general offices along with warehouse and manufacturing space, this style of building is very popular among smaller private companies that lack the size or scale to support separate office and manufacturing space.

- *Special purpose.* This category is normally reserved for any building that does not fit into the preceding classifications. For the most part these are either manufacturing buildings that are custom-built to meet a specific need, such as cold storage warehouses, or obsolete buildings that have been recycled for industrial use. Loft buildings, which may have started as industrial buildings in the early 1900s and subsequently have been converted into live-work areas or studio space for artists or advertising agencies, are a prime example of special-purpose buildings. *Incubator buildings,* which are normally large obsolete manufacturing facilities that have been subdivided into multitenant structures with very affordable rents aimed at new small businesses, are another example of special-purpose buildings.

Unlike most other commercial structures, industrial buildings are not classified by quality level for investment purposes. Instead, they are normally classified by age and use. For example, a building might be referred to as a newer flex building or an older warehouse. Local market standards are very much a part of the industrial building description. What is considered older in some markets would be considered obsolete in other locales. These classifications are almost completely subjective and leave much room for interpretation.

Market Dynamics

Industrial markets are among the most stable when it comes to the supply of and demand for space. Because of the special nature of industrial space, most space is not created until a demand exists. And, due to the very short amount of time required to construct industrial space, the supply can be very responsive to demand or lack of demand. For example, in an area zoned for industrial use, construction permits can usually be obtained within 60 days, and a building can be constructed in three to six months. Contrast that with an office building, which can take two years (or more) from permit to completion. Because of the short cycle time, supply and demand for industrial space does not normally get too far out of balance. This supply and demand constancy translates into very stable occupancy patterns. Historically, industrial vacancies usually run in the 5 to 6 percent range. In extreme periods, vacancies have run up to 11 percent, but rarely do they exceed these levels for long, even in very competitive local markets.

Final demand for industrial space is highly correlated to the growth of the U.S. economy. An expanding economy produces increasing demand for products and services. Economic growth also tends to stimulate corporate profitability. Increased profits often lead to increased capital spending among businesses, which also translates into demand for more and often better or newer industrial space. Conversely, any general slowing in the economy will usually quickly translate into a decline in demand for industrial space. But, because of the long-term capital-intensive nature of most industrial projects, end users, whether owners or renters, normally project their need for space based on long-term projections of final demand. This long-term characteristic of industrial users also tends to stabilize the supply-demand cycle in the industrial sector by moderating spikes in the final demand for space.

The special nature of certain industrial operations often creates locational factors that affect the demand for space at the local market level. For example, the Chicago area, with its geographically central location, its major hub for interstate highways, large international airports, multiple railroad operations,

TABLE 14.1 Historical Sector Data for Industrial REITs

	2001	2000	1999	1998	1997
Total return on sector	8.90%	28.6%	3.9%	−16.3%	19.0%
Dividend yield	6.97%	8.84%	7.94%	4.58%	6.27%
Estimated NAV	95.0%	93.0%	79.0%	100.0%	122.0%
Market cap of sector ($B)	19.6				
Index weight	12.6%				
All other sectors	87.4%				
Volatility	16.97%				
Five-year return	7.71%				

Source: NAREIT; Uniplan Real Estate Advisors, Inc.

and easy access to the Great Lakes and Mississippi river waterways, is a favorite location among distribution-intensive businesses. Other industries that require large amounts of raw materials or power will consider these needs in their location decision. Industrial space users such as commercial baking and bottling operations will want to locate near their final markets to reduce transportation costs. These locational factors can create particular demand dynamics in the local marketplace.

Because of the stable nature of the demand profile in industrial space and the general correlation of demand to economic growth, forecasting long-term future demand is less difficult for industrial space than for other real estate sectors such as office or retail. Over the long term, the U.S. economy is expected to demand, on average, about 270 million square feet per year. This is a reasonably stable number and includes approximately 40 million square feet of annual obsolescence.

Summary Data

The nature of the supply and demand cycle for the industrial sector make it one of the more stable and predictable segments of real estate. Over the last five years the industrial REIT sector has produced an average annual return of 7.1 percent (see Table 14.1). The volatility of the sector as measured by the standard deviation of returns was 17 percent, making it among the most stable sectors. The demand for industrial real estate and the performance of the sector will rise and fall primarily with general economic growth.

Interview with Hamid R. Moghadam

Hamid R. Moghadam is chairman, CEO, and director of AMB Property Corporation. He cofounded AMB's predecessor in 1983 and held similar positions in it prior to the company's initial public offering in November 1997. Moghadam holds S.B. and S.M. degrees in engineering from the Massachusetts Institute of Technology and an M.B.A. from Stanford. He is treasurer and a member of the Board of Governors of NAREIT and a member of the Real Estate Roundtable, the Young Presidents Organization, and several MIT Advisory Committees. He also serves as a director of Stanford Management Company and Plum Creek Timber Company and is a trustee of the Bay Area Discovery Museum. In 1998, Moghadam was named as the Ernst & Young Entrepreneur of the Year in Real Estate.

Richard Imperiale: In your opinion, what characteristics distinguish industrial real estate as a property group within the real estate world and within the REIT world?

Hamid Moghadam: First would be the return profile and the financial characteristics of the sector, which are characterized by high cash returns, low levels of capital expenditures in relation to NOI [net operating income], and low volatility of returns. Also, industrial real estate provides the highest absolute returns of any asset class with the lowest level of volatility. The return profile has been very stable, and, on a risk-adjusted basis, very high.

In terms of operational aspects, two things stand out. One is that the occupancy level has been relatively stable over time. In the last 20 years, I believe the lowest levels of occupancy were experienced in the last recession, and they were in the area of 89 percent. The peak vacancy was 10.5 percent, and the lowest vacancies, which were about a year ago, were about 6.5 percent. This is a very narrow range compared to most other asset classes. The other operational aspect which is related, is a short development cycle. This enables supply to be better matched with demand, so the market doesn't get quite as out of kilter as it does in some other real estate categories.

Finally, there are the rental or tenant-based characteristics of the industry, which are extremely diversified. If you look at who uses industrial real estate, you'll find that it ranges all the way from manufacturers to distributors to service companies. So the tenant base is extremely diversified, and, because the rents are relatively low, most companies that operate industrial assets have extremely diversified rent rolls. In the case of AMB, our largest customer only accounts for 1.5 percent of our rental revenue.

As far as industrial REITs, I think REITs provide an excellent way for investors to get exposure to the industrial category. Private investment in industrial real estate is very difficult. It's very difficult to get meaningful exposure to industrial REITs by investing privately.

Imperiale: Why is that?

Moghadam: Well, let's say you're an institutional investor for a typical $10 billion pension fund, and you have a typical asset allocation program, which calls for a 10 percent allocation to real estate. That would be $1 billion. Let's say you decide to have 40 percent of that in office, 20 percent in industrial, 30 percent in retail, and 10 percent in apartments. If you buy 10 office buildings for $30 million apiece, you can get your exposure filled to office space pretty quickly, and by buying a couple of malls and neighborhood shopping centers, you can do the same for retail. This also goes for apartments. But to get a 20 percent exposure in industrial, at an average cost of $40 a square foot you would have to buy 5 million square feet of property. With an average building being 100,000 square feet, that means you have to buy 50 buildings.

Imperiale: That's a lot of buildings.

Moghadam: Exactly. To get the same dollar exposure, you have to do a lot of deals. These transactions are usually small in size, they come from goofy sources, and it takes a lot of pick and shovel work to get meaningful exposure to the sector. So most people are underinvested in industrial simply because they can't reach their allocations through the traditional ways. Now factor in that the management firms that help institutional investors get exposure to real estate operate on an assets under management model, where they get paid in acquisition fees and asset management fees. You will very quickly figure out that these advisors will gravitate away from industrial because it's not a very profitable product type for them. That's just one factor that is unique to industrial because it comes in small packages.

Another thing that is worth noting about industrial real estate in the public form is that industrial companies have a wide range of accounting policies. They often use radically different accounting policies when it comes to calculation of FFO [funds from operations], which provides some real opportunities for investors and some real risks for investors. For example, there are some companies that include all sales and all gains on sales in their FFO, there are some that include none of it, and there are some that are somewhere in between. That puts a big burden on investors to figure out meaningful comparisons between these companies. Another point regarding industrial REITs is that companies in this sector, more so than in other sectors, derive their income from a broader range of activities with different qualities attributed to each activity. Most office and retail companies, for example, derive virtually 99 percent of their income from rental operations. But once you get to industrial, you'll find that there are some companies where 20 to 40 percent of the income comes from ancillary activities. The sources of income are more varied in industrial, and therefore the quality of the income streams is more varied, so investors have to be careful about what they're really buying when they invest in the industrial sector.

Imperiale: We often hear that industrial REITs have a lower expense structure because they're just roofs and parking lots. Is that really true?

Moghadam: Yes, and the reason is that we operate in a world where people measure FFO as a primary driver before cap X, and to the extent that certain property categories have much higher cap X ratios across the cycle, there are meaningful differences in valuation that the market doesn't fully appreciate in pricing these assets. We found that for industrial companies a good benchmark is the ratio of cap X to NOI, which ranges between 8 and 10 percent within a fairly narrow band. So it is mostly roofs and parking lots—which have long useful lives. For some other property types, like offices and malls, cap X is as much as 20 to 30 percent of NOI. So this is not a trivial difference, it's pretty substantial.

Imperiale: What drives the supply and demand dynamic within the industrial segment?

Moghadam: The biggest driver of demand is GDP [gross domestic product] growth. It is very hard to have growth in demand without GDP growth. Within GDP growth, at least in hub and gateway markets where we happen to focus, the foreign trade aspect of GDP is a big driver of demand. So even if you had flat GDP but you had significant imports and exports, you could still see significant demand for industrial real estate, at least in hub and gateway markets where there are ports and airports. Unfortunately industrial real estate does not grow as rapidly as GDP because for the last 50 years there has been a very strong trend of declining ratio of inventory to final sales or to GDP. In other words, there has been a speeding up of the supply chain, which has reduced the need for industrial real estate per unit of GDP. There have been brief interruptions in that long-term trend, mostly in recessions. What happens is that inventory builds up as demand falls off and that ratio goes the wrong way for brief periods of time, but then it gets back in line. So as GDP grows at 2.5 to 3 percent, industrial demand grows at 1.5 to 2 percent per year because of this declining ratio of inventories to GDP. Every time that pattern reverses itself, either because of a recession or now because of September 11, people say that this time it's different and maybe we need to think about just in case as opposed to just in time. But those debates are academic and are just distractions from a very basic long-term trend. Nobody's going to pay for and consciously carry any more inventory than they absolutely have to, and therefore industrial, by definition, grows at a lower rate than GDP.

There are two things that I can think of that paint a brighter picture than demand growing at a lower level than GDP. One is demand for replacement or substitution of obsolete real estate. A lot of industrial real estate just wears out, or is in the wrong place after a while, or is going to be converted for some higher and better use, and that stock needs to be replaced. The other is network reconfiguration. When a company goes from 40 warehouses in the wrong places to 5 warehouses in the right places, that creates net new demand for real estate, because basically a bunch of the product becomes obsolete and not useful.

All of this needs to be looked at through a different lens, however, because we talked about aggregate concepts in terms of demand. We actually think that what's going on below the surface is a bifurcation of the marketplace. We think that demand for pure storage is actually declining in absolute terms and that flow-through demand for industrial real estate is increasing. We've positioned our strategy along this high-throughput distribution model because we really want to take advantage of the growth in demand that's coming for facilities that are built for rapid distribution of products, as opposed to facilities devoted exclusively to the long-term storage of products. By the way, those two functions don't necessarily have to take place in different buildings—often they're combined under the same roof. Over time, storage is in absolute decline and distribution is growing, and it's supported by a lot of the trends we talked about earlier.

Imperiale: What about the supply side of the equation?

Moghadam: Supply basically is driven by demand. It's easy to create supply because industrial buildings are simple to build.

Imperiale: So there really isn't a lot of speculative building going on in this sector.

Moghadam: That's right. To the extent there is speculative building going on, it's very easy to turn off the spigot if supply and demand get out of whack.

Imperiale: What are the major thematic trends currently in the industrial sector?

Moghadam: There are three trends that I think are important. One is the debate between just in time and just in case. I think just in time wins in the long term with a few setbacks. But if you can get comfortable with your strategy in a just-in-time environment, where levels of demand for industrial are growing at a lower rate than GDP, then you will be in good shape if you're wrong and just in case kicks in, because then you've built your business assuming that demand will be lower than GDP and you'll have a nice bonus surprise. The second big trend is network reconfiguration. It's giving a great deal of importance to build-to-suit development. The third trend is conversion to higher and better use. Inner-city industrial properties are now becoming very interesting sites for conversion to other uses—usually office, but sometimes residential. Infill industrial is becoming a really good way to carry land with a return on it until you get to the point where you can redevelop it to higher and better use. That's another thing that I think is generally not understood very well in the marketplace. If you have a company that owns primarily industrial assets in secondary markets in places where land is unconstrained, you're never going to have the upside conversion possibilities because the land is not a scarce resource. But if you own good infill industrial real estate in places like Boston, New York, San Francisco, or L.A., and you can justify it based on its current industrial use and later convert it to something with double or triple the value, you've really created some shareholder value. I don't think this is being priced into anybody's industrial REIT models.

Imperiale: Do you think the long-term outlook for the industrial sector and its participants is going to rise and fall with GDP?

Moghadam: Yes, although I think this storage versus speed thing is really important. A lot of people either don't understand that or think it's window dressing, but over time, we've made most of our money in places with scarce land, barriers to entry, and high demand for people who are using the property for something other than storage. Storage can go anywhere, whereas distribution can only occur near major modes of transportation.

Imperiale: What cap rates are available for investors and developers in the industrial sector?

Moghadam: First of all, let's define cap rates. If we define cap rate as first-year stabilized NOI—meaning after a 5 to 7 percent vacancy allowance—divided by the purchase price, I would say the cap rates for industrial property are between 8.5 and 10 percent. There are certainly industrial properties that you can buy at a higher cap rate than that, but I think they tend to be special-purpose properties, or they're in the middle of nowhere, or there's something wrong with them. To build, the premium yield I would want to take the development risk would be somewhere between 100 and 200 basis points above that, depending on whether it's built to suit. In other words, if the leasing risk has been eliminated and I'm just dealing with construction risk, I'd do it for a 100-basis-point premium return. But if I'm taking speculative risk, I would want to build for a 200-basis-point premium in cap rate.

Imperiale: Do you believe developers are making those kind of premiums in general when they engage in development activity? Are they earning the risk premium that they deserve?

Moghadam: I think they make the numbers in a good market and fall short in bad markets. To the extent that they make more money than that, it's usually because of their land profit. So I think by and large people are underpricing development because they're pricing the average so that if everything works they get the average return that they expect. Then, if things don't work, they're underperformed.

Imperiale: Do you think the market in general has trouble recognizing that?

Moghadam: Yes, because there are different ways that companies calculate cap rate and costs. For instance, in calculating development costs, some people just capitalize third-party construction interests. If they build totally with the REIT's equity, they don't attribute the cost of capital to the finished product. That really understates the true cost of the project, because it doesn't include any interim rental charge for capital and that makes the free and clear returns higher than they would be otherwise. Some people count historical cost of land in their development projects as opposed to what they could sell the land for to a third party the day before they start construction. They're really minimizing land profit as opposed to engaging in profitable development activity. There are all kinds of quirky things like that that go on.

Imperiale: What performance benchmarks do you believe should be used in measuring industrial REIT performance?

Moghadam: Well, for the core of the business, which is how much money a company is making renting properties, I think the most relevant measure is the return on invested capital plus same-store NOI growth. Total unleveraged return on capital is the most important measurement. I think most of the analytical community either misses half of that equation or flips it around. In other words, they never get both parts of it. Either they're very focused on growth and same-store NOI growth and miss the fact that they may be paying too much for that growth up front, or they get upset because of a low return on invested capital and low current yield and forget that these assets perform differently over time in terms of same-store NOI growth. I think the real challenge is to put the two halves of that together and measure total return on invested capital, which is a combination of current return on invested capital plus same-store NOI growth.

Imperiale: Why do you think the investment community at large misses that?

Moghadam: Because it's too much work and people don't really use consistent ways of reporting these things. For example, people have different definitions of same-store NOI growth. One company throws all development projects into their same-store pool the day they are opened for business. For example, let's say a company has two assets, one that is 100 percent leased and one that is 0 percent leased because it just got completed. If they throw both these assets in together, and the 0 percent asset leases up the next day, that would show tremendous same-store NOI growth, but that's just because of a one-time leasing up. That really distorts the numbers.

Imperiale: So how do you deal with that as an investor?

Moghadam: I think if companies had standard definitions it would help. There are 190 public REITs out there and industrial is just a small component. Who has time to really get into all these nuances of all that REIT accounting? But I think over time most people understand what's going on. That's why I don't pay a lot of attention to short-term performance, because that will hype what's going on at that moment. Long-term performance is pretty hard to arrive at.

Imperiale: Is there anything else you'd like to add?

Moghadam: There is the issue of being vertically integrated in property management and development versus doing it through alliance relationships. There have never been good national companies that have survived over decades in any kind of real estate and certainly not in industrial real estate, and I think the reason is that there's tension between the big companies and the local entrepreneurs. Local people are good at identifying local development opportunities. They have the political relationships to be able to process them and the local tenant relationships to be able to lease them. The big national companies bring to the table the ability to access and allocate capital more efficiently, and to manage national relationships more efficiently. There's a lot of debate about whether the local sharp-shooter model or the national model is better, but I think there are good things about each one of those models, and the best model is the one that takes the best elements of both and marries them together.

Retail REITs

Chapter Summary

- Retail properties represent 30 percent of all investment-grade commercial real estate.
- There are approximately 43,000 retail properties across the country, comprising over 6 billion square feet of gross leasable space.
- Retail real estate investment trusts (REITs) are the largest sector in the National Association of Real Estate Investment Trusts (NAREIT) Index, representing approximately 20 percent of the entire index.
- There are 45 publicly traded REITs that focus exclusively on retail properties. In addition, approximately 50 percent of the investment activity of diversified REITs (REITs that own properties in more than one sector) is focused on retail properties.

If you think the United States has stood still, who built the largest shopping center in the world?

—Richard Nixon, 1969

For purposes of the National Association of Real Estate Investment Trusts (NAREIT) Equity Index, the retail property sector is broken down into three broad categories. Shopping center real estate investment trusts (REITs), which number 28, are the largest single category. There are 10 REITs that specialize in regional malls and 7 REITs that focus on freestanding retail properties. Retail REITs make up about 20 percent of the NAREIT Equity Index (see Figure 15.1).

It is estimated that publicly traded REITs own an equity interest in over one-third of all regional malls. Real estate investment trusts represent the ownership of approximately 50 percent of super-regional malls (regional malls with over 800,000 square feet of gross leasable area) and approximately 14 percent of all nonmall retail properties in the country.

Due to the size of the retail real estate sector and the complex nature of retail operations, description of retail REITs and retail properties could fill a book by itself. This chapter will try to generally quantify and categorize the various aspects of retail real estate. The retail sector can be broken down into three large subgroups, each of which comprises a number of smaller categories. The regional mall category includes super regional malls, regional malls, destination or theme malls, specialty malls, and outlet centers. Shopping centers include two broad groups, neighborhood centers and community centers. Freestanding retail is divided into two groups known as power centers and big box retail.

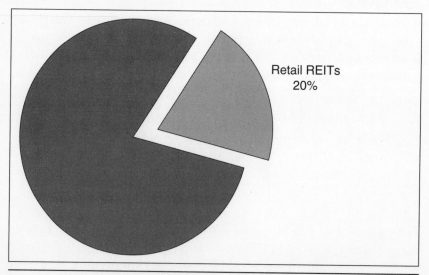

Retail REITs
20%

FIGURE 15.1 Retail REITs as a Percentage of the NAREIT Equity Index as of December 31, 2001

In the United States, the consumer, as defined by the U.S. Department of Commerce, represents over two-thirds of the domestic economy. Nowhere in the world, except perhaps Japan, is retail activity such a large part of the domestic economy. Each month, nearly 200 million U.S. shoppers visit shopping centers. American culture is dominated by consumerism, and the United States has by far the highest amount of retail space per person of any country in the world. The American landscape is covered with shopping centers of various shapes and sizes. Because of the vast array of different shopping centers, it can be difficult to classify these into groups and subgroups.

In general terms, the quality of retail property is judged by the quality of the retail tenants that occupy the property. Large, high-quality retail organizations tend to have an excellent ability to understand local markets and trade areas. Therefore, when they commit to a particular location, it tends to be a primary driver of retail traffic to a particular location. Thus, the type and quality of tenants can be one way in which a retail property can be classified. From a financial point of view, the best tenants are frequently referred to in the real estate industry as *credit tenants*. In general, these are retail operators that are part of a large, national, publicly traded retail organization with access to the public credit markets as well as an investment-grade credit rating from a major credit rating agency such as Moody's, Standard & Poor's or Fitch Investor Services. Credit tenants tend to represent the best and most successful organizations in the retail industry and tend to attract other credit tenants of a complementary nature to a retail real estate project. Thus, in general terms, a retail project that is dominated by credit tenants will normally be described as a class A retail property. Retail properties that are generally dominated by noncredit tenants are normally classified as class B retail properties.

The size and age of a retail complex is also used as a method of categorizing retail properties. Larger and newer properties tend to receive a higher quality rating than smaller and older properties. Older, smaller properties often face with what is known as the *death spiral*. The typical situation involves an older mall that begins to lose its prime credit tenants. These credit tenants tend to move into newer, larger space that might be within the local market area of the older property. The older property then has difficulty in attracting new tenants of either credit quality or noncredit quality as a result of the vacant space left behind by the credit quality tenant. This tends to be the beginning of a downward spiral as the obsolete property is slowly abandoned by the retail tenants. The decline makes it increasingly difficult to attract new tenants or new investors and thereby ultimately results in high, if not complete, vacancy of the mall and often abandonment of the property.

Malls or retail properties can also be classified in terms of their market location and the distance from which they are able to draw shoppers to the retail center. Neighborhood shopping centers tend to be located in or near residential neighborhoods and have a primary trade area of 3 to 5 miles. Community shopping centers tend to be in larger urban neighborhoods and have a trade area of 3 to 8 miles. Regional shopping centers tend to rely on a metropolitan region for most of their retail activity and have a primary trade area that can be 5 to 20 miles in range.

The various classifications of retail shopping centers and their age, size and location characteristics are summed up in Table 15.1.

- *Neighborhood shopping centers.* Neighborhood shopping centers tend to be the smallest in size, ranging from 30,000 to 150,000 square feet. The primary concern of the neighborhood shopping center is convenient access for local market users to obtain the necessities of daily life. Neighborhood shopping centers tend to be anchored by grocery stores and are located on sites that range from 3 to 15 acres in size. They normally encompass a primary trade area of 3 to 5 miles.

- *Community shopping centers.* Community shopping centers tend to be approximately 100,000 to 350,000 square feet in size, located on sites of 10 to 50 acres. They usually focus on general merchandise, with convenience of daily necessities being the primary motive. The community shopping center may be considered a one-stop shopping center for daily needs and may include a department store, a drugstore, and a grocery anchor on the same site. The primary trade area is a 5- to 10-mile range.

TABLE 15.1 Retail Property Subcategories and Related Data

Name	Size	Market area	Primary Function
Neighborhood shopping centers	230,000–100,000 ft²	3–5 mi	Convenient access to local population
Community shopping centers	100,000–300,000 ft²	5–10 mi	One-stop shopping for most daily needs
Regional malls	250,000–650,000 ft²	Up to 25 mi	Enclosed shopping with general merchandise
Super-regional malls	800,000 ft² or larger	25+ mi	Entertainment and destination shopping
Outlet malls	50,000–400,000 ft²	As much as 75 mi	Focus on manufacturer-direct off-price items
Power centers	300,000–600,000 ft²	5–15 mi	Dominant anchor tenant located on major roads

- *Regional malls.* Regional malls tend to cover general merchandise, fashion and some type of entertainment as well. Regional malls are normally enclosed, whereas neighborhood and community shopping centers are frequently not enclosed and have a more uniform design. Regional malls tend to be from 250,000 to 600,000 square feet in size and occupy sites that range from 50 to 100 acres in size. The primary trade area for a regional mall can extend to as much as 25 miles.

- *Super-regional malls.* Super-regional malls are very much like regional malls in terms of merchandise mix. They have a larger variety of merchandise than regional malls and also tend to have more entertainment activities. Super-regional malls are defined generally as 800,000 square feet or larger, located on sites of 60 to 120 acres or more. The super-regional mall's market area is 25 miles or perhaps even farther depending on its location.

- *Fashion or specialty malls.* As the name implies, these properties are fashion or clothing oriented and tend to attract higher-end retail tenants. Because of their specialty nature, fashion malls tend to be 100,000 to 250,000 square feet in size and are located on sites of 5 to 25 acres. Their primary trade area can extend for as much as 25 miles and is largely dependent on competition from regional or super-regional malls.

■ *Outlet malls.* Outlet malls tend to focus on off-price merchandise being sold directly through manufacturers' outlet stores. They are normally 50,000 to 400,000 square feet in size and occupy sites of 10 to 50 acres. Because of the specialty nature of outlet malls, they tend to draw from even larger market areas than super-regional malls. Consumers are often willing to drive as much as 75 miles to visit outlet malls.

■ *Theme or festival malls.* Also termed *lifestyle malls,* these malls focus on leisure activity or tourist-oriented activities and tend to have a high percentage of space dedicated to restaurants and other types of entertainment. The size tends to be 100,000 to 250,000 square feet on a 5- to 25-acre site. They are often located in or around areas with high levels of tourist activity. For example, a large number of leisure or lifestyle properties are found in locations such as Orlando, Florida, and the Las Vegas, Nevada, area.

■ *Power centers.* Power centers have a category-dominant anchor tenant and may have a few smaller inline tenants as well. They are familiar as big national chain stores like Wal-Mart or Home Depot. Power centers are typically 300,000 to 600,000 square feet in size and are located on 25- to 100-acre sites. Power centers tend to have a trade area of 5 to 15 miles and are generally located on the edge of higher-density residential areas with nearby access to major highways.

Supply and Demand in the Retail Sector

As with other categories of real estate, demand for retail space is driven by the general growth of the domestic economy, with a high sensitivity to growth in demand for retail and consumer goods and services. The demand for retail goods and services is a function of household income and growth in the demographic segments that tend to be higher consumers of retail goods and services—generally the 15- to 25-year-old and the over-50 segments. However, it should be noted that demographic and consumer spending habits change over time and that good retail property operators are very sensitive to the impact of changing lifestyle demographics on their retail properties. Normally, a healthy domestic economy will produce a consumer who is willing to spend at a higher level and at a higher rate than that of a slowly expanding or quiet economy.

The seemingly ever expanding supply of retail property is part of the retail property cycle. Since 1996, on average 250 million square feet of retail space have been delivered into the U.S. real estate market. With approximately 6 billion square feet of existing space, the base of retail space is expanding nearly twice as fast as the U.S. economy. However, it is important to note of that 250 million square feet of annual delivery, approximately 125 million square feet replaces obsolete retail property that is in some stage of the death spiral and ultimately will be vacant and off the market for practical purposes. It is estimated that over the next seven years, nearly 1 billion square feet of the aggregate retail market total will become functionally obsolete and be removed from the aggregate retail property pool. The long-term demand for retail space over the same period is estimated to be approximately 290 million square feet per year. However, it is important to note that the overall demand for retail space will be directly impacted by the level of economic growth as well as the financial health of the consumer and changing trends within the retail industry. Any of these factors could have a large impact on the overall demand for retail space.

Industry Dynamics

The dynamics of the U.S. retail property industry are inextricably intertwined with the dynamics of the U.S. retail sector. In general terms, much like hotel operators, retail real estate operators provide a very high-value-added management component. Retail property owners must know and understand the dynamics of the retail sector, which they deal with from a tenant basis. They generally have a marketing plan for their entire portfolio of retail properties as well as a specific marketing plan for each individual property and perhaps even for each space within a property. These marketing plans are often driven by the marketing plans of one or more anchor tenants that may dominate the location of the retail property. In addition, the overall marketing plan will consider factors such as property location relative to population density, the current and projected population growth, local household income levels and buying habits, and the age demographics of the area. Competitive retail centers in the same market area, as well as land available for retail expansion within a retail center's marketing area, are also taken into account. Thus, the retail property owner will tend to analyze all the market factors and attempt to position a retail property for maximum value in the local real estate market. This high-value-added component of retail operations can be critical in extracting value on the margin from the retail property. Because each retail property operates at such a different level, the best way to examine the industry dynamic is by property type.

Dynamics of Regional Malls

Regional and super-regional malls tend to be the largest retail structures, typically having two or more anchor tenants that may account for as much as 60 percent of the gross leaseable area. The anchor tenants draw retail traffic to a location, and the malls are configured so that the majority of retail shoppers enter the mall through an anchor store. Anchor tenants are generally credit tenants and are very sophisticated in their ability to analyze the local real estate market. In addition, they understand and recognize their traffic-drawing ability and use it to their advantage. In a typical regional or super-regional mall, the anchor tenant pays little or no rent to the landlord and generally makes a below-average per-square-foot contribution to cover maintenance expense. In general, anchor tenants own their own stores, which they build on the mall site on land that is leased from the landlord over a long period.

The specialty tenants, often referred to as *inline tenants,* represent the majority of the income available to the retail regional or super-regional mall operator. In most situations, the heavy promotional activity of the anchor tenant in turn draws the foot traffic which is of interest to the inline tenants that populate the balance of the gross leaseable area of the mall. Specialty tenants provide the majority of mall income, which is usually based on a minimum per-square-foot rental rate, with fixed periodic increases that are indexed to the Consumer Price Index or a minimum annual rate increase. In addition to minimum rents, a shopping center owner sets a base rental rate that increases as the tenant's sales volume increases. This is typically known as the *percentage rent clause* in a lease. In many ways, the percentage clause creates a powerful incentive for the shopping center owner to contribute to the success of the retail tenant. These percentage rents typically run in the range of 6 to 8 percent over a base amount of aggregate revenues on an annual basis. In addition, specialty tenants pay a common area maintenance and insurance charge that represents their pro rata share of all maintenance expenses for the shopping center. Real estate taxes are also handled on a pro rata share based on square footage. In addition, tenants are required to make a fixed contribution on an annual basis to a marketing and promotion fund, which is generally used to develop the marketing plan for the specialty tenants in a mall or regional mall. In many ways, the mall owner is attempting to align the financial success of the mall with the financial success of the retail tenants. Tenants' ability to pay rent is determined by their level of sales and profitability. In general, rents run at an average level of 8 to 10 percent of sales. Rents plus all other tenant costs typically run from 12 to 15 percent of sales. The mall owner, of course, enjoys the benefit of having higher productivity tenants or tenants with more popular products and services. In some lease situations, tenants with per-square-foot sales that fall within a target range might pay 7 to 8 percent of sales as a minimum rental payment; as sales increase to higher levels this may grow to 9 to 10 percent or more. As the sales and success of the property grow, the rents grow as well.

This unique relationship between the retail landlord and the retail property user requires some special analysis. Of all property types, retail properties are most likely to generate long and detailed lease negotiations prior to the actual signing of a lease for space. The retailer in general understands that every dollar in percentage sales or every expense that is not paid to the landlord will essentially fall to the bottom line for the retailer. National credit tenant organizations that lease retail space across the country normally have an experienced real estate department that will negotiate every aspect of a retail lease. Independent real estate brokers generally handle rental activities in smaller properties. Rental activities in major regional malls and large retail complexes are typically handled by the local office of the mall, or, in the case of national credit tenants, directly between the tenant's organization and the national real estate organization. In many circumstances, it is not uncommon for a national credit tenant to arrive at a standard lease structure for all locations with a large owner of multiple retail properties. In many instances, lease negotiations are bundled to cover a portfolio of retail centers and administered on a uniform basis. These factors suggest that skilled retail property management can add a high level of value in the area of property management and lease negotiations.

Regional mall owners are very focused on the sales performance of their properties. Mall owners monitor very closely the same-store sales levels for tenants that have occupied the mall for a period of 12 months or more. This year-by-year performance in same-store sales is a measure of the mall's retail activity as well as of the performance of the individual tenants. In monitoring the same-store sales levels of individual tenants, the landlord may begin to develop a profile of underperforming tenants that occupy the retail portfolio. This can lead to selective targeted negotiations at the time the space is re-leased, or to a mall owner simply making the decision not to re-lease space to an underperforming tenant. In general terms, mall management measures total sales for all tenants on an average per-square-foot basis, regardless of their tenure at the mall, in order to provide a comparative measure of the mall's ability to draw consumer traffic. Retail malls that generate higher levels of per-square-foot activity as a result of location, tenant mix, or other factors will demand a rental premium over malls whose performance is more average. Because the leases of inline retail tenants contain a percentage clause that requires the tenant to pay the higher of a base rent or a percentage of sales that is fixed in advance, the mall operator is truly a partner of the tenant.

Dynamics of Shopping Centers and Freestanding Retail Markets

There are three major subcategories of shopping centers. Neighborhood and community shopping centers are anchored by promotional tenants that tend to be discount retails or power retailers. In these instances, the anchor may use as much as 70 percent of the entire gross leaseable area of the center. Power centers, which are anchored by similar discount retailers, are in the same category; however, power centers tend to be 90 percent occupied by anchor tenants with only a few or no other retail tenants. These are often referred to as *freestanding* or *big box* retail centers. Finally, there are neighborhood and community shopping centers, anchored by supermarkets or drugstores, that typically find as much as 70 percent of their gross leaseable space occupied by one or two major anchor tenants. The supermarket and drugstore may be separate or combined.

As in malls, the anchor tenant in shopping centers tends to be the tenant that relies on heavy promotional activity to stimulate retail traffic to the property. However, anchor tenants pay their share of property expenses. In a typical strip shopping center, anchor tenants pay a minimum annual rent and a percentage of sales that in total produce a minimum rent level for the landlord. The major distinction is that, unlike mall tenants, anchor tenants at strip shopping centers pay a much smaller percentage of sales as rent—typically in the range of 2 to 5 percent. In many instances, these anchor tenants build and operate their own units, and in fact may directly own the real estate. Although shopping centers may not obtain the rental revenue growth component that regional mall operators enjoy, well-anchored shopping centers enjoy a highly stable rental stream. In addition, grocery- or drugstore-anchored shopping centers tend to have very long-duration lease structures. It is not unusual to find a grocery-anchored retail center with an initial lease term of 15 to 20 years with extensions of up to 10 years available. Thus, although the rental growth for these units may not be as rapid as that for regional malls, they tend to have longer, more predictable cash flow durations.

Trends in Retail Real Estate

In the long run, a shopping center will be successful only if it is able to create and maintain a competitive position in its local market. In many ways, this success is driven by a property owner's ability to reinvent the real estate on a periodic basis. One issue that continues to be at the forefront in the retail property sector is the level of maintenance capital an owner must spend to maintain or increase existing rental cash flow from a property. In particular, this is a big challenge for the mall sector, due to the dynamic and ever changing nature of the U.S. retail economy. In the last 10 years, the amount of capital expense required to maintain a regional mall in a competitive way has been increasing. In the early 1990s, capital expenses of 3 to 5 percent of net operating income were typical for regional malls. This number has increased substantially to 7 or 8 percent, and many experts believe that on a long-term basis, 10 percent of net operating income will be required. Most mall owners agree that in order for a regional mall to remain competitive, a capital renovation of the property must take place every 8 to 12 years. Based on the current cost of construction, it is not unusual for mall owners to spend between $12 and $24 per square foot every 8 to 12 years in order to reposition, reinvent, or remodel their retail properties. It is generally believed that this trend toward redeveloping existing properties helps them avoid the death spiral. Investors and retail REITs should consider the increasing level of capital expenditures required to maintain properties as a situation that could lower cash flow available for distribution to REIT shareholders.

Like regional malls, shopping centers are also faced with recurring capital expense items that need to be considered. Over the last decade, capital expense reserves for shopping centers have grown from about 4 percent to about 7 percent of net operating income, and many experts believe this trend will continue until levels reach approximately 9 to 10 percent. Functional and competitive obsolescence are primarily to blame for increasing capital expense in the shopping center sector.

Obsolescence results from a physical property requiring a major structural overhaul in order to remain competitive in a local market. *Competitive obsolescence* is a function of having to retool an existing property in order to accommodate a new tenant that may be replacing a major tenant that is leaving the property. It also results from changing retail dynamics. For example, a well-maintained grocery-anchored shopping center can become competitively obsolete when a new Wal-Mart opens just several miles down the highway. This competitive obsolescence often requires a major capital expenditure to retool the property in order to become competitive again. This form of obsolescence accounts for the generally higher level of capital expense in the shopping center area. *Functional obsolescence* can be seen throughout the retail real estate community and is embedded in a number of trends within the retail property sector. For example, supermarkets now tend to be much larger than just a decade ago. It is not unusual for an average store to be over 70,000 square feet, whereas just 10 years ago the average figure was about 28,000 square feet. Drugstores, another major tenant of community shopping centers, have also revised their operating strategy. Today, drugstores prefer to be freestanding units based on the edges of large shopping complexes rather than being a part of the inline tenant mix. Part of the reason is to accommodate the newest trend in pharmacy delivery—the drive-through pharmacy. Big box retailers are also getting bigger. Wal-Mart's average per-store square footage has grown from about 55,000 square feet 10 years ago to about 130,000 square feet today. As retail formats change, properties with older formats become functionally obsolete and require capital expenditures in order to bring them up to date and keep them competitive.

The low-inflation environment of the mid- and late 1990s has also been a problem for retail REITs. As mentioned, most retail leases contain a clause stating that the tenant will pay the higher of a base rent or a percentage of sales. In an environment where retail prices have been stable or even declining, inflation-driven increases in rental revenue have not materialized as many retail owners may have anticipated in the early 1990s. However, it should be noted that this tame inflationary environment has been somewhat offset by very strong consumer demand, which has translated into higher general retail sales.

Another interesting trend in the retail sector is that sales of goods typically purchased in stores and shopping centers has been growing at a rate slower than the growth rate of consumer income. This makes the notion the growth in personal income drives demand for retail space problematic. In addition, growth in retail sales has been about half that in retail space. This trend has contributed to a lower level of growth in per-square-foot sales for most major retail operators. Due to the participating nature of most retail leases, lower growth and per-square-foot sales have negatively impacted the returns in the retail real estate sector.

The Internet and Retail

There is much debate about the impact of the Internet on retail sales and therefore on the value of retail real estate. Internet sales are building at a steady pace. Industry reports put Internet retail sales as follows:

1999: $17.5 billion

2000: $37.9 billion

2001: $56.5 billion (estimated)

This is impressive sales growth, and holiday-related sales has been the fastest. These sales gains occurred because more people became Internet users during 1999 and 2000. That increase, however, was somewhat mitigated by a slight decline in the average amount purchased by Internet shoppers. It may be that the increase in Internet shoppers lowered the average purchase amount as more new shoppers entered the marketplace during the course of 2000.

Projections of longer-term e-commerce sales continue to rise. A number of forecasters have raised their Internet retail sales projections for 2002 and 2003 from an average of $67 billion and $87 billion to $79 and $102 billion, respectively. The strongest e-commerce categories include books, video, and music; computer hardware and software; and gifts and flowers. These three categories could capture a double-digit market share of total retail sales by 2003. Other categories such as apparel, housewares, and food look to achieve low- to mid-single-digit penetration over the next five years. As mentioned, holiday purchases are very strong on the Internet. The following is an estimate of the top online holiday purchases as projected by several different surveys:

Books and magazines: 58 percent

Music and movies: 55 percent

Computers and related: 42 percent

Toys and video games: 42 percent

Electronics: 40 percent

Clothing: 36 percent

The bursting of the Internet bubble has been the most notable setback for the e-commerce business. The diminished funding prospects for business-to-consumer Internet companies have slowed the growth of sales in the sector. Many existing Internet companies are in a cash squeeze, as cash burn rates are exceedingly high and profitability in most cases is a long time out. Without funding, the competitive threat to store-based retailers from pure-play e-commerce companies will be significantly reduced.

To the surprise of the Internet elite, old bricks-and-mortar retailers are often proving to be better equipped than their e-commerce competitors in developing Internet business in their respective product categories. These store-based retailers are leveraging their established brand names and retail distribution presence online without spending millions on incremental marketing and distribution. Although this is great news for existing retailers, it is only good news for the landlords. Although it is preferable for clicks-and-bricks business models to prevail over pure plays, a significant shift in volume away from traditional formats would still result in store closings.

Although the Internet's emergence may have a negative impact on the sales of retail tenants, it seems books, music, videos, and electronics are the categories that will suffer the most. Many REITs and their retail customers are implementing Internet initiatives to aid in the efficiencies of their operations, increase the availability of product information to consumers, and in some cases enhance top-line growth through the convergence of the Internet and shopping centers.

Overall the Internet continues to grow as a new channel of retail sales. It's not unlikely that ultimately Internet sales will have a penetration rate in the range of 7 to 10 percent of total retail sales. This emergence might negatively impact both existing mail-order and store-based retailers. Experts estimate that e-commerce will reduce retail rental growth by 50 to 60 basis points over the next five years. Not a disaster, but certainly a trend that bears watching. Investors in REITs should be aware of the risk that e-commerce poses to retail real estate. However, the tactile and social nature of much shopping activity should also be considered. It seems that e-commerce has yet to produce a measurable impact on prospective retail leasing activity, but the Internet will remain a topic of debate in the retail property sector for many years to come.

Summary Data

Returns and volatility for retail REITs are average (see Table 15.2). Over the last five years the retail sector has produced an average annual return of 6.3 percent, the lowest for the major REIT sectors. The volatility of the retail sector as measured by the standard deviation of returns was 19.1 percent. The basic characteristics of the retail sector make it very sensitive to economic and business conditions. The long lead times on major

TABLE 15.2 Historical Sector Data for Retail REITs

	2001	2000	1999	1998	1997
Total return on sector	27.60%	18.0%	−18.9%	−4.9%	17.0%
Dividend yield	6.97%	10.24%	7.12%	5.93%	7.12%
Estimated NAV	115.0%	79.0%	75.0%	106.0%	116.0%
Market cap of sector ($B)	31.7				
Index weight	20%				
Volatility	19.06%				
Five-year return	6.30%				

Source: NAREIT.

retail construction along with general competitive conditions in the retail community make the outlook for this sector less favorable than in the recent past.

Interview with Glenn J. Rufrano

Glenn J. Rufrano is chief executive officer and president of New Plan Excel Realty Trust, Inc. (NYSE: NXL). He joined the company in February 2000, following 17 years as a partner at The O'Connor Group, a diversified real estate investment firm where he most recently served as president and chief operating officer. Early in his career, Rufrano was a senior vice president in the Appraisal and Property Dispositions Department at Landauer Associates. He currently serves on a number of boards at New York University's Real Estate Institute, where he is an adjunct professor, and is a member of the board of directors of TrizecHahn Corporation, an integrated real estate operating company. He holds an M.S.M. from Florida International University and a B.A. from Rutgers University.

Richard Imperiale: What characteristics distinguish retail real estate as a property group within the real estate world and the REIT worlds?

Glenn Rufrano: Well, as Milton Cooper would say, there are retailers, there's retail real estate, and then there's a REIT, which is an operating company that runs retail real estate. All three are different but all are very related, and you really can't talk about the last two unless you start with the first one.

Imperiale: OK, so what is a retailer and how do we house them?

Rufrano: I'd say the retailer is probably the classic entrepreneur capitalist in our society today—the trader of goods that basic economics hinges on. Retailers are in a unique business that the people vote on every day by either buying or not buying the goods. It's interactive with consumers, it's an everyday capitalist process, and it's a very dog-eat-dog world. Retailers who can conform to that form of capitalism and who understand their market and how to merchandise that market thrive, and the ones who can't go away very quickly. So we have to recognize that we are housing businesses that can be obsolete if their form of distribution doesn't work within the current distribution network. Retail real estate is unique because these businesses are in large part dependent upon the location of the real estate and the bricks and mortar that surround them. This is different from an office building, where you can house a tenant and it makes no difference whether the tenant is on the north or the south side of the street. It can make a real difference if a retailer is on the north side or the south side.

Imperiale: So in retail real estate the old mantra of location, location, location is perhaps more important.

Rufrano: By a lot. In many cases, the retailer can make the real estate, which is almost never true in other forms of real estate. And so there's this unique bond between the owner and the retailer. If they cannot succeed in our housing, our properties won't succeed. That's why we've always thought of retail real estate as more of an operating business than pure real estate. We are 100 percent dependent on the sales volume and the productivity of our tenants. We can tell based on that whether or not they're going to be successful. If they are not successful, our real estate is not successful. So our business relationship as a partner with them is far closer than the business relationship with other tenants in other functions of real estate, and I think that's a distinguishing difference. We can never just put a tenant in and say they'll pay the rent. If they close, the rest of our tenants don't look good. So everybody's got to work for our real estate to work.

I think the difference between real estate, which is truly a partnership between the retailer and the owner, and a REIT is that the REIT is an operating business. It has a whole series of the components stores do, and at any given time it can create or lose value by making a portfolio decision, and that portfolio decision is more important than just that piece of real estate. In a REIT, we need a direction and a strategy that fit the capital we're attracting. That capital strategy, along with understanding between the capital and the sales, is paramount. If you're a high-risk venture that may be buying empty real estate, leasing it up, and selling it, you need to make sure the capital understands that and is looking for a higher-risk, higher-return investment. If you're a low-risk operator, you're not going to have the high returns of the old tech era, so you have to make sure your capital base understands that what they're investing in is a stabilized, slow- to mid-growth, but understandable income structure.

As an operating company, we have to operate the real estate, but also we have to catch the trends in the capital market to make sure we're coordinating with those trends. So I go from the retailer, who's got to run a business, to a partnership between the owner of the real estate and that retailer, who have to make sure jointly that they've run the business well, to an operator of many properties who not only has to run that business well but make sure there's a relationship with the capital base in terms of risk in the investment.

Imperiale: If a tenant is not being successful, would you be proactive in getting rid of them if you don't think that they're ultimately going to succeed?

Rufrano: In that case, we have to try to perfect their business. It may not mean getting rid of them, it may mean analyzing the situation and advising them. In shopping centers, that's less functional than in malls. But even in our largest centers, we effectively have to work with our tenants the first time we see the metrics not working. If they're not helpable, we have to think about what we can do to replace them.

Imperiale: To what degree is that driven by your responsibility to the shareholders?

Rufrano: Well, if you know that ultimately that tenant could fail, and if it stays 50/50, you have no choice but to try to represent your investors and to try to make sure that that 50/50 is 90/10 and up.

Imperiale: Are there hidden risks in REITs that public real estate owners might not be aware of?

Rufrano: I think there are, because we run a business that they're not in, so there's no way our REIT sales constituency truly understands the risks of our business. As a public company, we have more obligation to expose those risks than a private company would, and we do that as part of the way we interact with our shareholders, whether it's in the annual report or in our 10K.

Coming from the private market, for a long time I thought the public market was more disclosive than it is. From the outside, you say, "Wow, those public guys, they have the supplemental report, they have to expose a lot." And that's true, but there are trends and interpretations that are probably not fully understood at any given time in the public market. Nobody's trying to deceive anybody, it's just too much to know or to get out. But I think in general, the risks are fairly represented.

Imperiale: In your opinion, what drives the supply and demand dynamic within the retail segment?

Rufrano: When we looked at supply and demand and tried to understand how any piece of given real estate fared, we looked at a capture rate as a concept and the capture rate was the result of an analysis we called a gravity model. Let's demonstrate with a mall. If you had a market with three malls, you would be able to measure GAFO [general merchandise, apparel, furniture, and other] sales volumes in that market. That information is available, so you would know the total amount of GAFO sales at any given time. From that you'd be able to establish a GAFO for stores in each of the malls—the capture rate. With three malls in a market, you may have one very good one. You'd know that because you'd be able to find the capture rate in the market and understand the strength of the retailing capability of the property. So you should be looking at capture rate for every property in order to understand these dynamics. If you have a capture rate of 5 percent, that sounds bad, but it may not be bad, because you may find that you're missing certain merchandise formats. If you have 40 percent, sometimes that sounds terrific, but you might lose market share due to new forms of retail in the market.

So when we look at supply and demand, we always look at capture rates. We always dive down into the merchandise mix and look at it each year to determine whether or not it was optimum for the market so we could plan ahead. We would look at gravity model, capture rate, and merchandise mix. The other very important element is that supply is the tool, and we always overbuild supply.

Imperiale: The argument is made that we have more square footage of retail per capita than any country in the world and we're overbuilt, which hurts the return on capital in retail, but in many locations A quality retail properties seem to be doing fine. How do you explain that?

Rufrano: Well, from 1986 to 1990, we were building a tremendous amount of space—about 5 percent a year. We really minimized that in the five years after that, and we haven't gone overboard since. Your number was about 250 million square feet a year, and we're pretty close to that, if you look at the differentials that we're showing in growth. But the key is that we built about 2 percent a year in inventory, whereas in the 1980s we were building 5 percent a year. The flip side, which really caused the problem back then, is sales. We were increasing sales at about 2 percent a year while we were building at 5 percent. But recently—up until September—we had been growing at about 4 to 5 percent a year. In the last 10 years we've been growing faster than we've been building, so our supply and demand equilibrium has gotten much better.

Imperiale: What are the major thematic trends currently in play within the retail sector?

Rufrano: Well, I would define thematic trends as distribution, because the way I look at it, you've got retailers and they're trying to find the most efficient and profitable way to distribute their merchandise. Some are interested in having some stores in malls, some in urban centers on street corners, and some in regional shopping centers. Others want one specific type of property. Understanding distribution by the tenants in our universe is an important concept, and I'd say it's a matter of trend because our tenants are looking around and finding that the world's changing and that they need to be much more efficient. That's one reason why malls are becoming more difficult, because their occupancy costs are very high. And if they can't get the sales volume to satisfy the occupancy costs, that form of distribution becomes a very difficult frame unless they see something changing. Thematically, the obvious change has been for the discounters who are either in community shopping centers or stand-alone businesses where their primary form of distribution is a four-wall box and what really counts is price. Their value is distributing simply and cheaply with price maximizing profitability.

Imperiale: What kind of an impact does that have on the rest of the distribution network?

Rufrano: It varies. The world's so different that there's always going to be someone who loves a given store and someone else who doesn't. So now it's a question of degree. There's probably a market share for everybody, but it's in degrees. Nordstrom's market share is shrinking. The Gap can't continue to put its store on every corner and make it work; the fair market is shrinking. Ames can't continue to buy companies, even in the discount business, and think they can run them; they're going to shrink back. There's form of consumer for each of their distribution networks, but it's clear to me that the discount distribution network is getting larger right now, high-end apparel is shrinking, and in between everybody's fighting for market share. Distribution and moving merchandise to the proper consumers has changed dramatically in the last five years.

Imperiale: Would you characterize it as being a revolution?

Rufrano: Yes, and the result of that revolution is functional obsolescence and the functional obsolescence in all forms of retail. If you have a 30,000-square-foot grocer and in order to compete and distribute effectively against Wal-Mart and others, it has to be 50,000 square feet, you have functional obsolescence. If you have a 400,000-square-foot outlet center with a shrinking tenant base and fewer customers, you have functional obsolescence that is built into that industry.

Imperiale: That leads into the death spiral. In Milwaukee there was a regional mall that went through a death spiral, and ultimately somebody bought it for less than the land value and knocked it down. How does that kind of thing happen, and how do you deal with it if you're a property owner?

Rufrano: In regional malls, the death spiral happens primarily when one or two people build better mousetraps, and you're the third mousetrap. The better mousetraps are probably bigger and have more stores, a greater ability to attract tenants, better anchors, and maybe entertainment. Whatever they have, it's a form of tenancy that better serves the market. Not only is your third mall being out-performed by a better mousetrap, but that better mouse-trap probably stole one of your anchors. So now you've got two malls that are better mixed and larger, you've lost one of your tenants, and your other tenants are probably think-ing about getting to the better mousetrap. The result of all this is that your sales will start dropping, your tenants will become less profitable and ultimately look for another home, and the highest and best use of your property is no longer a regional shopping center. But it always starts with someone else doing a better job. And sometimes, that someone does a better job because you're not doing your job.

Imperiale: How do you defend against that?

Rufrano: The best defense is to make sure you've got the best anchors. If you've got three and you think you're in good shape, you should be looking for number four. Always be thinking that someone else can outmaneuver you. Many mall owners didn't do that, because there was this theory that the department stores would always base themselves first upon malls so they wouldn't eat up market share. That didn't always happen. Department stores would go 3 miles away to another site because their current store was only 90,000 square feet and they really wanted 240,000. They knew it would cannibalize the malls, but they were going to write that off. That happened an awful lot. And then in the 1980s there was a huge proliferation of department stores, and many of them died through mergers. Because of that, malls could be built with department stores, and then in many cases, someone else bought the stores, so now the malls had two of the same store. The death spiral occurred in large part because department stores were restructuring.

There is also a death spiral in community shopping centers. For example, let's say you have a grocer and a discount Wal-Mart that has 100,000 square feet. Now Wal-Mart says, "We want to put in a superstore." So you tell Wal-Mart you want to put a superstore on your site. But that's a problem because now the grocer (unintelligible) or you may not have enough land. So Wal-Mart says, "Okay, we're going to buy a lot across the street and build a superstore there." They leave your property. They're paying rent, but they leave. Across the street, put in the superstore with a 55,000-square-foot food store and not your food store. So now you've got a piece of property with a food store that's doing very poorly and an empty Wal-Mart, and that is a sign of obsolescence. You now have to remerchandise this whole parcel. If it's dense market, you'll find tenants to replace it, but if you're in the boonies, that's a death spiral.

Imperiale: What's the best way to handle the property in a situation like that?

Rufrano: You need to control the Wal-Mart space somehow and find another tenant. Hopefully somebody can come in and remerchandise or replace that tenant, and if you can do that, then you're probably okay. But you need another major tenant. If you can get one, you can go from an obsolete property to a great property. But if you can't get from A to B, there's not a lot of middle there.

Imperiale: Any other things out there that could impact retail real estate?

Rufrano: Well, one thing is that retail real estate belongs in the hands of a well-operated company. Let's assume that's a REIT. It doesn't have to be—it could be a private company—but by our very nature, REITs are operating companies. I think that's a very good place for retail real estate to be because as the retail environments change, if you just own a building, and something goes wrong, all you have is that building. But if you have an operating company, you should be able to get ahead of the trends because you've got tenants throughout the country and you've got an operation that should be watching those trends. You can maneuver around the negatives more easily with an operating company than if you just own pieces of real estate. And that's the significance of a REIT, that the shareholders should be expecting that the operator should be able to take advantage of some negative situations that could occur and not just sit there and be deluged by it. The REIT management should be able to see the trends and position the REIT to take advantage of those trends. If you just own a piece of real estate, you don't have that. So I think from a long-term perspective, owning retail real estate in an operating company is far better and should be more profitable than just owning pieces of real estate.

In terms of general trends, I would discount the Internet. I think it's a good distribution network, and if we ever get to the point where security becomes a real issue and we worry that some crazy will walk into a mall and blow himself up, we may see more use of the Internet than we have in the past. That could be a trend in the event security becomes an issue. And security as an issue has been important. One good part about the community shopping center business is that most of our security is run by local police. We don't have the problems of enclosed malls, where we have worry about the HBC and anthrax and everything. I can see that driving some retail to open air.

As far as other trends, the Wal-Mart trend is the one that everybody needs to watch now. There are people who say that eventually there's only going to be Wal-Mart and distributors to Wal-Mart. I don't think that's right, but Wal-Mart is not our friend. They're not our friend, and they don't care about us. So understanding the extent to which the Wal-Marts of the world will take over retail is extremely important. If you have a big enough consumer base and there's a lot of geography, they can't get into some markets. But, if you ever saw a Wal-Mart doubling in size, you'd really have to worry about how your whole distribution would work. I think that's far issue, but it is something people need to think about because Wal-Mart is still doing very well. They shot through Sears—I know Sears was the number one retailer for a long time, they shot right through them. But I'm not sure I could say there are any distribution forms that are going to go away. I don't think malls are going to go away. Actually I think they're a good form of retailing. There may be fewer, and they may even be designated from a merchandising standpoint so there are product differentiations that people care about, but I don't see malls going away. I think community shopping centers are not going to go away. Power centers are a reasonable concept. You may not see as many big boxes—there may be more smaller and larger space interspersed—spaced, but I think that's tweaking, not really any changes. Lifestyle centers are just large community shopping centers with higher-end goods. So I don't see anything going away, and I don't think there's anything on the horizon that's a brand-new form of distribution.

Imperiale: How about cap rates?

Rufrano: I think cap rates for community shopping centers have been 10, plus or minus, since the beginning of time. There's a rationale for it. By their very nature, 60 to 70 percent of the space is occupied by large tenants that don't have a lot of growth. There will never be a big growth concept here, so you have to have a higher initial return. Probably the cap rates that have really changed dramatically were the malls. In the 1980s, we were pricing malls in the six percent range. That was a time of great consumer spending, great rent increases, and high inflation, so there was some real growth. But now a mall in the eights is unusual because the growth is not there and we paid too much for them in the past.

Imperiale: And part of that is that property categories like regional malls seem to become the darling of institutional direct investors, and they drive the cap rates down to unbelievable levels.

Rufrano: The basis for that was always that malls are so hard to field, and in fact that's true. There are many stories of malls taking 10 years from the time the land is bought until the mall opens. Institutional investors like to hear that a mall is not a commodity, it's a franchise, which would mean you couldn't replace a mall, so it should always hold or increase its value. That's how malls were thought of, but in the 1990s it was proven wrong because the demand diffused into open-air shopping centers, outlets, and the Internet. I don't think there is much mall construction going on now.

Imperiale: Anything else you want to cover?

Rufrano: I would like to come back to one topic, which is the concept that the world should recognize that companies that own large pools of real estate are not stagnant. They are not passive, and they can change and evolve. You can start out as a mall company and end up as a community shopping center company because you have management that is looking ahead. What most people don't understand is that not only do you have core assets that have value, but management teams can maximize the value of those core assets. People think of real estate as stagnant, like one house just sitting on a piece of land. They don't think about the fact that you could have 300 of them and sell a hundred, then buy 200 more and capitalize it different ways, and that it's truly corporate finance as well as real estate. In the private market, we were doing opportunity funds, and we saw capital come in and turn 20 percent, but at huge risk. Then you look at the REIT market and you see 6 to 8 percent return dividend and 3 to 4 percent growth. I make the case that 11 to 14 with a good operator is way better than 20 with zero income, all residual, buying some of the most difficult stuff you could think of outside the United States. That's why I think the public market makes sense in real estate. The operating nature of REITs and their ability to provide liquidity are very important.

Hotel REITs

Chapter Summary

- Hotels represent about 4 percent of the total commercial real estate market.

- Publicly traded hotel real estate investment trusts (REITs) represent about 5 percent of the National Association of Real Estate Trusts (NAREIT) Equity Index.

- Real estate investment trusts own about 19 percent of all U.S. Hotel properties.

- Hotels are usually classified by room price, size, and location.

- Operations are more critical to the overall success of hotel properties than properties in any other real estate sector.

- Hotel properties are among the most volatile in the commercial real estate market but have high relative returns.

- Demand for hotel rooms is largely related to the state of the economy.

- There are 15 publicly traded hotel REITs.

When I feel like getting away from it all, I just turn on the TV to a Spanish channel and imagine I'm on vacation in a hotel in Mexico.

—Charles Merrill Smith, 1981

Hotel properties have an aggregate total value of approximately $225 billion. The hotel investment universe represents approximately 5 percent of all investment-grade commercial real estate. Hotel REITs make up about 5 percent of the NAREIT Equity Index (see Figure 16.1). The hotel sector has historically been the most volatile sector of the commercial real estate universe; however, demand for hotel rooms is easily predicted because it tracks very closely with general levels of economic activity. The problem in the industry has long been supply, which is prone to boom and bust cycles driven by overbuilding.

Hotels have a real estate component that contributes to their performance. To the extent that location and property type contribute to a successful hotel, the real estate component is obvious. However, mastering the hotel operating business is the key factor for success in the hotel sector. Operations are more critical to the overall success of hotel properties than properties in any other real estate sector. The other major challenge for hotel owners and operators is their near-total dependence on the economic cycle, which provides ongoing incremental demand for

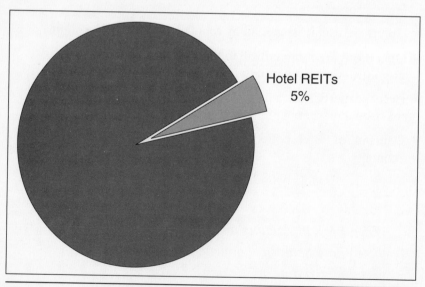

FIGURE 16.1 Hotel REITs as a Percentage of the NAREIT Equity Index as of December 31, 2001

rooms. Management is the one critical element over which a hotel owner has a high level of influence. (The other critical element is the economy, over which the hotel owner has little or no control.) Thus, more than in any other sector of real estate, the opportunity presents itself in the hotel sector for a high level of operational skills to enable an owner to add value in the sector. These excellent operational skills are often translated into hotel brand names such as Marriott or Hilton. Poor management of hotel operations will not only hurt a brand name, but will likely attract well-managed competitors into the local market of the inferior operator. Therefore, management skill and the hotel REIT's ability to capitalize on that management skill are critical in determining what kind of a return profile can be expected from a hotel REIT.

The revenue stream of hotels clearly has the shortest duration of all real estate. Room rates (rents) are literally reset on a daily basis as guests come and go from a property. When demand declines, room rates decline right along with it. When demand increases, room rates rise with it and can be repriced very quickly, literally overnight. Therefore as mentioned, hotel REITs are very highly leveraged to economic growth, which represents final demand for hotel rooms. If demand is increasing in a supply-constrained market, a hotel has the ability to immediately reprice rooms and leverage rental returns. A successful hotel REIT operator will affiliate with hotel brands and management teams that have the ability to manage through economic downturns as well as capitalize on upturns.

There are a wide range of investors in the hotel sector. As a result, there are a wide range of deal structures. Both property companies and hotel companies invest in hotel properties along with hotel REITs and private investors. In a typical private situation, a local real estate investor may build and own a hotel and then contract with a national hotel company for management services. In other cases, the investor and the hotel company might form a joint venture to share in the equity and return on investment. In another common format seen in the 1980s, pioneered by the Marriott Corporation, the hotel company develops the property and then spins off the real estate into a syndication while retaining a management contract. Moving the real estate into a limited partnership is a way of reducing the amount of capital needed to expand or grow a hotel business. The management company in turn creates a predictable earnings stream which makes it more attractive to Wall Street.

Traditional hotel REITs cannot operate the assets they own. Because of the operating company rules, assets must be leased and managed by a separate company. This makes analysis of the hotel REIT sector more difficult, because it often has to be taken in the context of an operating company or several affiliated operating companies. In addition, brands or assets that normally do not have a legal or ownership affiliation with the hotel are also an important factor to consider when analyzing hotel REITs.

Asset Quality

Hotels are not assigned class rankings like apartment and office buildings. Normally, a proxy for quality in the hotel industry is the price range or price segment of rooms that the hotel provides. Hotel room price segments are typically grouped into three broad classifications know as *budget* or *economy, mid-priced,* and *upscale* or *full service.* Economy rooms are the least expensive and full-service hotels tend to have the most expensive rooms. However, local markets play a role in the actual room price. For example, a $150-a-night room in New York City is likely to be in an economy-class hotel. But $150 a night in Des Moines is likely to be a full-service or upscale hotel room.

Hotel asset types are also broken into descriptions of property types. The following are some of the more common property descriptions in the hotel sector.

- *Conference center* or *convention hotels.* Have 500 or more rooms.
- *Full-service hotels.* Offer restaurant and bar facilities, room service, catering, and banquets and may provide meeting space.
- *Limited-service properties.* Do not have food and beverage operations and may or may not offer meeting space.

- *Extended-stay properties.* Resemble apartments; have studio and suite accommodations that are designed for the business traveler who may have a lengthy stay in a given location.

Hotels are also classified by the local market they serve or their location within a local market. This can add another level of description when dealing with hotel properties. The following are some of the local market classifications often applied to hotels:

- *Urban hotels.* Generally located in downtown central business districts.
- *Suburban hotels.* Often located in suburban areas contiguous to large groups of office and industrial buildings.
- *Motor inns.* Usually located at the intersections of major highways to accommodate auto travelers.
- *Airport hotels.* Typically located at or near airport locations for ease of meeting and transportation purposes.
- *Tourist or resort hotels.* Normally provide a full compliment of resort and luxury services at a single location.

Brand affiliation is another way to position or describe hotel properties. Users can easily identify a price point or property type that is normally affiliated with a particular brand. There are numerous national hotel brands that offer access to reservation systems, advertising programs, and management on a national scale. A number of regional brands focus their operations in specific geographic regions. To further confuse the process of hotel description, industry observers may use compound classifications to describe properties. For example, a property may be classified as a budget-priced suburban hotel or a limited-service mid-priced urban hotel. Any compound description might also be associated with a brand. For example, a property might be described as a budget-priced suburban Holiday Inn. This shows how highly segmented the market has become.

Supply and Demand for Hotel Rooms

Estimating aggregate demand for hotel rooms in the United States is relatively straightforward. There are three basic types of travelers who use hotels: the business traveler, the convention or meeting traveler, and the leisure traveler. For each type, demand is largely related to the state of the economy. A robust economic environment leads to more business travel as a result of a higher level of business activity. In addition, higher economic growth leads to more leisure travel, resulting in a greater demand for resort hotel rooms. Higher levels of economic activity also tend to create larger turnouts for business conventions, which also translates into more demand for hotel rooms.

The high correlation between growth of the domestic economy and hotel room demand can be affected by a number of factors. The cost of oil, which drives the underlying cost of most modes of transportation, will generally impact hotel occupancy rates. The value of the dollar will also have an impact on U.S. domestic hotel operations because a higher dollar tends to discourage foreign tourism whereas a lower dollar makes U.S. destinations more affordable to foreign tourists. Bad weather can also create a negative environment for certain hotel operators. The profitability of a particular industry can have an impact on its policy toward employee travel. For example, the dot-com industry was booming in the late 1990s, precipitating a high level of business travel among members of the industry. Since the industry has experienced severe downturn, travel policies have been focused on a reduction in travel expenses and therefore have translated into less business travel by a large sector of the business economy.

The supply of hotel rooms is also impacted by a number of economic factors. In some markets, crowded urban areas with little available land and difficult entitlement processes create a local market that is generally supply constrained. Many resort destinations fall into this category during the tourist season. For example, the Napa Valley wine region of California is generally supply constrained during the wine season. The local market and infrastructure do not lend themselves to new hotel development, and growing grapes is a higher and better economic use of land than hotel development. Thus, room demand generally exceeds supply in Napa at all times except the off-season. Supply-constrained markets tend to be highly profitable in an economic expansion and tend to be more insulated from an economic downturn because of the generally limited supply in the local market.

This set of factors is less true in nonurban areas or locations that are not supply constrained. Hotels in the economy, mid-range, and budget price ranges are simple and easy to build, especially in suburban areas where land and zoning provide few barriers to entry. Hotel construction can begin quickly in response to strong economic demand. This new supply can quickly erode profit margins of all hotels in a good economic environment and can create a supply gut glut in a bad economic environment.

Hotels tend to track their occupancy level in a figure called *RevPar,* which is an acronym for *revenue per available room.* This figure is calculated by taking the average daily room rate and multiplying it by the occupancy level of the hotel level on a given day. These daily revenues are then aggregated to come up with the average RevPar per period. A hotel that operates at 75 percent occupancy is considered to be nearly fully occupied. Few hotels are strong in both weekday and weekend operations and will tend to have more success either during the week with business travelers or on the weekends with leisure travelers. There are often seasonal differences in occupancy as well. As mentioned, resort hotel locations my be overbooked during the tourist season and may be virtually empty during the off-season.

Demand at the local level for a given hotel is often linked to its physical proximity to local attractions or businesses that generate travel. Airport hotels, for example, often provide a convenient location for groups of business travelers to meet. Being next to or part of a convention center can also be a positive factor. In addition, resort hotels depend heavily on their natural or man-made attractions such as golf courses and water parks, and on ease of access.

The operating component is more critical in the hotel business than in any other category of real estate. The benefits of economies of scale have been tested and proven within the hotel industry, and all of the leading hotel companies having a national portfolio tend to perform well in both economic expansions and economic declines. Being national in scope creates buying power, but the real key to economies of scale in hotels is a recognizable and well-respected brand name. Branding gives hotel operators leverage in booking reservations and in attracting and creating relationships with a large number of customers who identify the brand with a particular quality level. These factors provide a real advantage when the hotel company expands its market or brand into other locations. The extension or presence of strong brands in a particular market niche often serves as an effective barrier to entry for potential competitors in a particular market segment.

The hotel business and the airline business share many of the same operating characteristics. Both hotel and airline operators require large capital investments in plant and equipment. In addition, both involve large fixed operating expenses for staff and infrastructure such as reservation call centers. Both airlines and hotels have to fill the seats or rooms on a daily basis in order to remain economically viable. The more complex issue for operators of both hotels and airlines is a concept called *yield management*. This requires finding the right combination of price and occupancy level to maximize profits. Airlines were the pioneers of yield management systems, often charging dozens of different prices for seats of the same type on the same flight. Hotel operators and rental car companies have also adopted this practice. The idea is to selectively adjust the offering price until a particular economic result is achieved. It is better financially to fill a seat or a room with a lower-paying customer than to have that seat or room be vacant. That unused room-night or seat can never be recaptured. Yield management is slowly making its way into the residential real estate sector, with the owners of some apartment REITs beginning to price available units on a yield management basis.

Technical Aspects to Remember

There are a number of technical aspects to examine when looking at a hotel REIT and its relationship to a hotel operating company. The following are the key items that should be reviewed when examining hotel REITs.

- The lessee must have a legitimate business goal in terms of the hotel project.

- The Hotel must be leased to a company that is separate from the REIT.

- Gross revenue leases must be designed to deliver most of the economics to the REIT.

- Leases must be based on percentage or participating rents not net income.

- Hotel REITs collect 15 to 25 percent of room revenues up to a predetermined break point and 60 to 70 percent beyond that point.

- Food and beverage rent may be approximately 5 percent of revenues if the business is operated by lessee, or 95 percent of rent from a subcontractor.

- Break points adjust upward annually by a formula normally based on the Consumer Price Index.

- Leased revenues may represent 30 to 35 percent of hotel revenues, but beyond the break point, the REIT collects rent at twice the level of the typical weighted average margin. This situation creates a high level of operating leverage for hotel REITs.

- Typically a 1 percent change in RevPar may result in a 1.5 to 2 percent change in lease revenues to the REIT.

- Lease leverage disappears when hotel revenues and break points change at the same rate.

- Seasonality amplifies quarterly volatility, as a lease formula is applied to each quarter's annualized rents.

- Hotel REITs may collect excess rent during seasonally strong second and third quarters, but differences are made up during the seasonally slow fourth quarter.

- The affiliated lessee is separate from the REIT but is owned and operated by senior management—in many cases the REIT's founders.

- An independent lessee reduces the potential for conflicts of interest.

- The lessee may pay franchise, licensing, and management fees to the owner of a hotel flag for use of a brand, reservation system, and property management.

- Hotel REITs are responsible for insurance and property taxes.

- Hotel REITs or lessees typically reserve 4 percent of hotel revenues for furniture and equipment replacement, but 6 to 7 percent may be a more appropriate long-term level.

- Very few hotel REITs do any development work.

Performance

On a long-term basis, the performance of hotel REITs has been among the best relative to other REIT asset classes. However, the volatility of earnings or return, when measured by standard deviation, has been very large when compared to the growth rate. Profits in the hotel business are very difficult to maximize because of the need to return capital into the enterprise to refine and upgrade hotel facilities. In addition, high volatility of returns is due to a combination of very high operating leverage and very high financial leverage, which are often present in the hotel sector. The significant fixed cost of hotel operation as well as high leverage make hotel operators very vulnerable to excess supply or a downward shift in demand. Hotel financing is generally a more specialized form of funding, which means fewer lenders are willing to become involved in the sector. Generally, for hotel REITs, this allows for a higher operating margin on invested capital.

Summary Data

Returns on hotel REITs are the most volatile of those for all property REIT sectors. Over the last five years the hotel sector has produced an average annual return of −7.8 percent (see Table 16.1). This is the worst five-year return of any single property sector other than specialty REITs, which include a number of different property types. The volatility of the hotel sector as measured by the standard deviation of returns is 39.3 percent, making it the most volatile of the property REIT sectors. The basic characteristics of the hotel sector make it extremely sensitive to economic

TABLE 16.1 Historical Sector Data for Hotel REITs

	2001	2000	1999	1998	1997
Total return on sector	−11.12%	45.8%	−16.2%	−52.8%	30.1%
Dividend yield	6.97%	14.92%	7.92%	2.18%	6.78%
Estimated NAV	89.0%	107.0%	74.0%	89.0%	146.0%
Market cap of sector ($B)	8.0				
Index weight	5%				
Volatility	39.28%				
Five-year return	−7.79%				

Sources: NAREIT; Uniplan Real Estate Advisors, Inc.

and business conditions. Whether hotel REITs have an up or a down year, the performance tends to be very extreme.

Interview with Rod Petrik

Rod Petrik is vice president of Legg Mason Wood Walker, Inc. He covers hotel and lodging REITs as part of his research universe with the Legg Mason Real Estate Research Group. During his 15 years in the business Petrik has worked on public and private debt and equity markets transactions, workouts, and strategic financial advisory assignments. He earned a B.A. and M.B.A. in finance from Loyola College in Baltimore, Maryland.

Richard Imperiale: In your opinion, what characteristics distinguish hotel real estate as a property group within the real estate world and the REIT world?

Rod Petrik: Well, hotel leases are short-term—daily, in essence—compared to apartments, which theoretically have 1-year leases, shopping centers with 3 to 5 years, and office buildings with about 5 to 10 years. Because you're filling up your property on a daily basis, it's much more management intensive. Hotels also have a number of ancillary businesses, such as restaurants, bars, catering businesses, golf courses, and spas. This makes hotels very unique as both an asset class and in the REIT arena.

The conventional wisdom back at the beginning of this REIT wave in the early 1990s was that you could not put hotels into a REIT format because of the furniture fixtures and equipment, particularly in the upscale properties where you did not meet the real estate test. Then the other thing was that all the ancillary business was bad income coming out, and so the theory was that you could not do hotels. The first hotel REITs were generally limited-service, which had more asset dollars in real estate, but also did not have food and beverage outlets. The way the investment world got around some of the issues was by creating convoluted lease structures where the hotel owner formed an affiliated lessor with no substantial dollars behind it that would then lease the hotels. By doing that, all the bad income was filtered through this affiliated company, which had little capital behind it. The lease payments were scaled to the lease revenues—when hotel revenues went down, your lease payments went down, and when hotel revenues went up, you shared in it. It was a really convoluted structure. When most of these hotel REITs were formed—1993 to 1994—the business was still in a recovery and they were very active on the acquisition side. As it got past the recovery, this sector became one of the more volatile sectors and had the most difficulties. When we go back to around the third quarter of 1996, the relative multiple for the hotel REIT sector was slightly over 100 percent of that of the Equity REIT Index. Since that time, it slid down to 61 percent by the end of 1999.

Imperiale: So the market's valuing hotel REITs differently relative to other REITs?

Petrik: Yes, it's because of the volatility in the earnings stream. In a hotel REIT, you have an operating business where there are multiple entities that can spend your money. You are a passive investor in an active business. First and foremost, was that there is revenue leakage that goes to the lessor. Some of that has been fixed, but not completely. There are some REITs that have bought in all their leases, but some have bought in half of them, so you're actually getting property-level revenue and expenses on half your portfolio and lease revenue for the other half, and there's no performing numbers to track. New investors, find this very complicated.

Also, you have to have full-party management in a REIT. Whether you're dealing with the major operators or an independent, you have to have a separate management company. Then, on top of that, you have the brands, the flags—the Marriotts, the Hiltons, the Sheratons—which can also dictate to you. They can spend your money by telling you that you have mandated capital expenditures in the branded hotels—for example, they might tell you they're changing the colors of their signs, so you've got to put new signs at all your properties. Well, if you have 15 properties times $5,000 for a new sign, it adds up. I think the structure has been improved with the REIT Modernization Act at the end of 2000. I would think the majority of these leases have been brought into taxable REIT subsidiaries, which kind of washes the bad income because if there's taxable income from your restaurant, you're paying it in that entity and then passing the after-tax dollars into the REIT. You still have outside management and you still have the franchises, which is unlike other sectors. If you own a mall, you run the mall. If you own an office building, you run the office building. With hotels, you own the Marriott but Marriott runs it. That makes hotels a very unique class and probably the most volatile class, both as an asset class and in the REIT world. And obviously the events of September 11 have exaggerated that issue.

Imperiale: Which is a natural segue into talking about what drives the supply and demand dynamic within the hotel segment. Do you think it's prone to overbuilding and boom and bust cycles?

Petrik: Yes. Of course, the demand drives the supply in that travel is a growth business. When you look over the past 30 years, demand has been pretty constant at just below 3 percent a year. It doesn't mean that you don't have down periods, and we're certainly experiencing that now. But over the longer term, demand has grown at a constant rate, and I don't think that's going to change. You have the macro demographics working in your favor when it comes to the Baby Boom generation. They are the wealthiest generation America has ever seen. First, they are at or just past their peak earning years, and second, their inheritance is the biggest America has ever seen. The leading edge of the Baby Boom is 55 years of age, and soon they'll have a lot of time on their hands, so their travel will increase, so you have the major demographic in this country entering huge travel years.

On the business side, the concern a couple years ago was that technology would reduce travel because we'd have videoconferencing, e-mail, voice mail, and all that. But what actually happened was that all that technology has allowed people to work more efficiently when they do travel, so it actually allowed business travelers to travel more, not less. Now we're in a fear of flying period. I hope we get over that, because the economy can't pick up without travel. Generally in economic downturns, you see the big slump in travel, and then when you get into recovery, people make up for lost travel.

The other interesting thing is that historically the downturn in travel was a trailing indicator—the gross domestic product would be negative one quarter and within the next three to six months, travel would be down. In 2001, January was a decent month, February moderated, and in the middle of February, business fell off a cliff. It will come as no surprise to anybody in the lodging industry that the economists who actually determine when we're in a recession have now come back and said the recession started March or April of this year. Most of the lodging companies can pinpoint that day. In this information age, the market is much quicker to react on the downside, and I think we're also going to see it on the upside.

Imperiale: Do you think the hotel sector is going to lead the economy in terms of signaling a recovery?

Petrik: Historically, the lodging industry generally starts to recover about midway into the recession, as investors start positioning their portfolios for the recovery.

Imperiale: And they look at lodging as being sensitive to the economic upturn?

Petrik: Exactly. Lodging industry should react relatively favorably in 2003 and 2004.

Getting back to supply and demand, while demand has been constant over the last ten 30-year periods, supply has been erratic. In 1988, we had over 4 percent annual supply growth, which you don't need when demand is at 2.8 percent. That was due to the supply of capital, but the supply of capital spigot has been turned off. Prior to September 11, trying to find capital for hotels was very difficult; today it's next to impossible. So while over extended periods of time supply growth has averaged about 3 percent, it could be 2 percent one year and 5 percent the next. We anticipate supply growth of less than 1.5 percent in 2002, and it could be less than 1 percent in 2003. And the only reason it's going to be over 1 percent in 2002 is the fact that a lot of full-service hotels that are under construction today will be finished then. After that, we're going to see very few starts. This industry generally gets in trouble with supply, and supply will not be a factor over the next two to three years. That's mostly because it takes two to three years to get through an entitlement process for large urban resort hotels, and another two to three years to build them. So a hotel that conceived today doesn't get delivered for four or five years.

Imperiale: If I'm a developer versus a buyer of hotels, what kind of cap rates should I expect?

Petrik: Prior to September 11, they were up 200 to 250 basis points in the last two years. Cap rates can run anywhere from 8 to 13.5 percent. Generally, older properties are at the top end of that range—limited-service will probably trade in the 12 to 13 percent range, full-service maybe 10 to 11, extended-stay maybe 11 to 12. Certain older properties, though—the one-of-a-kind properties and locations—go for 8 caps lower or they don't get sold. There will be very few transactions in those trophy properties.

Imperiale: What are the major thematic trends in play in the industry and going out into the future?

Petrik: I think there will always be more of a bias toward the full-service hotels. They're larger and more institutional in nature, and there's much more of an institutional market-place. Their cycles tend to be longer than for extended stay and limited service. If you want to go to a downtown loca-tion and build a Marriott, it takes four years, whereas if you wanted to go out by the airport and build a Fairfield Inn, it may take a year. Therefore, when things are good in lim-ited service, it is much easier and quicker for supply to come on line. It's a lot easier to get a bank loan on an 80-unit property that costs $50,000 a room to build as opposed to a 500-room hotel at $200,000 a room. It's not that one sector is better or worse than the other, it's just that the cycles tend to be shorter on the limited-service side due to the low cost to build the smaller properties. So supply can have an impact there much quicker than it can on the other side.

Another trend that also stands out is that through all this, one of the best-performing types of hotel REITs has been hospitality property trusts. I wouldn't bring them up as the poster child, because they are externally advised, which is a reason why a number of institutional investors would steer clear of their stock. There are potential conflicts because the external advisors get paid under management, so every time they do a stock or bond offering to increase their assets, they're increasing their pay. Therefore they are encouraged to constantly come to the market. Their leases are long-term triple-net operating leases, which means they take a higher base yield and hand the operating risk to the operator. So they take the 10 percent plus return—it's a base yield, it's guaranteed by the operator—but what they give the operator is 90 percent of the upside. To date, that has looked to be a much better way to play hotels in a REIT structure, because historically REITs have been income vehicles and two-thirds of your return has come from the dividend. I think the triple-net structure may prove to be much more accepted, because if you want hotels to be an income vehicle with any kind of stability in the cash flow stream, then you're going to have to look at that kind of structure.

If you want an operating business, you're not going to have an income vehicle. You'll have more of a growth vehicle and maybe more of a value vehicle today. If you want an income vehicle, you're going to need a much better lease structure. There are some partnerships within private REITs, and they're doing joint ventures using a very similar structure. Next year we'll see lodging REIT prices trading at a discount to net asset value because they do not have currency in their share price. When we're in a recovery, they'll be left on the sidelines if they aren't the targets, because on the private side a number of opportunity funds are being formed either within real estate opportunity funds or as separate lodging opportunity funds. I'm not so sure that the opportunities aren't sitting in some of these REITs for people to come in and throw a bid over the transom.

I believe that the hotel business gets hit in anticipation of recessions because historically hotels relate to lodging stock. Investors have gotten to the point where they anticipate a poor performance on the operating side during a recession, so stocks actually start to decline in anticipation of a recession. When you look back, they're really getting hit in the third quarter of 1998. There were problems in Asia and Russia, the long-term capital debacle, and a crash in the real estate capital markets. In September of 1998, there were comments that we were entering a recession in late 1998 into 1999, and the hotel stocks got hammered at the end of 1998. In 1999 stocks did poorly, and it was punctuated by a lot of tax selling in December of that year. People were still calling for a downturn, but in 2000 we not only didn't have a downturn, we had the most profitable year in the lodging business. Despite that, the valuation stayed at the bottom end of the ranges on an EBITDA [earnings before interest, taxes, depreciation, and amortization] multiple basis, and an earnings multiple basis. We never got premium value, and when we got to the third

quarter of 2000, there was another selloff, again in anticipation of the recession, and then it finally came. Getting
the recession behind us will ultimately be one of the best
things for this industry because I believe that investors
have been waiting for the recession for a two- to two-and-
a-half-year period, and they never were going to move off
of the low end of their valuation ranges unless there was an
economic recovery. And generally what that means is that,
while historically hotel companies trade at 9 to 12 times
EBITDA, they'll stay down at that low end of the range
until they're out of the trough.

Imperiale: As a REIT investor, what performance benchmarks
should I be using when I'm measuring hotel REIT performance?

Petrik: I mean, you can look at the FFO [funds from opera-
tions], or, more important, you can look at an adjusted
FFO number. The problem is there's no consistency in the
way analysts report adjusted FFO numbers. Do you just
take out cap X, do you take out amortization—how do you
adjust it? So what happens with a company is you'll get a
group of analysts that may be within a penny or two on
FFO estimates, but their FAD [funds available for distri-
bution] numbers might be 10, 12, or 15 cents off. But looking at adjusted numbers is important because cap X is
significant and you should be applying at least 5 percent
and maybe even 6 percent of revenue as cap X. The industry studies show that that's not constant—that you might
have 0 percent one year and 12 percent the next—but on
the average it's 6 percent, and when you're in a recession,
it's generally when you're closer to the zero—when you're
only putting cap X dollars that really need to be spent.
Then you spend the dollars in a recovery.

Imperiale: So if somebody's spending less than that on cap X
over a longer period, that's a warning sign for investors?

Petrik: Absolutely.

Imperiale: Is there anything else we should cover?

Petrik: Well, the other metric people are going to look at for
REITs is dividend. Most of the hotel REITs have suspended

their dividend in the fourth quarter, so dividend payments of 2002 will be dramatically reduced. Until they bring dividend back up to prior levels, they won't get back to prior pricing, which probably means it will take until 2003 to get back to where we were. And then I think over that course of time, the lodging sector of the REIT industry is going to have to find ways to produce a more stable cash flow stream. There are certain risks we haven't had to confront yet, but I think that there will be continued improvements in the structure over the course of the next 12 to 18 months when it comes to that dividend stream. Without that, the investing public discounts the dividend for the inherent risk. Now hopefully, when we talk about nonrecurring events, September 11 is the biggest nonrecurring event we've seen. This industry was heading for the bottom and the events of September 11 got us there a lot quicker and a lot deeper than anyone imagined. Now we're digging out from that hole, and we're looking for flat to negative growth in the first half. I think we'll have negative growth in the first half, possibly flat performance into the third quarter, and positive growth beginning late in the third quarter and into the fourth quarter of 2002.

Imperiale: So the recovery's still a ways out for the sector?

Petrik: Right.

CHAPTER 17

Health Care REITs

Chapter Summary

- Health care real estate investment trusts (REITs) represent approximately 5 percent of the National Association of Real Estate Investment Trusts (NAREIT) Equity Index.

- Health care REITs are typically an overlooked sector of the REIT universe.

- Health care makes up 13 percent of the U.S. gross domestic product.

- Health care REITs operate in a complex regulatory environment.

- The aging U.S. population should drive continued growth in the health care sector.

- Health care REITs offer the chance to participate in the growth of health care services with less risk.

- One-half of all health care REIT investments are in nursing homes.

- One-half of health care REIT investments are in medical office buildings, hospitals, and clinics.

A hospital's reputation is determined by the number of eminent men who die there.

—George Bernard Shaw

Health care properties are generally not as familiar to the investing public as the properties that other real estate investment trusts (REITs) might invest in. In addition, many of the health care providers that operate these properties are not really well known and the regulatory environment in which they operate is often very complex. These factors can make health care REITs seem more difficult to analyze than other property sectors. There are several common misconceptions about the health care REIT segment. First is the popular belief that health care REITs lack value-adding ability because they do not actively manage their properties. This idea is not based on fact. In addition, health care REITs often add value largely through the careful selection and negotiation of their ultimate investment in a health care property. The sector has experienced a fair amount of growth over the last decade and its returns in general have been better than those for many other sectors of the REIT industry. The health care REIT sector represents about 5 percent of the National Association of Real Estate Trusts (NAREIT) Equity Index (see Figure 17.1) and has a market capitalization of approximately $7 billion. The sector's capitalization grew steadily through the 1990s at an average annual rate of approximately 15 percent and then declined through 1998 to 2000 as changes in Medicare and Medicaid reimbursement and highly fragmented ownership in the health care industry caused some dislocations of capital.

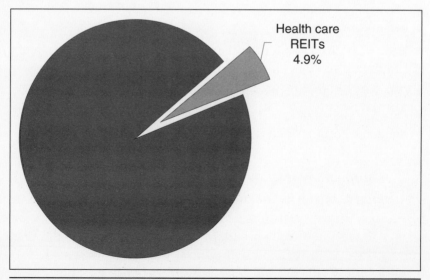

FIGURE 17.1 Health Care REITs as a Percentage of the NAREIT Equity Index as of December 31, 2001

Real estate investment trusts represent an opportunity for investors to participate in the growth of the health care or services industry but remain one level removed from the operational and regulatory risks that face front-line health care providers. Health care, as a percentage of gross domestic product, is about 13 percent of the U.S. domestic economy, and health care services account for about two-thirds of that 13 percent. Investor interest in the health care industry in general has increased over the last decade because of a number of factors. First, reform of the government health care system has provided an opportunity for many fragmented sectors of the health care industry to consolidate. Second, growth in the health care industry is expected due to demographics. The aging of the U.S. population also creates a level of investment interest in the sector.

Real estate investment trusts are impacted by government policy and government regulations regarding the payment process and other market dynamics, but the share prices of health care REITs generally experience less volatility than the shares of publicly traded health care providers, largely because of the recurring earning streams and the long-term structure of leases and mortgages from REITs to health care providers. The trade-off for investment in health care REITs versus in the health care industry directly is a lower total return.

The Economics of Health Care

Health care REITs generate profits by providing capital to the health care services industry. Generally this capital is gathered by the REIT at a lower cost and provided to the health care industry at a higher cost. The nature of health care REITs would be termed *spread investing,* and it is possible because health care real estate trades at yields from 50 to 500 basis points over the cost of capital for a well-run REIT. In turn, a REIT that carefully structures each transaction with a health care provider to create increasing future cash flows can also increase its total rate of return above the initial spread. In this way a health care REIT may add value in its capital structure. While health care REIT providers can often find capital sources such as banks and finance companies, these REITs provide a stable source of long-term real estate capital for the health care industry. Their superior understanding of the industry and the economics of health care properties allow REITs to provide better capital resources than other financial competitors in the health care sector.

Demographics for the aging population in the United States have been instrumental in creating demand for additional health care properties. Approximately half of all health care REIT investments are directed toward the nursing home property sector. The high percentage of investment in this property type has resulted from the supply and demand characteristics of the nursing home industry. Many health care REITs started as spin-offs of property portfolios from nursing home operators. The other half of health care REIT investment dollars have flowed to a wide range of properties in the health care sector, including assisted living, which provides long-term care for the elderly and is the fastest-growing segment of the health care infrastructure industry. The health care REITs have also financed acute care hospitals, psychiatric and substance abuse hospitals, rehabilitation hospitals, freestanding medical and surgical hospital facilities, medical office buildings, and physicians' clinics.

The financing possibilities in the health care sector for REIT operators generally take one of two structures. First is the sale/leaseback structure, which is put in place as a long-term renewable triple-net lease in which the tenant pays property taxes, insurance, maintenance, and upkeep on the building. The second structure is the long-term mortgage loan to the direct health care provider. Under either form of financing, the health care facility operator benefits by being able to reinvest capital into the growth of its operations rather than tying up capital in its physical plant and facilities or buildings. There are positives and negatives that go along with each financing structure. Under the sale/leaseback approach, the operator wishing to improve the financial statement by lowering leverage can remove depreciation charges from the income statement and leverage from the balance sheet, resulting in higher net income and lower leverage. Conversely, under the mortgage loan scenario, an owner/operator wishing to defer taxes on a low-basis investment can generate capital from that asset by mortgaging it. Therefore the incremental capital from the mortgage becomes available to finance continuing operations of the health care REIT. Mortgages may also be preferred in states where operators might incur limitations on medical reimbursement for lease payments under the state's Medicaid plan structure. Economic terms tend to be structured in a similar manner for underlying leases and mortgage loans. The lease or loan typically has a 10- to 15-year term with one or more renewal options of 5 or more years. Payments escalate in future periods in accordance with a number of different formula computations. A percentage of the operator's revenue at the facility may be payable under a lease or mortgage finance arrangement. There may also be fixed percentage increases in either the interest rate or the lease payment. Finally, there may be some kind of indexing to the Consumer Price Index (CPI) or another measure of inflation. Escalation clauses in many deals have what are termed *transition points*. Once the total cost structure reaches a transition point, there are limits on future escalations. In any case, growth of cash flow is built in from the owner/operator to the capital provider for the real estate services.

In addition to sale/leaseback structure or long-term mortgage structure, some health care REITs offer development financing options. These options often come in the form of equity extended to the health care provider through the REIT, which allows the health care provider to complete a capital project. The project is then subject to a long-term sale/leaseback agreement upon completion. A number of REITs provide small amounts of accommodation financing as well, which allows health care operators to leverage some personal property and even accounts receivable in some instances as a package with their real estate financing arrangements.

An important distinction between health care REITs and REITs that invest in other property sectors is that, for a given investment, health care REITs receive rent or lease payments from a single operator and not a number of tenants using a single property. Health care REITs are therefore a step removed from operational risk at the property but also very much exposed to the credit quality of the property operator, which allows them to hedge or lower their exposure to single-property-level operational issues that health care operators have to deal with. For example, an owner/operator of nursing homes may have a large portfolio of several hundred facilities. While the occupancy of any particular nursing home may drop, causing the health care operator to have financial difficulty at the unit level, the health care

REIT that has financed that facility will not suffer a drop in revenue because the operator is required to pay through on the overall portfolio that is financed. The REIT's fixed base rent or lease revenue cushions the impact on total revenue, which is only affected by percentage rents that may be precipitated at a property-level basis, but the base rents or lease revenues generally are not subject to these property-level adjustments. Therefore the real risk for the REIT is in a default by the operator because of poor results across the whole portfolio.

Health Care Service Industry Economics and Demographics

As mentioned, health care makes up about 13 percent of the nation's gross domestic product. The health care services industry accounts for about two-thirds of that total. From a demographic point of view, there are two segments of the population that are growing faster than the population in total (see Figure 17.2). First, the over-85 segment is the fastest-growing segment of the overall population. Its growth rate is currently running at about 4 percent, whereas that for the overall population is running at a little over 1 percent. In addition, over the next 15 years, it's expected that the 65- to 85-year-old segment of the population—

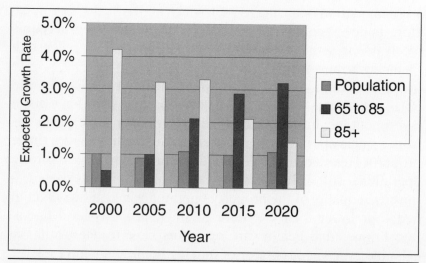

FIGURE 17.2 Growth of Population versus Expected Growth of Seniors

essentially the front end of the Baby Boomers—will begin to grow at a very rapid rate. The growth rate for this segment will rise from approximately 1 percent in 2000 to 4 percent by 2015. Therefore, many of the services required by an aging population will need to be provided through health care services.

The primary feature of the current health care service industry is a high level of uncertainty regarding future growth and operational issues. This uncertainty is due to high fragmentation within the industry and very high levels of competition among providers, which have resulted in low margins for health care service providers. In addition, cost control efforts by managed care companies and state and federal providers have helped keep margins in the health care area very slim. Increasing competition from new forms of health care delivery, such as assisted living facilities or out-patient medical/surgical centers, also raises issues about which modes of health care delivery are most likely to succeed and therefore about which type of capital investment in plant and equipment will ultimately be rewarded from an economic point of view and which will become obsolete and therefore essentially of little or no value. These issues have resulted in a lower-quality financial profile for many operators in the health care services industry. This is of concern to the health care REIT community because managing credit exposure is the primary objective of the health care REIT.

In light of the current uncertainty, it is only fair to point out that the industry does have a number of positive characteristics from an investment point of view. Consolidation, which is going on at a furious rate, is creating financially stronger and larger participants. Demand for health care services is generally inelastic, and therefore on the margin when people need health care services, price is not going to stop the demand for services. Also, a major portion of industry revenues come from government programs, primarily Medicare and Medicaid. These are essentially low-risk programs from a credit point of view because they tend to pay the bills to the health care providers. Because Medicare and Medicaid have an ever increasing number of complex rules and requirements for program providers to meet, the number of health care providers that operate under those programs is declining, leaving larger operators with more scale and capability to administer large, complex programs. These providers tend to have higher credit profiles than smaller, more fragmented providers. Finally, the continued growth in the older segments of the population will require higher amounts of health care services and therefore a larger number of physical facilities to service this growing number of older adults.

Medicare and Medicaid Economics

Two federally mandated programs provide approximately half of the revenues of the health care services industry. Medicare, which is federally funded, provides for health care other than long-term care for all Americans over age 65. Medicaid, which is jointly funded by federal and state programs, provides health care for the poor and also provides long-term skilled nursing home care for those who cannot afford it. Although officially designated for the poor, Medicaid winds up paying the majority of all bills for the nation's nursing home care and continues to provide an increasing level of support for the nation's population in nursing homes. Because of increasing scrutiny of costs by the federal and state governments and managed care companies, the delivery of health care services has been shifting from higher-cost settings to lower-cost settings. Treatment for less complex conditions has been moving from hospitals to outpatient clinics or skilled nursing facilities. Even complex treatments such as heart surgery and related cardiac care are now even being delivered in lower-cost specialty care facilities such as heart clinics and outpatient surgical centers. In addition, custodial care for the elderly has been moving from nursing homes to assisted living environments. Where feasible, care has been even shifting into the home setting of the person being cared for. Health care consumers often prefer these new settings because they are easier to use than traditional settings and they also have a greater focus on better outcomes for the patients. The competition in the health care services industry will be won by the lowest-cost provider of the highest-quality services. Health care REITs are aware of this and have invested in industry segments that tend to be low-cost providers. In many ways, health care REITs are providing capital to service providers who are creating alternative, lower-cost channels to provide health care in nontraditional forms.

REIT Underwriting and Investment Criteria

For health care REITs, the credit quality of the health care provider is a major factor in the underwriting decision. In addition, the quality of the underlying real estate becomes secondary when analyzing a health care real estate transaction. Well-located and functional properties can be of value even if their operating performance is substandard. For example, if an existing operator fails, a high-quality property can often be transferred to a new operator or a serviceable property can be readapted for other uses. Any poorly located or structurally inadequate property will always create problems for the real estate owner. Health care REITs look to property level cash flow coverage of a lease or debt payment as a principal ratio in determining the credit quality of the property and the operator. The target ratio depends on several factors such as the credit quality of the operator, any credit enhancements that may be a part of the financing package, and the property location; however, the coverage ratio for a typical pool of nursing homes is usually a 1.5 to 1.9 multiple of the total rent, based on cash flow, before deducting the operator's management fees.

Because the credit characteristics of most health care providers are subject to the difficult operating environment discussed earlier, health care REITs have developed a number of property-level strategies either in the sale/leaseback or mortgage area to help protect their investment portfolios. It is not unusual for health care REITs to bundle leases or mortgages of a single tenant into a unified portfolio and to preclude the tenant from "cherry-picking" the best leases or mortgages upon renewal or expiration. This structure forces the tenant to renew all of the leases or none of them, making it a single decision on the part of the health care operator. Real estate investment trusts also typically cross default lease arrangements. For noninvestment credits, REITs often require a cash deposit or letter of credit to cover three to six months of lease or mortgage payments. In addition, REITs typically retain the authority to approve any changes in tenant or borrower, including those occurring due to mergers, acquisitions, or spin-offs. These credit protections have helped health care REITs manage credit losses and reduce the negative impact of leases rolling over or mortgage maturities in a given health care portfolio. In addition, they often provide opportunities for the health care REIT to revisit terms and conditions of a deal with a health care operator that may be involved in a merger or acquisition and become affiliated with a higher-quality credit provider.

Increasing Competition Among Health Care Capital Providers

Historically, health care REITs have succeeded in part because of their ability to offer niche financing to health care operators that may have been overlooked by other capital providers. Currently, health care REITs face increasing competition from various non-REIT capital sources. Finance companies, mortgage companies, commercial banks, insurance investment portfolios, pension funds, and opportunity funds sponsored by investment banking firms have all become active in the health care property financing sector. These non-REIT investors and lenders are seeking to finance attractive elements of the health care industry at higher cost-of-capital spreads than are available in other, more traditional real estate sectors. The uncertainty of legislation concerning the health care reform that has lingered around the industry seems to be subsiding. In addition, the continued consolidation among existing health care providers is in the end creating more creditworthy health care operating companies. Over the last five years there have been initial public offerings by 25 assisted living or nursing home providers that continue to add legitimacy to the industry segment and also create larger and better-financed pools of capital for these operators. When you combine these factors with improvements and profitability in many of the health care provider segments, the continued availability of capital from more traditional sources should increase rather than decrease in the future.

Although REITs have always had competition from other capital suppliers in the health care segment, such as commercial banks and investment banking companies, there are new sources of competitors that could possibly make things more difficult for health care REITs in the future. One new competitor is existing REITs that are diversifying into the area of financing health care assets. These REITs hope to increase their growth rate and total return on capital by moving into what appears to be the higher-margin area of health care specialty financing. In addition, health care operators who are spinning off their real estate assets are also becoming competitors in the health care real estate financing arena. These operators create an operating affiliate that owns and manages the health care properties and normally attempt to expand their business by owning, operating, and financing health care properties of other nonaffiliated health care operators. These two new sources of competition for traditional health care REITs will probably pose more problems than the more mainstream commercial banks and investment companies, which tend to operate under far more limited capital allocation criteria. The fact that there are additional competitors for mainstream health care REITs indicates that the margin on capital may continue to decline in the future.

Health care REITs offer a type of financing not typically available from other capital sources. Health care REIT financing is generally long-term in nature, with initial terms of 10 to 15 years that extend through renewal options for another 10 to 20 years. Health care REITs offer a range of deal structures, beginning with conventional mortgage loans and sale/leasebacks and extending to hybrid financial structures such as participating mortgages and direct finance leases. Health care REITs also provide a high ratio of leverage, which is normally not available through more conventional real estate lenders. Sale/leasebacks are usually for 95 to 100 percent of asset value and thus require very little equity on the part of the real estate operator. Mortgages are generally higher than typical loan-to-value requirements for commercial banks, and it is not unusual to see leverage of 90 to 95 percent on conventional mortgages. Historically, health care REITs have developed functional working relationships with key industry participants, and they generally understand the health care provider's business model and weaknesses better than other financial institutions that may compete for the investment. This leaves health care REITs with a continuing competitive advantage over more traditional financial sources, which is not easily overcome by existing outside financial providers.

Physical Property Characteristics

Health care REITs finance a wide variety of health care property types. Each property type constitutes a separate group within the health care services industry, and although some common analytical themes carry between the segments, each segment requires its own analysis in order to evaluate the credit implications from a REIT investment standpoint. The following is a review of the major property categories in which health care REITs are involved.

Long-Term Care Nursing Homes

Nursing homes, usually referred to as *skilled nursing facilities* by the industry, represent about half of the total investment of REITs in health care properties. Long-term care facilities have been a very stable property sector, making them attractive to health care property investors. The nursing home industry provides long-term ongoing care to elderly persons who require frequent medical supervision and attention. The industry consists of about 2.1 million skilled nursing beds in facilities that average about 120 beds apiece. Skilled nursing homes compete with hospitals for long-term treatment of patients and with assisted living facilities for the care of residents who may not require medical supervision but rather assistance in conducting day-to-day living activities. The average daily cost of skilled nursing care runs roughly at $118 per day, making skilled nursing homes far less costly than acute care hospitals but more expensive than assisted living facilities. It should be noted that in response to changes in reimbursement policies, many large acute care hospitals with excess capacity have restructured some of their existing space into subacute treatment centers. At these hospitals, subacute treatment can be competitive in terms of price with average nursing home costs. In general terms, nursing home operators favor sicker patients over patients that you would typically find in assisted living, because sicker patients essentially generate higher revenue streams through additional services such as physical therapy and pharmacy services.

Although the nursing home industry has gone through a tremendous consolidation over the last 10 years, half of all nursing homes are still run by single-facility operators. The other half of the industry is run by multiple-facility operators. The four largest public operators own and control approximately 15 percent of the total industry beds. The remaining public operators comprise roughly another 20 percent of available industry beds.

Medicaid reimbursements account for over half of the revenues of the skilled nursing home industry. This high level of government funding has had mixed results for the industry. On the one hand, profit margins in the industry are very small, averaging 3 percent after taxes. Because state governments pay approximately half of the Medicaid reimbursements, they attempt to set their cost and reimbursement levels as low as possible while still providing a marginal return on capital for nursing home operators. Reasonably efficient operators, however, have largely been assured of long-term survival due to the cost-based reimbursement structure found at the state level. Thus larger nursing home operators with higher scales of economy are able to survive better on the average cost-based reimbursement system that exists in most state-funded programs. Although the nursing home industry has historically attempted to fight low reimbursements through various lobbying and legislative efforts, it has lost out to the cost containment methodologies that continue to proliferate in the health care reimbursement area. The supply and demand situation in the nursing home industry has been the attraction for the involvement of health care REITs. On the supply side, the number of nursing home beds has historically grown at about a rate of about 2.5 percent per year. This slow growth rate reflects the attempts by state and local governments to slow the reimbursement costs of their Medicaid programs by restricting the development and construction of new nursing homes. This process, which is known as the Certificate of Need process, is often required by states before they will allow developers to create incremental supply in nursing home beds. Thus, many states have effectively limited new supplies of beds at levels that support very high average occupancy rates in existing facilities. On the demand side, the rapid increase in the population over 85 years of age and the soon-to-be increasing level of 65- to 85-year-olds should continue to support the demand side for nursing home beds for the next 5 to 15 years. As a result, the national average occupancy among nursing homes has remained in the mid- to high 80 percent range, depending upon the time period.

Long-Term Care Assisted Living Facilities

Assisted living facilities make up about one-third of the investment of health care REITs in the health care property segment. This has grown from a level of less than 5 percent just seven years ago. The development of the assisted living industry continues to be a growth-oriented area for health care REITs seeking new venues for the placement of capital. The industry, it should be noted, is still in a growth phase and is less mature and less regulated than the skilled nursing home segment, but offers a higher growth rate than the traditional skilled nursing care industry.

Assisted living projects cater to older persons who want to retain their independence but who also need assistance with one or more activities of daily living (ADLs). These ADLs may take the form of bathing, dressing, or assistance in mobility. Typical residents in assisted care facilities are about 83 years of age and ambulatory but are frail and often require a high level of assistance with daily tasks. These residents tend to have stays of about three years before they either move into a skilled nursing care environment or require hospitalization that may result in not returning to the facility. Residents in assisted living facilities live in a homelike apartment environment but are assisted with daily activities by staff members. Meals are served in a communal dining room, and transportation for other activities is often provided by the facility's operator. The industry consists of approximately 500,000 beds in 4,800 facilities across the country, although it is difficult to get exact numbers because the industry is largely unregulated and the definition of assisted living spans other nontraditional elderly residential structures. The typical assisted living facility has 70 living units with shared common areas such as dining and activity areas. Costs average between

$70 and $80 per day, making assisted living generally less costly than nursing homes and competitive with home health care for patients who require more than three visits per week.

The assisted living industry has grown very rapidly because there are very low barriers to entry. A typical facility may cost $4 million to $7 million to construct and equip. Employees are not required to have any certifications or high levels of health care skill, and therefore are easily found. Minimal regulations exist because revenues come primarily from private pay situations rather than Medicaid reimbursements. The assisted living industry remains highly fragmented, with the top four operators controlling less than 5 percent of the total industry beds. Including nursing home operators that also run assisted living facilities, the total market capture of all the public companies is approximately 16 percent of beds.

Continued consolidation among assisted living operators will create and achieve economies of scale and consistency of delivery in addition to some level of brand identity among operators. In many ways, because the industry is largely unregulated, operators are focusing on the consumer, who will ultimately be making decisions about assisted living care. The net outcome is likely to be an industry that looks to some degree like the hotel industry where scale and brand are well established.

It is expected that government involvement in assisted living will continue to increase. State governments seeking to reduce Medicaid costs are starting to view assisted living as an attractive, lower-cost alternative to nursing home care. Care provided at assisted living facilities typically costs two-thirds of the total cost of nursing home care, and, assuming that even just 10 percent of current nursing home patients could be eventually moved into assisted living facilities, the savings could be several billion dollars a year. It is not unusual to find that Medicaid has provided waivers that permit states to use long-term Medicaid funds outside of nursing homes and specifically for assisted living. The transition from private pay to government pay is already under way in the assisted living facilities sector, and over time a higher percentage of revenues will probably flow to this sector from state and federal programs. The assisted living industry has been very active in lobbying state and federal governments for receipt of these funds. The growing level of state and federal funding will provide a primary growth vehicle for the industry. If the 10 percent of nursing home patients eventually migrate into the assisted living environment, it will increase the industry's current size by about 40 percent and provide an ongoing level of industry growth in the future.

Retirement Care Communities

Retirement care communities, also known as *continuing care communities,* account for approximately 10 percent of health care REIT investments and health care properties. This area deserves some analysis because it has a different operating imperative than the assisted living or skilled nursing sectors. When reviewing the spectrum of senior housing alternatives, retirement communities lie in the middle. At the beginning of the spectrum is senior housing, where adults rent units in an age-restricted community but receive few or no additional services. Retirement communities provide basic services such as meals, transportation, and housekeeping, but otherwise allow residents to conduct their lives in a fairly independent manor. Therefore they provide fewer services than assisted living but more than age-restricted or adult communities. The retirement care industry consists of approximately 5,500 communities across the country, many of which were built in the 1980s as a result of anticipated market demand. This demand was expected from a demographic segment that would have suggested a rapid growth in the over-65 population in the late 1980s and mid-1990s. Market demand was largely overestimated during that period because residents were typically much older than originally anticipated. The overbuilding of retirement communities resulted from the expectation of demand from people in the 65-to-75 age group, when the reality was the average age of the retirement community resident was 82 years or older.

Retirement communities have found that they are subject to a certain softness in demand in the spectrum of housing available to senior citizens. Many elderly persons do not consider a retirement community as a desirable residential situation. Most seniors who might live in a retirement community could also live independently in their home. Thus, many older people are reluctant to leave their homes and only do so when there is no alternative in terms of their required assistance in daily activities. This tends to move seniors further down the spectrum into either assisted living or skilled nursing care, and they largely avoid retirement communities all together. Those seniors who do move to retirement facilities often do so as a lifestyle choice and find the atmosphere from a social and economic perspective more beneficial than maintaining their own separate residence. Because retirement community care is more elastic than the demand for long-term care, it is difficult to quantify the acceptable investment return levels. Therefore, selective investments in retirement care communities may provide acceptable returns but REITs have been reluctant overall to invest in this sector.

Many retirement care communities have transformed themselves into *congregate care retirement communities*. These communities combine retirement care, assisted living, and nursing facilities all in one building or in a single campus setting. The goal is to provide an environment in which the elderly can remain in place throughout their senior years. There are an estimated 2,200 congregate care retirement communities nationwide. The economic risk of these communities often requires that they be run more like an insurance vehicle rather than a real estate vehicle. Congregate care retirement communities provide for a large prepayment or endowment in exchange for a guarantee of continuing care for the balance of a resident's life. As a result, these communities generally appeal to elderly persons of higher financial means who plan to stay for the remainder of their lives. The more stable private pay nature of these communities can make them unattractive investment opportunity for health care real estate investors.

Acute Care Hospitals

Acute care hospitals make up about 10 percent of the investment of health care REITs. In recent years, health care REITs have generally focused on lower-cost providers rather than acute care hospitals. This is primarily because Medicare, Medicaid and managed care companies have targeted acute care hospitals as part of their cost cutting.

Acute care hospitals provide medical and surgical care for the population as a whole. The acute care hospital industry consists of about 5,300 hospitals with about 875,000 beds nationwide. One-third of all health care service spending takes place in acute care hospital facilities. The costs of acute hospital care are high, averaging about $1,200 per day, making the acute care industry one of the primary targets for cost cutting. There has been a trend among acute care hospitals for shorter stays and lower occupancy levels. As a result, revenues from inpatient services have been largely flat or only consistent with CPI for the last five years. In contrast, outpatient revenues have been growing at a rate of 10 to 12 percent per year as hospitals have responded to the requirements to provide more cost-efficient services and therefore have moved many procedures to outpatient status. The acute care hospital industry is somewhat fragmented, but not as fragmented as other health care sectors. Publicly held acute care hospitals account for about 14 percent of all hospital beds, with the top 10 acute care hospital systems accounting for about 15 percent of all hospital beds. Although publicly traded for-profit hospital companies account for a large percentage of hospital beds, the majority of the industry consists of nonprofit hospitals affiliated with religious and secular organizations. Consolidation is ongoing among for-profit and not-for-profit hospitals because of the large cost savings normally generated by economies of scale in the hospital industry.

Because of the economic trends impacting acute care hospitals, health care REITs have not been actively investing in this sector. Because of their high cost structure, hospitals remain very much the target of competitors attempting to provide less costly delivery systems. Even in such areas as surgery and critical care, other providers are now available to provide less costly and more focused businesses such as outpatient surgery or specialty care hospitals. These facts tend to leave health care REITs largely uninterested in investing in acute care hospitals.

Rehabilitation Hospitals

Rehabilitation hospitals make up approximately 8 percent of health care REIT investments. These investments originated in the 1980s, when rehabilitation hospitals were viewed as a lower-cost alternative to acute care hospitals. During the 1990s, however, rehabilitation hospitals have come under some level of scrutiny.

Rehabilitation hospitals provide treatment aimed at correcting physical and cognitive disabilities often due to work or sports injuries or accidents. The industry consists of approximately 200 facilities with about 18,000 beds. Rehabilitation hospitals compete with outpatient treatment centers and inpatient rehabilitation centers located at acute care hospitals. Rehabilitation hospitals are generally subject to Medicare cost reimbursement systems, in contrast to Medicare's perspective payment system, which is a fixed-fee system applicable to acute care hospitals. Managed care plans have been exerting pressure on rehabilitation hospitals to keep costs down by contracting for large, continuous blocks of service for certain procedures. Unlike other areas of the health care services business, which are highly fragmented, the rehabilitation health care service sector has several dominant players. It is unlikely that REITs will make any new investments in the rehabilitation hospital area, given that the high-cost segment is subject to many of the same managed care pressures as the acute hospital sector.

Psychiatric Care Hospitals

Psychiatric care hospitals make up about 3 percent of the assets of health care REITs. Psychiatric hospitals provide inpatient treatment for behavioral disorders, drug addiction, and alcohol abuse. The industry consists of about 340 facilities with 34,000 beds. Facilities compete with outpatient treatment programs and with acute care hospital segments dedicated to the same services. The fallout from the industry's excess capacity has decreased the number of operators; four operators now account for about 60 percent of the total beds. Occupancies are low and operators continue to report pricing pressures from managed care plans.

Medical Office Buildings/Physicians' Clinics

Medical office buildings make up on average about 9 percent of the assets of health care REITs. Medical office buildings are properties that contain physicians' offices and diagnostic service providers. These buildings come in two varieties. Some are located at or near acute care hospitals and are leased entirely to the hospital, which in turn releases space to individual physicians, often at a low cost, as an incentive for physicians to locate their practices within the building. In these cases, the medical office buildings are really a part of the hospital's health care delivery system. As a result, investment in this type of medical office building is completely dependent on the credit strength of the hospital operator. In the other situation, medical office buildings are leased directly to medical practitioners and small group practices on a multitenant basis. These medical office buildings may be located near a hospital or may be independently located within a community. In either case, these buildings carry a somewhat higher level of risk from an investment standpoint due to the lower credit quality of the independent physician tenant. In addition, these types of buildings experience greater leasing turnover and probably have a higher level of reccurring capital expenditures. In addition, managed care is driving many small physician groups to lower margins or even to affiliation with larger managed care providers, therefore making the credit quality of medical office buildings populated by individual physician tenants to be a declining proposition at best.

Physicians' clinics are facilities leased to a single physician's practice, rather than to several solo group practices. These practices may be longstanding local or regional business enterprises, or they may be newer affiliates of national physician practice management companies. The tenant credit quality is generally better than that of unaffiliated group practices.

Ancillary hospital facilities, typically adjacent to a hospital, are medical office buildings that contain not only physicians' offices but also space for additional services such as outpatient surgery, medical labs, or rehabilitation. These facilities may also house hospital administrative departments or hospital pharmacies and are typically leased to hospital operators but may be leased to a third-party investor that in turn subleases space to the hospital and the physicians. The investment quality depends on the credit strength of the tenant or subtenants and on the long-term stability of the adjacent hospital. There are an increasing number of ancillary hospital facilities in remote locations from hospitals. These facilities are designed to provide a spectrum of medical services in a different market while drawing on the brand recognition or regional dominance of the hospital system. These are most typically leased to investor managers who in turn sublease the space to the hospital.

Because these medical office buildings and ancillary hospital facilities are such an integral part of the hospital health care delivery system, REITs are likely to continue to increase their exposure selectively to this segment. While medical office buildings in general carry a higher level of risk than other health care properties, the total return on a medical office building tends to be somewhat higher than that for other health care real estate segments.

Expected Returns for Health Care REITs

Unlike other REITs, which actively manage property, REITs in the health care area create a structural rate of return at the time of their initial investment in a specific health care property. The management of a health care REIT has little ability to create any more internal growth than is initially structured into the deal. In the past, the most common arrangement for payment escalation was a percentage of operating revenue above a base level, which typically resulted in internal growth rates of 3 to 6 percent. Percentage of revenue escalations frequently include a cap such that, after a certain transition point, the health care REIT will participate at a lower level in rental growth—usually 1 to 2 percent. More recent deals have been structured with fixed percentage increases of 2 to 3 percent that are constant throughout the life of the financing. This is driven by competition among REITs and also by the desire of health care REITs to obtain more predictable cash flows. Across the health care real estate spectrum, it is expected that unleveraged internal growth should run in the 2 to 3 percent range for health care REITs. As a result, health care REITs are looking more and more to external projects to help stimulate growth.

External Growth

In view of the slower pace of internal growth, health care REITs, are looking more toward external growth projects to provide added value for their shareholders. Several key management factors determine a health care REITs ability to create high risk-adjusted returns through external growth projects. Management's knowledge of the health care segment is very important to sustaining external growth at a reasonable risk level. Another factor is management's ability to access low-cost capital from the capital markets. In addition, management's ability to manage the risk exposure level of a given new project is also important when evaluating health care REIT operators. The final factor is management's ability to evaluate the credit quality of a health care service provider when reviewing the external growth prospects of a health care REIT.

The fragmented nature of health care real estate ownership and operation suggests that health care REITs will have ample opportunities for future investment in a consolidating health care industry. In addition, external growth in the health care REITs' traditional niche—long-term care—is becoming more difficult as health care REITs grow larger and outside competition for these financings grows more intense. This has fueled a trend in which health care REITs will increasingly turn to more diverse opportunities such as medical office buildings or specialty care facilities involved in faster-growing segments of the health care arena in order to create added value for shareholders through higher external growth rates. It should be noted that these alternatives tend to carry a higher level of risk, both financial and market risk and may be more management intensive when taken in total.

Summary Data

Like hotel REITs, health care REITs tend to have big up and down price movements. Unlike the hotel sector, however, the health care sector has managed to deliver modestly good incremental returns. Over the past five years, returns on health care REITs have averaged 7.2 percent (see Table 17.1). The volatility

TABLE 17.1 Historical Sector Data for Health Care REITs

	2001	2000	1999	1998	1997
Total return on sector	56.50%	25.8%	−24.8%	−17.5%	15.8%
Dividend yield	6.97%	15.87%	7.14%	6.20%	8.20%
Estimated NAV	99.0%	91.0%	72.0%	108.0%	132.0%
Market cap of sector ($B)	7.8				
Index weight	4.9%				
Volatility	33.19%				
Five-year return	7.19%				

Source: NAREIT; Uniplan Real Estate Advisors, Inc.

of the sector as measured by the standard deviation of returns is 33.2 percent, making it the second most volatile of the property REIT sectors behind hotels. The political outlook for the health care delivery system and the demographics of the local population drive the performance of this sector.

CHAPTER

18

Self-Storage REITs

Chapter Summary

- The total value of all self-storage facilities in the United States is estimated to be $6 billion.
- Real estate investment trusts (REITs) own an estimated 12 percent of all self-storage units.
- Self-storage REITs represent 4 percent of the National Association of Real Estate Investment Trusts (NAREIT) Equity Index.
- Demand for self-storage is driven by a more mobile population living in smaller dwellings.
- Location and ease of access are the features that local self-storage consumers deem most important.
- Returns for self-storage REITs are stable and higher than those for many other REIT sectors.

Only in America would people rent a place to store boxes packed full of stuff they can't remember.

—Yakov Smirnov, 1998

Self-storage real estate investment trusts (REITs) represent about 4 percent of the capitalization of the National Association of Real Estate Investment Trusts (NAREIT) Equity Index (see Figure 18.1). There are four publicly traded REITs in the self-storage sector, with an aggregate market capitalization in excess of $6 billion. According to the self-storage industry association, there are 58,000 self-storage locations across the country, totaling 8.5 million self-storage units.

The real estate segment known as self-storage is very much like the manufactured housing community segment. By first appearance, self-storage seems to be far less interesting and less dynamic than other segments of the real estate market. However, once economic occupancy is achieved, the self-storage center becomes a very stable and consistent money-making opportunity. The origins of the self-storage industry in the United States can be traced back to the late 1950s, when a number of self-storage facilities were built in the Southwest. These facilities were targeted at military personnel who were required to relocate frequently. Since then, the demand for self-storage space has been driven by the general nature of the American consumer to accumulate large quantities of material goods. In addition, the increased mobility of the American population, along with higher numbers of apartment and condominium residential units, has created a need for easily accessible storage of consumer items.

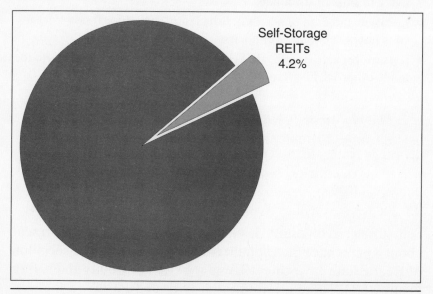

FIGURE 18.1 Self-Storage REITs as a Percentage of the NAREIT Equity Index as of December 31, 2001

Self-storage operations are generally located at high-visibility intersections and along high-traffic corridors in major urban areas. In the early era of the self-storage industry, these complexes were designed to help create a revenue stream from vacant land. The intention was to populate a vacant parcel of real estate with self-storage units that created a rental income stream. The idea was to create revenue for a certain period of time and then to develop the real estate into a higher and better use. Interestingly, the landowners found that, over a long period of time, the return on capital invested in self-storage was often very competitive with the returns of other real estate investment activities. This not only led to a proliferation of new self-storage properties, but also to the conversion of older multilevel buildings, which were often obsolete, into self-storage facilities.

The practical market area for a self-storage property is usually a radius of 5 to 7 miles around the existing site. Because of the limited market nature of the self-storage property, it is important that a high level of care be taken when selecting the self-storage site. Self-storage operators attempt to locate their properties on high-visibility roads with access to small business as well as high-density residential areas. This allows the self-storage operator to target the two primary users of the facility. Residential customers typically comprise two-thirds to three-quarters of unit users, and one-quarter to one-third of unit users tend to be small business customers.

In general, self-storage units appear to be large, continuous units of garagelike structures with separate overhead garage door access for each tenant. Self-storage customers rent fully enclosed storage units for their personal use. These units generally range in size from 5×5 feet up to 20×20 feet, with varying sizes in between. Most self-storage facilities are fully enclosed by fencing and have on-site management. Access is provided 24 hours a day, seven days a week through digitally controlled security gates that allow renters to enter and exit using a security code system. Access to individual units is controlled by the unit renter through the use of padlocks or combination locks provided by the renter.

The renters of self-storage units indicate that the primary consideration when looking for self-storage locations is a location that is nearby the self-storage user. The security provided at the property tends to be the second most important factor, followed by the ease of accessibility and availability of the suitable rental space. Rental rates in most markets are not among the top five factors listed by self-storage users. This relatively low sensitivity to rental rates often translates into a high per-square-foot rental revenue when compared with other property types.

The self-storage business is a highly fragmented industry with many different quality levels and many different types of owner/operators. The vast majority of self-storage operations are owned and operated by individuals. It is estimated that REITs own approximately 12 percent of all self-storage units. Other estimates suggest that as much as 48 percent of units are owned and operated by individuals. The remaining 40 percent are owned and operated by small businesses, limited partnerships, and real estate operating companies. Institutional investors other that REITs own less than 2 percent of all self-storage units.

Because of the low barriers to entry into the self-storage business, along with the modest capital requirements to begin a self-storage operation, competition within this segment of the real estate industry is quite high. The image of the industry has kept most traditional institutional real estate investors from participating at a significant level. The low barriers to entry have kept the industry relatively fragmented.

Trends in the Self-Storage Industry

During the last five years, the self-storage industry has moved toward building climate-controlled units in various markets. Climate-controlled spaces offer tenants the option of leasing storage space within which the storage operator will guarantee a constant temperature and humidity. This lends itself to the storage of items of higher value. The demand for climate-controlled space started in the Southeastern United States, where demand has been the highest, and has spread throughout the country. Currently climate-controlled space represents about 3 percent of the self-storage space available but is growing much faster than regular self-storage space.

The self-storage industry has struggled with many of the same issues as the manufactured housing industry. The primary concern is the creditability of self-storage as a long-term real estate option. As the self-storage industry has spread, the general consumer market has become more familiar with the industry. In some places, familiarity has led to a higher level of consumer acceptance than in others. Again, the Southwestern United States, the region where self-storage in the United States began, is also the region with the highest level of self-storage awareness among consumers.

Newer self-storage facilities emphasize esthetics and construction designs that attempt to blend with the nature of the neighborhood which they serve. Landscaping has also become a prime consideration in the development of new self-storage facilities. In addition, the development of self-storage has been tailored to work in conjunction with planned office, industrial, and retail parks, combining office space or industrial space with storage as a part of the overall design concept.

Summary Data

The nature of the self-storage sector makes it behave like a blend of industrial and residential real estate. The physical nature of the buildings is much like that for industrial real estate. The lease structure—typically an annual term—is similar to that of the residential sector. Over the last five years the self-storage REIT sector has produced an average annual return of 7.9 percent (see Table 18.1). The volatility of the sector as measured by

TABLE 18.1   Historical Sector Data for Self-Storage REITs

	2001	2000	1999	1998	1997
Total return on sector	44.80%	14.7%	−8.0%	−7.2%	3.4%
Dividend yield	6.97%	8.19%	5.96%	3.66%	4.66%
Estimated NAV	128.0%	78.0%	79.0%	108.0%	128.0%
Market cap of sector ($B)	6.7				
Index weight	4.2%				
Volatility	21.78%				
Five-year return	7.94%				

Source: NAREIT.

the standard deviation of returns was 21 percent, making it a stable sector with returns that exceed those for industrial real estate. The demand for self-storage and the performance of the sector will rise and fall primarily with general economic growth.

Interview with C. Ray Wilson

Charles Ray Wilson, MAI, CRE, has specialized in the appraisal and consultation of self-storage facilities worldwide for over 25 years. His company, Charles R Wilson & Associates, Inc., has appraised more than $3.5 billion worth of self-storage properties in the past five years. Wilson has been published in *Appraisal Journal, The Mini Storage Messenger, Inside Self Storage,* the Commercial Mortgage Insight newsletter, and the Korpacz Investor Survey. In 1992, he founded Self Storage Data Services, Inc. (SSDS), a research company with a database of over 30,000 facilities that includes the annual operating statistics on more than 2,000 facilities nationwide. It is the only private database of its kind in the United States. With the Self Storage Association, Wilson jointly publishes the *SSA/SSDS Market Analysis Report.*

Richard Imperiale: Tell us a little about the history of self-storage and how it developed as a real estate class.

C. Ray Wilson: Self-storage is still developing as a real estate class. It started in the late 1960s early 1970s, but word spread quickly about its profitability and soon it started to appear in virtually every city in America. Only a handful of astute large developers capitalized on the idea and started building portfolios. For the most part, self-storage was predominantly an investment of individuals, until the REITs came along in the early 1990s.

Imperiale: What features distinguish self-storage as a property group within the real estate world and within the REIT world more particularly?

Wilson: Self-storage is one of the newest of all property types, and there is the least amount of published information about it. One of the major features that distinguish self-storage from other property types is that it appeals to the need to save things, be it personal or business property. It's very similar to an apartment house as far as investments go, without the headache of tenants living on the premises. Eviction is much easier and operating expenses and construction costs are historically much lower.

Imperiale: In your opinion, what drives the supply and demand dynamic within the self-storage segment?

Wilson: The supply is driven by availability, cost of construction financing, and ease of the entitlement process. Barriers to entry into self-storage are changing because lenders are tightening lending practices and cities are making the entitlement process more difficult. In most major cities, the entitlement process is now taking 18 to 24 months. As the supply increases, the absorption period will lengthen and fewer investors will have the staying power to take a project from groundbreaking to stabilization—which can take more than five years.

Historically, projects filled up rapidly and become profitable quickly. Good management was not a concern because tenants just needed the space. The facilities rented themselves. Now that the markets are becoming more competitive, absorption can take longer and marketing the space is becoming more difficult and requires a more professional approach. Supply and demand has usually been measured in terms of the number of square feet per capita, typically within a three-mile radius or about a 15-minute driving time. It should be measured in terms of the number of square feet per household and per business establishment. The maximum number of square feet a single market can successfully absorb is still unknown. Some markets are overbuilt at 2 square feet, while others can handle upward of 10 square feet per capita. Additional research needs to be conducted before we know conclusively what the true demand perimeters are.

A large segment of the demand comes of disruption in people's lives—a death in the family, a divorce, the downsizing of family or business, the loss of a job, a job transfer. The types of things that happen during a down economy can be good for self-storage, and unfortunately, that includes war.

Imperiale: How important are branding and local market domination for a self-storage operator?

Wilson: Branding has not been proven in the self-storage industry. All else being equal, independent operators are able to maintain occupancies and rental rates as well as the REITs or large operators. Brand or market domination doesn't replace good management. With continued increase in total supply, professional on-site and off-site management is becoming more important.

Imperiale: Why are traditional institutional direct real estate owners not very involved in the self-storage sector?

Wilson: The total lack of current and reliable operating statistics prevents many would-be investors from being able to properly assess the risk of self-storage. There are no published stats on self-storage like there are for other property types. Self-storage is considered too small and is overlooked as an investment for this reason and this reason alone.

Imperiale: What types of cap rates are available for direct investors and for developers in self-storage?

Wilson: Until recently, overall capitalization rates for self-storage had not changed much over the years. Generally, investment-grade self-storage cap rates have historically been around 10 percent. Recently, trailing cap rates on portfolio acquisitions have dropped to the low 9 percent range. On forward-looking bases, investors are still looking for something closer to 10 percent. For the thousands of mom-and-pop facilities across the country, cap rates reach upward of 11 percent or more. This is due to the lack of barriers within those markets.

Specialty, Diversified, and Mortgage REITs

Chapter Summary

- Specialty, diversified, and mortgage real estate investment trusts (REITs) make up the balance of the National Association of Real Estate Investment Trusts (NAREIT) Index.

- Specialty REITs are engaged in various real estate–related activities but are more highly focused than other REITs.

- The specialty REIT sector has had operating problems in the past.

- Specialty REITs represent 3 percent of the NAREIT Equity Index.

- Golf course and timber REITs are the largest and fastest-growing groups within the specialty category.

- Returns for the specialty REIT sector have been more volatile than those for other REIT sectors.

- Diversified REITs own a portfolio of varied properties with a specific geographic focus.

- Diversified REITs are often smaller market capitalization REITs.

- Mortgage REITs have developed into vehicles that finance specific niche areas in the real estate industry.

- Mortgage REITs must manage credit risk and interest rate risk.

- Mortgage REITs have the most volatile returns of all REITs.

*The big house on the hill surrounded by mud huts has
lost its awesome charm.*

—Wendell Wilkie, 1940

Other than the types of real estate investment trusts (REITs)
already discussed, there are several other sectors contained
within the National Association of Real Estate Investment
Trusts (NAREIT) Index. These other REITs, which make up in
total 3 percent of the NAREIT Index, fall into three other categories: specialty REITs, diversified REITs, and mortgage
REITs.

Specialty REITs

Specialty REITs represent approximately 3 percent of the
NAREIT Equity Index (see Figure 19.1). The specialty REIT sector comprises eight publicly traded REITs. Specialty REITs are

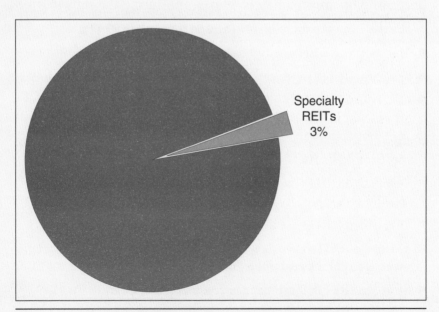

FIGURE 19.1 Specialty REITs as a Percentage of the NAREIT
Equity Index as of December 31, 2001

engaged in various activities, all of which are real estate–related but more highly focused than other REIT categories. For example, the ownership of timber-producing properties is represented in the specialty sector of the index. The ownership and operation of movie theaters, golf courses, prisons, gas stations, and automobile dealerships, and the rental of rooftops for the use in wireless communications, are other specialty REIT sectors.

The specialty REIT sector has had operating problems. Because these REITs are considered out of the mainstream and are very focused in their operational objectives, specialty REITs are often considered supplemental to more mainstream real estate opportunities.

Among the specialty REITs with the highest expectation are the golf course REITs. There are currently three publicly traded golf course REITs. The golf course industry has a number of characteristics that make it appealing to the specialty REIT segment: For instance, it shows positive demographic and growth trends. Between 1982 and 1995, the number of golfers increased from 16 million to 32 million, a 100 percent increase. The number of rounds of golf played in the United States increased by approximately 40 percent during the same period. Despite the tremendous growth in the number of golfers and the rounds of golf played, the number of golf courses only grew by approximately 10 percent. Since the mid 1990s, the situation has reversed itself. New golf courses continue to be developed while the number of golfers has remained relatively flat. The supply and demand equation has reached a state of equilibrium, and it is expected that demographic trends such as the retirement of Baby Boomers will continue to drive the demand for golf.

Table 19.1 provides historical data for specialty REITs.

Diversified REITs

Diversified REITs are REITs that own a portfolio of diversified property types. These REITs, which make up 8.6 percent of the NAREIT Index (see Figure 19.2), normally focus on a specific geographic region and own a diversified portfolio of properties within that geographic region. The idea behind the diversified

TABLE 19.1 Historical Sector Data for Specialty REITs

	2001	2000	1999	1998	1997
Total return on sector	12.40%	−31.6%	−25.7%	−24.3%	27.3%
Dividend yield	6.97%	3.14%	6.65%	4.38%	6.79%
Estimated NAV	79.0%	68.0%	71.0%	96.0%	129.0%
Market cap of sector ($B)	4.8				
Index weight	3.0%				
Volatility	26.46%				
Five-year return	−11.26%				

Sources: NAREIT; Uniplan Real Estate Advisors, Inc.

REIT is to focus on a specific property market from a geographic point of view and know and understand the dynamics of all the real estate activity within that market. This will lead the operator of a diversified REIT portfolio within a specific geographic market to gain a market knowledge advantage over

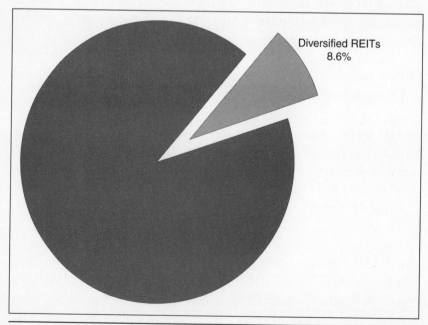

FIGURE 19.2 Diversified REITs as a Percentage of the NAREIT Equity Index as of December 31, 2001

other REITs or other real estate investors that may not be as focused on the region.

There are just a few larger diversified REITs, and their size and scale within a particular geographic focus makes them of interest. Smaller diversified REITs are typically too small to create any significant interest on Wall Street. They are likely to be merger candidates; however, because they maintain diversified portfolios, REITs that focus on specific property sectors may not be interested in acquiring them. The trend among diversified REITs is actually to focus more specifically on a particular property sector within a geographic region and recycle portfolio capital out of those noncore property types into the core property holdings. For example, a REIT that owns community shopping centers and apartment buildings within a specific geographic region may make the decision to sell its apartment holdings and recycle that capital into community shopping centers in order to more narrowly focus the investment activities of the REIT. Historically, many REITs began as portfolios of a single property category focused within a geographic region. These single-property-category REITs were eventually absorbed into larger REITs with the same single-property focus in other geographic regions. The result of this has been the creation of the super-regional and nationally focused REITs.

Table 19.2 provides historical data for diversified REITs.

TABLE 19.2 Historical Sector Data for Diversified REITs

	2001	2000	1999	1998	1997
Total return on sector	0.82%	24.1%	−14.4%	−22.1%	21.7%
Dividend yield	6.97%	8.89%	9.30%	3.92%	8.52%
Estimated NAV	99.0%	92.0%	84.0%	112.0%	131.0%
Market cap of sector ($B)	13.7				
Index weight	8.6%				
Volatility	20.78%				
Five-year return	0.30%				

Source: NAREIT.

Mortgage REITs

Mortgage REITs represent 3 percent of the NAREIT Index (see Figure 19.3). During the late 1960s and early 1970s, mortgage REITs dominated the REIT industry. Essentially, mortgage REITs stood in place of commercial banks as the primary lending source for real estate developers. Many mortgage REITs were in fact affiliated with bank holding companies. The joke within the industry at the time was that if you couldn't get construction financing by going through the front door of the bank, you could go in through the side door and talk to the bank's REIT about that same construction financing, and normally you'd get it. As mentioned in Chapter 2, the mortgage REIT era came to a bad ending in the recession of 1973 and 1974 when higher interest rates and the inability of developers to obtain permanent financing created widespread defaults in the mortgage REIT industry.

The mortgage REITs of today are vastly different from those of the 1960s and 1970s. It could be argued that there may be more efficient mortgage investment vehicles than REITs. However, mortgage REITs have developed into vehicles that finance

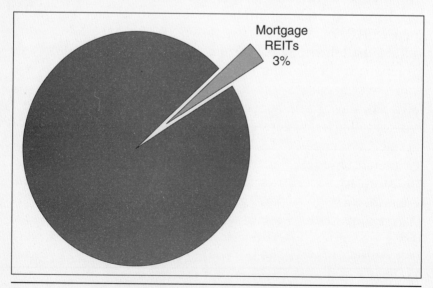

Mortgage
REITs
3%

FIGURE 19.3 Mortgage REITs as a Percentage of the NAREIT Index as of December 31, 2001

specific niche areas. Mortgage REITs may originate mortgage loans on income-producing commercial real estate, create syndications or pools of mortgages on commercial properties, or originate and package for resale mortgages on single-family residential homes. In general, mortgage REITs tend to specialize in what are known as *non-conforming loans*. These are mortgage loans on residential or commercial properties that do not meet the criteria to be packaged into pools of mortgage-backed securities that are then sold in the mortgage-backed securities markets. Nonconforming loans are typically held in the loan portfolios of the lenders that originate them with no opportunity to package and resell the mortgage. As a result, many mainstream lenders will not make nonconforming mortgage loans.

The focus of current mortgage REITs is far more conservative than that of the mortgage REITs of the early REIT era. The principal concern of mortgage REITs is typically with the quality of the borrower and the value of the underlying real estate, which the mortgage will collateralize. Real estate investment trusts that originate and create mortgage loans establish underwriting guidelines and criteria that define the risk level of the mortgages they undertake. The acceptable credit standard of the borrower and the value of the collateral varies widely between mortgage REITs. Some attempt to manage the risk in a mortgage portfolio by requiring government or private insurance on the underlying mortgage. Government mortgage insurance programs originated during the depression as part of the federal government's effort to stimulate the domestic economy. This mortgage insurance was made available through a federal agency called the Federal Housing Administration (FHA). Since the depression, the FHA has had a positive affect on the mortgage industry by helping to create an active, standardized market for mortgage securities and instruments. This has allowed lending institutions to package and sell their mortgages into the capital markets, thereby recycling capital and making more money available for real estate investment activities. Private mortgage insurance is also available through a large number of private mortgage insurance companies. Private mortgage insurers tend to offer products that are available to different segments of the mortgage marketplace. Private mortgage insurance is often preferred over government mortgage insurance because the terms and conditions required under private mortgage insurance are often more flexible than those of government mortgage insurance programs. Lower down payments and higher debt-to-equity ratios often make private mortgage the only alternative under some mortgage scenarios.

Some mortgage REITs accomplish risk management through the packaging and sale of their secured mortgages into the commercial mortgage–backed securities marketplace. In most instances, the REIT will package the mortgages and, in conjunction with the services of a debt rating agency such as Standard & Poor's or Moody's, will obtain an investment-grade debt rating on the pool of mortgages. This rating then allows the pool of mortgages to be easily sold into the commercial mortgage loan market.

In order to facilitate liquidity in the mortgage markets, there are several quasi-governmental agencies that are buyers of mortgage portfolios. The Federal National Mortgage Association (FNMA), often referred to as Fannie Mae, the Government National Mortgage Association (GNMA), often referred to as Ginny Mae, and the Federal Home Loan Mortgage Association (FHLMA), commonly called Freddie Mac, as well as private insurance companies, pension plans, and mutual fund portfolios are all potential buyers of securitized mortgage pools. The secondary market for mortgage portfolios is very large. Savings and loans, commercial bankers, mortgage bankers, and credit unions all participate to some extent in the commercial mortgage–backed markets. Secondary markets have developed not only for single-family mortgages, but for multifamily commercial properties as well. Fannie Mae and Freddie Mac have programs that guarantee mortgages on multifamily properties and commercial properties as part of their overall portfolio strategy.

The credit and collateral risk associated with specific mortgage loans is known as specific risks. In addition, there is market risk associated with mortgage loan investments. Market risk is principally interest rate risk in mortgage loan portfolios. Mortgage loan values move in the opposite direction of interest rates. Thus, as interest rates move higher in the market, mortgage loan portfolio values decline, and conversely, when interest rates decline in the marketplace, mortgage portfolio loan values increase. Thus, when analyzing mortgage REITs, the interest rate environment must be considered carefully.

Some mortgage REITs specialize in adjustable-rate mortgages (ARMs). An ARM is a mortgage that has an interest rate that is periodically adjusted according to a predetermined index. The interest rate is based on an index that typically reflects the cost of funds to the REIT. That index is then marked up or a spread is added in order to reflect a profit margin for the underlying mortgage REIT. Indexes for ARMs may be the London Interbank Origination Rate (LIBOR), which is the prime rate charged by commercial banks; the government bond yield; or any number of mortgage indexes that are published on a regular basis. Usually the only factor related to the index is that it must be broad enough to be out of the control of the lender and must be readily verifiable by both the borrower and the lender. The index is used to set the base rate on the loan and then an additional margin that represents the lender's profit is added to the index rate. The index rate may be adjusted monthly, quarterly, semiannually, or annually. Features known as *caps* and *collars* may be applied to the ARM loan. Caps limit the amount of interest rate increases over a specific period of time and collars limit the level of decreases in interest rates over a specified period of time. Caps and collars provide some level of certainty for the borrower and the lender with regard to the minimum and maximum interest rates that can be charged on the underlying mortgage loan. Through the use of ARMs with caps and collars, a mortgage portfolio can be protected to some degree from interest rate fluctuations.

Because of the highly sophisticated nature of the commercial mortgage–backed securities marketplace, it is possible for lenders to obtain interest rate protection on their portfolios through the use of derivative financial instruments and/or interest rate swaps. This is often referred to as *interest rate insurance* and may be affixed on a mortgage portfolio for a given period of time with a given level of protection for a predetermined price to be paid to the institution that will guarantee the insurance protection. Although a complete analysis of the mortgage-backed securities marketplace and derivative interest rate protection is beyond the scope of this book, an excellent discussion can be found in *Handbook of Financial Engineering* by Clifford W. Smith Jr. and Charles W. Smithson (Harper, 1990).

Another form of mortgage loan that attempts to mitigate the market risk of increasing interest rates is known as a *participating mortgage*. In this type of mortgage, the lender will participate in the increased value of the property over the term of the mortgage and may also participate in the increasing cash flow of the property over the mortgage period as well. The idea is that in an environment of rising interest rates, typically property values and cash flows are rising as a result of inflation. This rising property value and cash flow are captured as a part of the mortgage participation, thus mitigating the long-term effect of rising interest rates on the mortgage holder. As mentioned in Chapter 8, participating mortgages are one form of partnership and joint venture remedies that can help to facilitate the real estate investment process.

Participating mortgage loans were fairly common in the inflationary era of the 1970s and 1980s. In addition, during the same period, higher levels of leverage were used in real estate transactions. Participating mortgages allowed the lender to offer lower-than-market interest rates in order to facilitate mortgage lending and higher leverage levels on properties. The lower rates allowed borrowers to acquire properties profitably at higher leverage levels and provided lenders with certain protection against rising interest rates. In the lower interest rate environment of the 1990s, participating mortgages are less typical.

In addition to rising interest rates, investors and mortgage portfolios must also be aware of the risk in a decreasing interest rate environment. Decreasing interest rates tend to create a significant level of refinancing activity in the mortgage marketplace, resulting in higher-yielding mortgage instruments being refinanced at lower interest rates to capture the current declining interest rate environment. This results in the return of mortgage proceeds to the lender, which must then reinvest those proceeds in a lower interest rate environment.

To deal with the prepayment situation in the mortgage marketplace, collateralized mortgage obligations were created. These instruments divide a pool of mortgages into various tranches.

TABLE 19.3 Historical Sector Data for Mortgage REITs

	2001	2000	1999	1998	1997
Total return on sector	63.42%	16.0%	−33.7%	−29.3%	−3.1%
Dividend yield	16.62%	12.63%	7.10%	4.78%	6.96%
Estimated NAV	121.0%	92.0%	84.0%	98.0%	141.0%
Market cap of sector ($B)	4.8				
Index weight	3.0%				
Volatility	39.53%				
Five-year return	−2.96%				

Sources: NAREIT; Uniplan Real Estate Advisors, Inc.

The tranches receive the return of principal from prepayment activity at different time intervals based on which tranch is owned. Thus, holders of tranch 1 will receive prepayment principal as first priority, then prepayment principal flows to tranch 2, and so on. This division of mortgage pools into tranches provides the mortgage investor with a higher degree of certainty as to the final maturity range of their mortgage investment.

Major commercial mortgage lenders have devised an alternative method of dealing with the declining interest rate environment. Many large commercial mortgages are created on a nonprepayable basis. Thus, in the commercial mortgage marketplace, a lender may impose restrictions or prepayment penalties on a commercial mortgage in order to realize a certain fixed return on the mortgage over a given period of time.

Table 19.3 provides historical data for mortgage REITs.

Interview with Tony Edwards

It is widely believed that the taxable REIT subsidiary (TRS) will fuel the growth of specialty REITs. The ability to engage in a related business has many people within and outside the REIT industry studying the structure. Farm REITs have been the most commonly discussed possibility, but any real estate–intensive business operation could possibly benefit from the new structure. The following interview with Tony Edwards of NAREIT is designed to provide a more detailed understanding of the TRS.

As senior vice president and general counsel for NAREIT, Tony Edwards is involved in NAREIT's policy and political initiatives. NAREIT provides numerous programs, publications, and services including a voice and representation before national and state policymakers. Edwards has a B.A. from Lehigh University and a law degree from the University of Miami.

Richard Imperiale: Can you tell us the legislative background on TRSs and how they fit with current REIT practices?

Tony Edwards: Sure. It's important to view what happened to taxable subsidiary legislation as part of the overall evolutionary process. And you have to go back to the early days of the REITs to really appreciate it. When REITs were first authorized by Congress in 1960, they were viewed as a very passive vehicle—a way people could invest in real estate, but investing not really in companies but in real estate portfolios. So the REITs back then would own properties, but they had to hire outside independent contractors to operate the properties. Through the mid-1980s, there were a number of issues that came up when the REITs as landlords tried to provide normal services to their tenants and they couldn't do it through their own employees. Congress realized that this vehicle that was intended to let ordinary investors invest in real estate was instead penalizing those investors by not allowing the companies to do what landlords normally do. So in 1986, Congress changed the laws to let REITs provide normal, customary services that landlords provide to their tenants.

Imperiale: So it put the REITs on an equal footing with private property operators?

Edwards: In a lot of ways. What happened also was that REITs started to get some expertise in things like landscaping for their own buildings, and they got the opportunity to provide those types of real estate–related services for the owners of similar properties. In 1988, they came up with a structure that was actually the predecessor to TRSs in a lot of ways. The REITs wanted to set up taxable subsidiaries to provide services to third parties—everything from landscaping to buying and selling property on a regular basis. REITs could sell property on a regular basis, but all the income gained would be confiscated by payment of 100 percent excise tax. They wanted to shift this to a subsidiary and pay only their normal 35 percent tax. So they went to the IRS, and the IRS approved the idea, but the rules back then stipulated that REITs couldn't own more than 10 percent of the voting shares of a non-REIT company.

So the IRS approved a structure in which the REIT would invest in a company and own less than 10 percent of the common stock, but would have 95 percent or so of the economics of that company by owning nonvoting preferred stock. The common stock typically was owned by officers of the REIT, major shareholders of the REIT, or other friendly parties, and as long as the parties remained friendly, everything worked out fine. That structure was called either the third-party subsidiary or the preferred stock subsidiary.

Now shift into the modern era of REITs. By the 1990s, it wasn't just space, but all types of services, that tenants wanted. For example, tenants in class A apartments would expect everything from someone walking their pet to picking up their dry cleaning to providing a personal trainer. All this was beyond what is normal and customary. People were expecting these new types of services that a REIT couldn't provide, and REITs couldn't use a preferred stock or third-party subsidiary to do it, because these subsidiaries were only for providing services to a third party, not to their own tenants. Then in the late 1990s, the IRS got concerned that the REITs and the subsidiaries were arranging things so the subsidiaries weren't paying their fair share of taxes.

Imperiale: So they would structure things to gain the economic benefit, but because any profits of the subsidiary would be taxable, they tried to zero out the profits to avoid taxes?

Edwards: Precisely. And that started a dialogue between the industry, Congress, and the administration that eventually led to creation of TRSs.

Imperiale: How does this new structure improve the REIT as a business enterprise?

Edwards: Well, it allows REITs to provide the types of services that will benefit the tenant and to go into other areas that might be considered very tangential to real estate opportunities. For instance, in recent years some REITs have put money into technology companies and have written it off. The same thing can happen here too, but now the REITs get criticized, so the transparencies that work in the public marketplace make sure that if a REIT ventures too far from being just a regular real estate company, it's going to have to explain itself very closely if it doesn't succeed.

Imperiale: Are there any limitations on TRSs with regard to hotels?

Edwards: Yes, because hotels have always been a separate analysis area in the tax code. Whereas operating an office building, a shopping center, or an apartment building is considered an integral part of owning the real estate and collecting rent, operating hotels has always been viewed as operating a non–real estate business. The rental period is really just a day at a time, and you have a very high amount of personal property and services. So hotels are viewed as a business, not as part of the real estate rental business. TRSs have helped hotels by allowing hotel REITs to have the TRS as a lessee. Before that, hotel REITs would have to set up partnerships and lease to them. Sometimes the partnership would operate the hotels, but more likely they would subcontract with a management company. The profit that was embedded in the leases between the REIT and the partnership was considered "leakage" by the analysts, because that profit really belonged to the REIT shareholders but, because of the requirement in the tax code that there had to be a lease, it was taken away from the shareholders and given to the owners of the partnership. Since the partnership owners were typically officers or major shareholders of the REIT, there was conflict of interest.

Now you don't need an outside partnership anymore. The REIT that owns the real estate leases with its own subsidiary, which is usually 100 percent owned, but on the condition that the hotel TRS cannot operate the hotel business, so they have to have an independent contractor.

Imperiale: So for hotels, the TRS can eliminate the leakage of the economic cost of that relationship for compliance purposes?

Edwards: Yes.

Imperiale: That probably solved the issue of whether or not to be a hotel REIT.

Edwards: Yes, it did. Still, if you want to be an operating company, you can't be a REIT, but if you want to stay on the real estate side, then you can do it and it simplifies the structure. You can consolidate the subsidiary for capitalization purposes and keep the real estate lease element for the benefit of the REIT shareholders. Then you just pay the independent contractor and keep anything that's left, using that profit base.

Imperiale: How did the TRS structure shake out for the health care REIT industry?

Edwards: Health care has always been very triple-net. It's very passive. When NAREIT asked whether or not health care REITs wanted to be able to operate the nursing homes using the hotel lease structure, they said no, because they are very comfortable being very passive, traditional real estate. They were concerned that if TRSs were allowed to operate health care properties, some high flyers would come in and ruin the reputation they had worked so hard to gain.

Imperiale: Does the TRS structure open up any new opportunities for specialty REITs that wouldn't have been possible under the old structures?

Edwards: Not really. Typically, when a REIT owns 10 percent or more of another entity, and then that entity rents something from the REIT, that's not considered good rent under the REIT tax rules. Health care REITs got an exception to that, but other structures that might want to use this could very easily build up a lot of bad income and not be able to keep the REIT.

Imperiale: As an investor, what's the best way to assess the REIT's use of the TRS structure?

Edwards: The best thing is performance. Look at what the management has said they're going to do and then measure their performance. Read management's discussion of their vision and see if it agrees with the investor's expectations.

Imperiale: Let's say I'm a large apartment REIT owner and I decide I'm going to provide some high-level services to my tenants through my TRS. Is the REIT going to benefit in terms of increasing its multiple valuation by having TRSs valued identically to public market comparables of independent corporations?

Edwards: When you're talking about service to tenants, as opposed to third-party services, all the REITs I know of view it as purely a way of satisfying tenant demand. Most times the profit is secondary and the important thing is remaining competitive. You want to provide services that are satisfying, either to meet tenant demand or to create it. The focus is on using tenant services to maximize the rental stream. For third-party services, the situation is a little different. It's not about tenant demand, it's about business opportunity.

Imperiale: If a REIT is engaged in building development, would you agree with the argument that spreading the cost of development by engaging in merchant building through a TRS enhances shareholder value?

Edwards: It depends on the business plan. You have to look at cost of capital and the alternative revenues—how that cost of capital could alternatively correlate. If you're in an environment where you could build and get cap rates far in excess of anything you could do from buying, then it makes sense, although it comes with risk because if demand evaporates, you're left holding the bag. It all goes to cost of capital and how to maximize shareholder value.

Appendix

Company Name	Ticker Symbol	Address	Phone Number	Web Site
Residential REITs				
AMLI Residential Properties	AML	125 S. Wacker Dr., #3100 Chicago, IL 60606-4501	(312) 443-1477	www.amlires.com
Apartment Investment/ Management	AIV	2000 S. Colorado Blvd., #2-1000 Denver, CO 80222-4358	(303) 757-8101	www.aimco.com
Archstone-Smith Trust	ASN	7670 S. Chester St., #100 Englewood, CO 80112	(303) 708-5959	www.archstonecommunities.com
Associated Estates	AEC	5025 Swetland Ct. Richmond Heights, OH 44143-1467	(216) 261-5000	www.aecrealty.com
Avalonbay Communities	AVB	2900 Eisenhower Ave., #300 Alexandria, VA 22314	(703) 329-6300	www.avalonbay.com
BNP Residential Properties	BNP	3850 One First Union Center Charlotte, NC 28202-6032	(704) 944-0100	www.bnproperties.com
BRE Properties	BRE	1 Montgomery St., Telesis Tower San Francisco, CA 94104-5525	(415) 445-6530	www.breproperties.com
Camden Property Trust	CPT	3 Greenway Plaza, Ste. 1300 Houston, TX 77046	(713) 354-2500	www.camdenprop.com
Cornerstone Realty	TCR	306 E. Main St. Richmond, VA 23219-3820	(804) 643-1761	www.cornerstonereit.com
Equity Residential Properties	EQR	2 N. Riverside Plaza, #400 Chicago, IL 60606-2609	(312) 474-1300	www.eqr.com
Essex Property Trust	ESS	925 E. Meadow Dr. Palo Alto, CA 94303	(650) 494-3700	www.essexproperties.com

Gables Residential Trust	GBP	2859 Paces Ferry Rd., #1450 Atlanta, GA 30339-5701	(770) 436-4600	www.gables.com
Home Property of New York	HME	850 Clinton Square Rochester, NY 14604-1730	(716) 546-4900	www.homeproperties.com
Mid-America Apartment Communities	MAA	6584 Poplar Ave., Ste. 340 Memphis, TN 38138-0612	(901) 682-6600	www.maac.net
Post Properties	PPS	4401 Northside Pkwy., #800 Atlanta, GA 30327	(404) 846-5000	www.postproperties.com
Roberts Realty Investments	RPI	8010 Roswell Rd., #120 Atlanta, GA 30350	(770) 394-6000	N/A
Summit Properties	SMT	212 S. Tryon St., Ste. 500 Charlotte, NC 28281-0001	(704) 334-3000	www.summitproperties.com
Town & Country Trust	TCT	100 S. Charles St. Baltimore, MD 21201-2725	(410) 539-7600	www.tctrust.com
United Dominion Realty	UDR	10 S. 6th St., #203 Richmond, VA 23219-3802	(804) 780-2691	www.udrt.com
Manufactured Home Community REITs				
American Land Lease	ANL	3410 S. Galena St., #210 Denver, CO 80231	(303) 614-9400	www.americanlandlease.com
Chateau Communities	CPJ	6160 S. Syracuse Way Greenwood Village, CO 80111	(303) 741-3707	www.chateaucomm.com
Manufactured Home Communities	MHC	2 N. Riverside Plaza, #800 Chicago, IL 60606-2608	(312) 279-1400	www.mhchomes.com
Sun Communities	SUI	31700 Middlebelt Rd., #145 Farmington Hills, MI 48334	(248) 932-3100	www.suncommunities.com

(continued)

Company Name	Ticker Symbol	Address	Phone Number	Web Site
		Office REITs		
United Mobile Home	UMH	3499 Route 9 North, #3-C Freehold, NJ 07728	(732) 577-9997	www.umh.com
Alexandria Real Estate	ARE	135 N. Los Robles Ave., #250 Pasadena, CA 91101	(626) 578-0777	N/A
Amerivest Properties	AMV	1800 Glenarm Pl., Ste. 500 Denver, CO 80202	(303) 297-1800	www.amvproperties.com
Arden Realty	ARI	11601 Wilshire Blvd., #400 Los Angeles, CA 90025-1740	(310) 966-2600	www.ardenrealty.com
Boston Properties	BXP	800 Boylston St. Boston, MA 02199	(617) 236-3300	www.bostonproperties.com
Brandywine Realty Trust	BDN	14 Campus Blvd. Newton, PA 19073	(610) 325-5600	www.brandywinerealty.com
Carramerica Realty	CRE	1850 K St. NW Washington, DC 20006	(202) 729-7500	www.carramerica.com
Corporate Office Properties	OFC	8815 Centre Park Dr., #400 Columbia, MD 21045	(410) 730-9092	www.copt.com
Equity Office Properties	EOP	2 N. Riverside Plaza, 22nd Floor Chicago, IL 60606	(312) 466-3300	www.equityoffice.com
Glenborough Realty	GLB	400 S. El Camino Real, #1100 San Mateo, CA 94402-1708	(650) 343-9300	www.glenborough.com
Great Lakes REIT	GL	823 Commerce Dr., #300 Oak Brook, IL 60523-1226	(630) 368-2900	www.greatlakesreit.com

Company	Symbol	Address	Phone	Website
Highwoods Properties	HIW	3100 Smoketree Court, Ste. 600, Raleigh, NC 27604-1052	(919) 872-4924	www.highwoods.com
HRPT Properties Trust	HRP	400 Centre St., Newton, MA 02458-2076	(617) 332-3990	www.hrpreit.com
Koger Equity	KE	8880 Freedom Crossing Trail, Jacksonville, FL 32256	(904) 732-1000	www.koger.com
Mack-Cali Realty Trust	CLI	11 Commerce Dr., 1st Floor, Cranford, NJ 07016-3501	(908) 272-8000	www.calirealty.com
Parkway Properties	PKY	1 Jackson Pl., 188 E. Capitol St., Jackson, MS 39225-4647	(601) 948-4091	www.parkwayco.com
Prentiss Properties	PP	3890 W. Northwest Hwy., #400, Dallas, TX 75220	(214) 654-0886	www.prentissproperties.com
Prime Group Realty	PGE	77 W. Wacker Dr., #3900, Chicago, IL 60601	(312) 917-1300	www.pgrt.com
SL Green Realty	SLG	420 Lexington Ave., New York, NY 10170	(212) 594-2700	www.slgreen.com

Industrial REITs

Company	Symbol	Address	Phone	Website
AMB Property	AMB	505 Montgomery St., San Francisco, CA 94111	(415) 394-9000	www.amb.com
Banyan Strategic Realty Trust	BSRTS	150 S. Wacker Dr., Ste. 2900, Chicago, IL 60606-4202	(312) 553-9800	www.banyanreit.com
Bedford Property Investments	BED	270 Lafayette Circle, Lafayette, CA 94549-3751	(925) 283-8910	www.bedfordproperty.com
Centerpoint Property Trust	CNT	1808 Swift Rd., Oak Brook, IL 60523-1501	(630) 586-8000	www.centerpoint-prop.com

(continued)

Company Name	Ticker Symbol	Address	Phone Number	Web Site
		Industrial REITs (*Continued*)		
Duke Realty	DRE	8888 Keystone Crossing, #1200 Indianapolis, IN 46240-2182	(317) 808-6000	www.dukereit.com
Eastgroup Properties	EGP	300-1 Jackson Pl., 188 E. Capitol St. Jackson, MS 39201	(601) 354-3555	www.eastgroup.net
First Industrial Realty	FR	311 S. Wacker Dr., #4000 Chicago, IL 60606	(312) 344-4300	www.firstindustrial.com
Keystone Property Trust	KTR	200-4 Falls Corporate Center West Conshohocken, PA 19428	(484) 530-1800	www.keystoneproperty.com
Kilroy Realty	KRC	2250 E. Imperial Hwy. El Segundo, CA 90245	(310) 563-5500	www.kilroyrealty.com
Liberty Property Trust	LRY	65 Valley Stream Pkwy., #100 Malvern, PA 19355-1460	(610) 648-1700	www.libertyproperty.com
Mission West Properties	MSW	10050 Bandley Dr. Cupertino, CA 95014-2188	(408) 725-0700	www.missionwest.com
Monmouth Real Estate	MNRTA	125 Wyckoff Rd., PO Box 335 Eatontown, NJ 07724-0335	(732) 542-4927	www.mreic.com
Prologis Trust	PLD	14100 E. 35th Pl. Aurora, CO 80011	(303) 375-9292	www.prologis.com
PS Business Parks	PSB	701 Western Ave., Ste. 200 Glendale, CA 91201-2397	(818) 244-8080	www.psbusinessparks.com
Reckson Associates Realty	RA	225 Broadhollow Rd. Melville, NY 11747-4807	(631) 694-6900	www.reckson.com

Acadia Realty Trust	AKR	20 Soundview Market Pl. Port Washington, NY 11050	(516) 767-8830	www.acadiarealty.com
Aegis Realty	AER	625 Madison Ave. New York, NY 10022	(212) 421-5333	www.aegisrealtyinc.com
Agree Realty	ADC	31850 Northwestern Hwy. Farmington Hills, MI 48334	(248) 737-4190	www.agreerealty.com
Alexander's	ALX	210 Route 4 East Paramus, NJ 07652	(201) 587-8541	N/A
Burnham Pacific Properties	BPP	110 W. A St., #900 San Diego, CA 92101-3350	(619) 652-4700	www.burnhampac.com
CBL & Associates Properties	CBL	6148 Lee Hwy., Ste. 300 Chattanooga, TN 37421	(423) 855-0001	www.cblproperties.com
Center Trust	CTA	3500 Sepulveda Blvd. Manhattan Beach, CA 90266-3696	(310) 546-4520	www.centertrust.com
Chelsea Property Group	CPG	103 Eisenhower Pkwy. Roseland, NJ 07068-1029	(973) 228-6111	www.cpgi.com
Commercial Net Lease	NNN	455 S. Orange Ave. Orlando, FL 32801-2813	(407) 265-7348	www.cnlreit.com
Crown America Realty Trust	CWN	Pasquerilla Plaza Johnstown, PA 15901	(814) 536-4441	www.crownam.com
Developers Diversfed	DDR	3300 Enterprise Pkwy. Beachwood, OH 44122	(216) 755-5500	www.ddrc.com
Equity One	EQY	1600 NE Miami Gardens Dr. North Miami Beach, FL 33179	(305) 947-1664	www.equityone.net

(continued)

Company Name	Ticker Symbol	Address	Phone Number	Web Site
		Retail REITs (*Continued*)		
Federal Realty Investments	FRT	1626 E. Jefferson St. Rockville, MD 20852-4041	(301) 998-8100	www.federalrealty.com
General Growth Properties	GGP	110 N. Wacker Dr. Chicago, IL 60606	(312) 960-5000	www.generalgrowth.com
Getty Realty	GTY	125 Jericho Turnpike Jericho, NY 11753-1016	(516) 338-2600	www.getty.com
Glimcher Realty Trust	GRT	20 S. Third St., Ste. 200 Columbus, OH 43215-4206	(614) 621-9000	www.glimcher.com
IRT Property	IRT	200 Galleria Pkwy. NW, #1400 Atlanta, GA 30339-5945	(770) 955-4406	www.irtproperty.com
JDN Realty	JDN	359 E. Paces Ferry Rd., #400 Atlanta, GA 30305	(404) 262-3252	www.jdnrealty.com
JP Realty	JPR	35 Century Park Way Salt Lake City, UT 84115-3507	(801) 486-3911	www.jprealty.com
Kimco Realty	KIM	3333 New Hyde Park Rd., #100 New Hyde Park, NY 11042	(516) 869-9000	www.kimcorealty.com
Konover Property	KPT	11000 Regency Pkwy., #300 Cary, NC 27511	(919) 462-8787	www.facrealty.com
Kramont Realty Trust	KRT	128 Fayette St. Conshohocken, PA 19428-1879	(610) 941-9292	www.kramont.com
Macerich	MAC	401 Wilshire Blvd., #700 Santa Monica, CA 90401	(310) 394-6000	www.macerich.com

Company	Symbol	Address	Phone	Website
Malan Realty Investors	MAL	30200 Telegraph Rd., #105 Birmingham, MI 48025-4503	(248) 644-7110	www.malanreit.com
Mid-Atlantic Realty	MRR	170 W. Ridgely Rd., #300 Lutherville, MD 21093-5678	(410) 684-2000	www.martreit.com
Mills	MLS	1300 Wilson Blvd., Ste. 400 Arlington, VA 22209	(703) 526-5000	www.millscorp.com
New Plan Excel Realty	NXL	1120 Avenue of the Americas New York, NY 10036	(212) 869-3000	www.newplanexcel.com
One Liberty Properties	OLP	60 Cutter Mill Rd. Great Neck, NY 11021	(516) 466-3100	www.1liberty.com
Pan Pacific Retail	PNP	1631 S. Melrose Dr., #B Vista, CA 92083	(760) 727-1002	www.pprp.com
Price Legacy	XLG	7140 Bernardo Center Dr., #300 San Diego, CA 92128	(858) 675-9400	www.peireit.com
Ramco-Gershenson Properties	RPT	27600 Northwest Hwy., #200R Southfield, MI 48034	(248) 350-9900	www.ramcogershenson.com
Realty Income	O	220 W. Crest St. Escondido, CA 92025-1707	(760) 741-2111	www.realtyincome.com
Regency Centers	REG	121 W. Forsyth St., #200 Jacksonville, FL 32202-3842	(904) 356-7000	www.regencyrealty.com
Rouse	RSE	10275 Little Patuxent Pkwy. Columbia, MD 21044-3456	(410) 992-6000	www.therousecompany.com
Saul Centers	BFS	8401 Connecticut Ave. Chevy Chase, MD 20815-5803	(301) 986-6200	www.saulcenters.com
Simon Property Group	SPG	115 W. Washington St. Indianapolis, IN 46204	(317) 636-1600	www.simon.com

(continued)

Company Name	Ticker Symbol	Address	Phone Number	Web Site
Retail REITs (Continued)				
Tanger Factory Outlet	SKT	3200 Northline Ave., #360 Greensboro, NC 27408	(336) 292-3010	www.tangeroutlet.com
Taubman Centers	TCO	200 E. Long Lake Rd., #300 Bloomfield Hills, MI 48303-0200	(248) 258-6800	www.taubman.com
U.S. Restaurant Properties	USV	12240 Inwood Rd., #200 Dallas, TX 75244	(972) 387-1487	www.usrp.com
Urstadt Biddle Properties	UBP	321 Railroad Ave. Greenwich, CT 06830	(203) 863-8200	www.ubproperties.com
Weingarten Realty	WRI	2600 Citadel Plaza Dr., #300 Houston, TX 77292-4133	(713) 866-6000	www.weingarten.com
Hotel REITs				
Boykin Lodging	BOY	45 W. Prospect Ave., #1500 Cleveland, OH 44115-1027	(216) 430-1200	www.boykinlodging.com
Equity Inns	ENN	7700 Wolf River Blvd. Germantown, TN 38138	(901) 754-7774	www.equityinns.com
Felcor Lodging Trust	FCH	545 E. John Carpenter Freeway Irving, TX 75062	(972) 444-4900	www.felcor.com
Hersha Hospitality Trust	HT	148 Sheraton Dr. New Cumberland, PA 17070	(717) 770-2405	www.hersha.com
Hospitality Property	HPT	400 Centre St. Newton, MA 02458	(617) 964-8389	www.hptreit.com

Host Marriott	HMT	10400 Fernwood Rd. Bethesda, MD 20817	(301) 380-9000	www.hostmarriott.com
Humphrey Hospitality Trust	HUMP	12301 Old Columbia Pike Silver Spring, MD 20904	(301) 680-4343	www.humphreyhospitality.com
Innkeepers USA Trust	KPA	306 Royal Poinciana Plaza Palm Beach, FL 33480	(561) 835-1800	www.innkeepersusa.com
Jameson Inns	JAMS	8 Perimeter Center East, #8050 Atlanta, GA 30346-1603	(770) 901-9020	www.jamesoninns.com
LaSalle Hotel Properties	LHO	1401 I St. NW, #900 Washington, DC 20005	(202) 222-2600	www.lasallehotels.com
Meristar Hospitality	MHX	1010 Wisconsin Ave. NW, #650 Washington, DC 20007	(202) 295-1000	www.meristar.com
RFS Hotel Investors	RFS	850 Ridge Lake Blvd., #220 Memphis, TN 38120	(901) 767-7005	www.rfshotel.com
Winston Hotels	WXH	2626 Glenwood Ave. Raleigh, NC 27608	(919) 510-6010	www.winstonhotels.com

Health Care REITs

Eldertrust	ETT	101 E. State St., #100 Kennett Square, PA 19348	(610) 925-4200	www.eldertrust.com
Health Care Property	HCP	4675 MacArthur Court, #900 Newport Beach, CA 92260	(949) 221-0600	www.hcpi.com
Healthcare Realty Trust	HR	3310 West End Ave., Ste. 700 Nashville, TN 37203-1058	(615) 269-8175	www.healthcarerealty.com
Health Care REIT	HCN	1 SeaGate, Ste. 1500 Toledo, OH 43604	(419) 247-2800	www.hcreit.com

(continued)

Company Name	Ticker Symbol	Address	Phone Number	Web Site
Health Care REITs (*Continued*)				
LTC Properties	LTC	300 Esplanade Dr., Ste. 1860 Oxnard, CA 93030	(805) 981-8655	www.ltcproperties.com
National Health Investors	NHI	100 Vine St., Ste. 1402 Murfreesboro, TN 37130	(615) 890-9100	www.nhinvestors.com
National Health Realty	NHR	100 Vine St., #1402 Murfreesboro, TN 37130	(615) 890-2020	N/A
Nationwide Health	NHP	610 Newport Center Dr., #1150 Newport Beach, CA 92660	(949) 718-4400	www.nhp-reit.com
Omega Healthcare Investments	OHI	900 Victors Way, St. 350 Ann Arbor, MI 48108	(734) 887-0200	www.omegahealthcare.com
Senior Housing Property	SNH	400 Centre St. Newton, MA 02458-2076	(617) 796-8350	www.snhreit.com
Universal Health Realty	UHT	367 S. Gulph Rd. King of Prussia, PA 19406	(610) 265-0688	www.uhrit.com
Ventas	VTR	4360 Brownsboro Rd., #115 Louisville, KY 40207-1642	(502) 357-9000	www.ventasreit.com
Self-Storage REITs				
Public Storage	PSA	701 Western Ave., Ste. 200 Glendale, CA 91201-2394	(818) 244-8080	www.publicstorage.com
Shurgard Storage	SHU	1155 Valley St., #400 Seattle, WA 98109	(206) 624-8100	www.shurgard.com

Sovran Self Storage	SSS	6467 Main St. Buffalo, NY 14221	(716) 633-1850	www.sovranss.com
Storage USA	SUS	165 Madison Ave., Ste. 1300 Memphis, TN 38103	(901) 252-2000	www.sus.com

Specialty REITs

Capital Auto REIT	CARS	1420 Spring Hill Rd., #525 McLean, VA 22102	(703) 288-3075	www.capitalautomotive.com
Correctional Properties Trust	CPV	3300 PGA Blvd., #430 Palm Beach Gardens, FL 33410	(561) 630-6336	N/A
Entertainment Properties	EPR	30 Pershing Rd., #201 Kansas City, MO 64108	(816) 472-1700	www.eprkc.com
Golf Trust of America	GTA	14 N. Adgers Wharf Charleston, SC 29401	(843) 723-4653	www.golftrust.com
Pinnacle Holdings	BIGT	1549 Ringling Blvd., 3rd Floor Sarasota, FL 34236	(941) 364-8886	www.pinnacletowers.com
Pittsburgh & West Virginia Railroad	PW	2 Port Amherst Dr. Charleston, WV 25306-6699	(304) 926-1124	N/A
Plum Creek Timber	PCL	999 Third Ave., Ste. 2300 Seattle, WA 98104-4096	(206) 467-3600	www.plumcreek.com

Diversified REITs

Arizona Land Income	AZL	2999 N. 44 St., #100 Phoenix, AZ 85018	(602) 852-6800	N/A
BRT Realty Trust	BRT	60 Cutter Mill Rd., #303 Great Neck, NY 11010	(516) 466-3100	www.brtrealty.com/

(continued)

Company Name	Ticker Symbol	Address	Phone Number	Web Site
Diversified REITs (Continued)				
Colonial Property Trust	CLP	2101 6th Ave. North, #750 Birmingham, AL 35203	(205) 250-8700	www.colonialprop.com
Cousins Properties	CUZ	2500 Windy Ridge Pkwy., #1600 Atlanta, GA 30339-5683	(770) 955-2200	www.cousins-cuz.com
Crescent Real Estate Equities	CEI	777 Main St., Ste. 2100 Fort Worth, TX 76102	(817) 321-2100	www.cei-crescent.com
First Union Real Estate	FUR	551 Fifth Ave., #1416 New York, NY 10176-1499	(212) 905-1104	www.firstunion-reit.com
Income Opportunity Realty	IOT	10670 N. Central Expwy., #300 Dallas, TX 75231	(214) 692-4700	www.incomeopp-realty.com
istar Financial	SFI	1114 Avenue of the Americas New York, NY 10036	(212) 930-9400	www.istarfinancial.com
La Quinta Lodging	LQI	197 First Ave., Ste. 300 Needham Heights, MA 02194-9127	(781) 433-6000	www.reit.com
Lexington Corporation Properties	LXP	355 Lexington Ave., 14th Floor New York, NY 10017-6603	(212) 692-7260	www.lxp.com
Pennsylvania REIT	PEI	200 S. Broad St., 3rd Floor Philadelphia, PA 19102-3803	(215) 875-0700	www.preit.com
Shelbourne Properties I	HXD	5 Cambridge Center Cambridge, MA 02142	(617) 234-3000	N/A
Shelbourne Properties II	HXE	5 Cambridge Center Cambridge, MA 02142	(617) 234-3000	N/A

Sizeler Property	SIZ	2542 Williams Blvd. Kenner, LA 70062	(504) 471-6200	www.sizeler.net
Vornado Realty Trust	VNO	888 7th Ave. New York, NY 10019	(212) 894-7000	www.vno.com
Washington REIT	WRE	6110 Executive Blvd., #800 Rockville, MD 20852	(301) 984-9400	www.washreit.com

Mortgage REITs

America 1st Mortgage Investors	MFA	399 Park Ave., 36th Floor New York, NY 10022	(212) 935-8760	www.am1st.com
American Residential Investors	INV	445 Marine View Ave., #230 Del Mar, CA 92014	(858) 350-5000	www.amerreit.com
Amresco Capital Trust	AMCT	700 N. Pearl St., #1900 Dallas, TX 75201-7424	(214) 953-7700	www.amrescoct.com
Annaly Mortgage Management	NLY	12 E. 41st St., #700 New York, NY 10017	(212) 696-0100	www.annaly.com
Anthracite Capital	AHR	345 Park Ave., 29th Floor New York, NY 10154	(212) 409-3333	www.anthracitecapital.com
Anworth Mortgage Asset	ANH	1299 Ocean Ave., #200 Santa Monica, CA 90401	(310) 394-0115	www.anworth.com
Apex Mortgage Capital	AXM	865 S. Figueroa St., #1800 Los Angeles, CA 90017	(213) 244-0440	www.apexreit.com
Capstead Mortgage	CMO	8401 N. Central Expwy., #800 Dallas, TX 75225	(214) 874-2323	www.capstead.com
Clarion Commercial	CLR	335 Madison Ave. New York, NY 10017	(212) 883-2500	N/A

(continued)

Company Name	Ticker Symbol	Address	Phone Number	Web Site
		Mortgage REITs (Continued)		
Criimi MAE	CMM	11200 Rockville Pike Rockville, MD 20852-3103	(301) 816-2300	www.criimimaeinc.com
Dynex Capital	DX	4551 Cox Rd., #300 Glen Allen, VA 23060	(804) 217-5800	www.dynexcapital.com
FBR Asset Investment	FB	Potomac Tower, 1001 19th St. North Arlington, VA 22209	(901) 580-6000	www.fbr.com
Hanover Capital Mortgage Holdings	HCM	90 West St., #2210 New York, NY 10006	(212) 732-5086	N/A
Impac Mortgage Holdings	IMH	1401 Dove St. Newport Beach, CA 92660	(949) 475-3600	www.impaccompanies.com
Laser Mortgage Management	LMM	65 E. 55th St. New York, NY 10022	(212) 758-2024	N/A
Novastar Financial	NFI	1901 W. 47th Pl., #105 Westwood, KS 66205	(913) 362-1090	www.enovastar.com
PMC Commercial Trust	PCC	18111 Preston Rd., Ste. 600 Dallas, TX 75252-4026	(972) 349-3200	www.pmccapital.com
Rait Investment Trust	RAS	1845 Walnut St., 10th Floor Philadelphia, PA 19103	(215) 861-7900	www.raitrust.com
Redwood Trust	RWT	591 Redwood Hwy., Ste. 3100 Mill Valley, CA 94941	(415) 389-7373	www.redwoodtrust.com
Thornburg Mortgage	TMA	119 E. Marcy St., #201 Santa Fe, NM 87501-2046	(505) 989-1900	www.thornburgmortgage.com

Index

Index

369